The Secret of Cooking

Recipes for an Easier Life in the Kitchen

Bee Wilson

Photography by Matt Russell

W. W. NORTON & COMPANY

Celebrating a Century of Independent Publishing

For information about permission to reproduce selections from this book,
write to Permissions, W. W. Norton & Company, Inc.,
500 Fifth Avenue, New York, NY 10110

For information about special discounts for bulk purchases, please contact
W. W. Norton Special Sales at specialsales@wwnorton.com or 800-233-4830

Manufacturing by Toppan Leefung

ISBN 978-0-393-86763-3

W. W. Norton & Company, Inc.
500 Fifth Avenue, New York, N.Y. 10110
www.wwnorton.com

W. W. Norton & Company Ltd.
15 Carlisle Street, London W1D 3BS

1 2 3 4 5 6 7 8 9 0

For Tasha, for everything

Contents

A few notes on ingredients and equipment

"What people have in their pantry depends,
obviously, on what they like to cook and eat."
Yotam Ottolenghi, *Ottolenghi Simple*

Oil

You can drive yourself crazy with the complexity of deciding which cooking oil is the "right" one to use. But the answer is simple. Decide which oil you like best and use it up while it's fresh. You don't need dozens of different oils. For me, cooking oil means a good—but not too expensive—extra-virgin olive oil, which I use for almost all my cooking as well as raw in salads, because I like the taste more than any other oil, plus it's healthy. This keeps life simple—I mostly like having just one bottle of olive oil on the go at any one time so that I can use it up quickly. As well as using it as a finishing oil—drizzled over food raw at the end to add flavor—I use it for everything from sautéing to roasting to stir-frying. I got the idea of using olive oil to stir-fry from my friend Ping, who is from China. In her UK kitchen, Ping uses olive oil in all her Chinese wok cooking, partly because her husband, Rafa, is from Spain and olive oil is the taste of home to him.

For years, cookbooks warned us that olive oil must never be heated. The thinking was that it had a relatively low smoke point, meaning the temperature at which the fats start to smoke and break down and produce unhealthy chemicals. But actually, the smoke point of good quality extra-virgin olive oil is easily high enough for most cooking needs, though it partly depends on the age of the oil (a bottle that has been open a long time will have a lower smoke point). Overall, the smoke point of extra-virgin olive oil ranges from around 330°F to 420°F. If you bear in mind that sautéing happens at around 250°F and even deep-frying only requires oil to be around 350°F, you see that—as Italian cooks have long known—extra-virgin olive oil is perfectly fine for most cooking needs, including frying.

In this book, when I say olive oil, I mean extra-virgin olive oil. But if your oil and fat preferences are different, for goodness sake, ignore me. Perhaps you love the rich taste of coconut oil or the spicy tang of mustard oil. Lots of people I know in the UK are switching to unrefined canola oil because it's more sustainable and local than olive oil. Cold-pressed sunflower oil can also be delicious (and is completely different in flavor from the refined kind).

I will also sometimes refer to neutral oil or light oil. By this, I mean a refined or blended oil such as light olive oil, sunflower oil, canola, or grapeseed oil. These oils are cheaper and blander with a slightly higher smoke point than extra-virgin olive oil and they are what I tend to use for deep-frying and occasionally for making mayonnaise. I would ideally only ever have one of them open at a time, again for reasons of freshness. Nothing is nastier than rancid oil. I go to and fro in whether sunflower is better than canola or vice versa but in the end, I think what matters most with these oils is that the bottle is relatively fresh (an old bottle of sunflower oil tastes far from neutral). My current favorite is light olive oil, but ask me again in a year's time and I will probably give you a different answer.

Is all butter unsalted?

There is almost always a section in modern cookbooks that says something like: "all butter is unsalted, all eggs are large, all parsley is flat-leaf" and I think: "speak for yourself." It's all very well saying that "all eggs are large," but what if you went to a store that only sold medium? And what if you prefer your butter on the salty side?

All I can tell you is how things usually were in my kitchen when I tested the recipes, but please know that if you use different ingredients or experiment with what you have on hand, I will be cheering you on.

I try to buy only eggs that are free-range and preferably organic, and the same goes for meat. I used to buy extra-large eggs, but since reading a few things suggesting that laying larger eggs is not good for chickens' welfare, I have switched to buying cartons of mixed-weight eggs. I originally tested the recipes with extra-large eggs but they will still work with large. If you think your eggs are very small, add an extra one. The canned tomatoes I buy are always whole plum tomatoes—to me, the pre-chopped kind taste thin and metallic. I'd always rather buy canned tomatoes whole and then blend or chop them as needed. If you don't have a blender, you can turn a can of whole tomatoes into chopped ones simply by squeezing the whole tomatoes with your hands (satisfyingly squelchy) or chopping them still in the can with a butter knife. Salt is fine sea salt unless I'm adding it right at the end of a dish to adjust the seasoning, in which case it is flaky sea salt (Maldon for preference). And when I run out of salt half an hour before dinner, it's any tub of table salt I can find at the corner store. I always try to get good bronze-die dried pasta—it makes a huge difference. Canned chickpeas are the cheap but delicious ones that I can buy from my local Turkish grocery store. Lemons are unwaxed if I can get them, or waxed and scrubbed under a hot tap if not. Brown sugar can be light or dark, it really doesn't matter.

And yes, I do use mostly unsalted butter because I like it on my toast. If you buy salted butter, you might want to decrease the salt levels in the recipes a bit.

Oven temperatures

My oven is an electric oven with a convection setting. All the temperatures given are for conventional ovens and have been adapted and tested. But do check your oven with an oven thermometer, as ovens vary in how hot they run, which can make a surprising difference to timings.

My tastes and my pantry

We each have certain flavors and ingredients we gravitate toward more than others, which partly depend on the grocery stores we have access to. Just so you know, here are some of my current favorites. I love rice vinegar for its mildness and now use it in almost every recipe requiring vinegar. I buy it in big bottles from a Korean market where I also buy big jars of pickled sushi ginger—another ingredient I use constantly. And from the same store, I buy big bags of short-grain sushi rice and noodles. You can buy any of these online if you have trouble finding them in your local shops. You should also know that I am slightly obsessed with Dijon mustard and with lemons, so you may find they feature in a lot of the recipes. I've included quantities for salt in most of the recipes because I like being told how much salt to add. As mentioned above, when I say salt, I mean fine sea salt. If you are using a flaky salt such as Maldon, you might want to add a bit more by volume. Or just leave it out, if you are like my friend Sarah, who somehow—I don't understand how—makes delicious meals without a speck of salt.

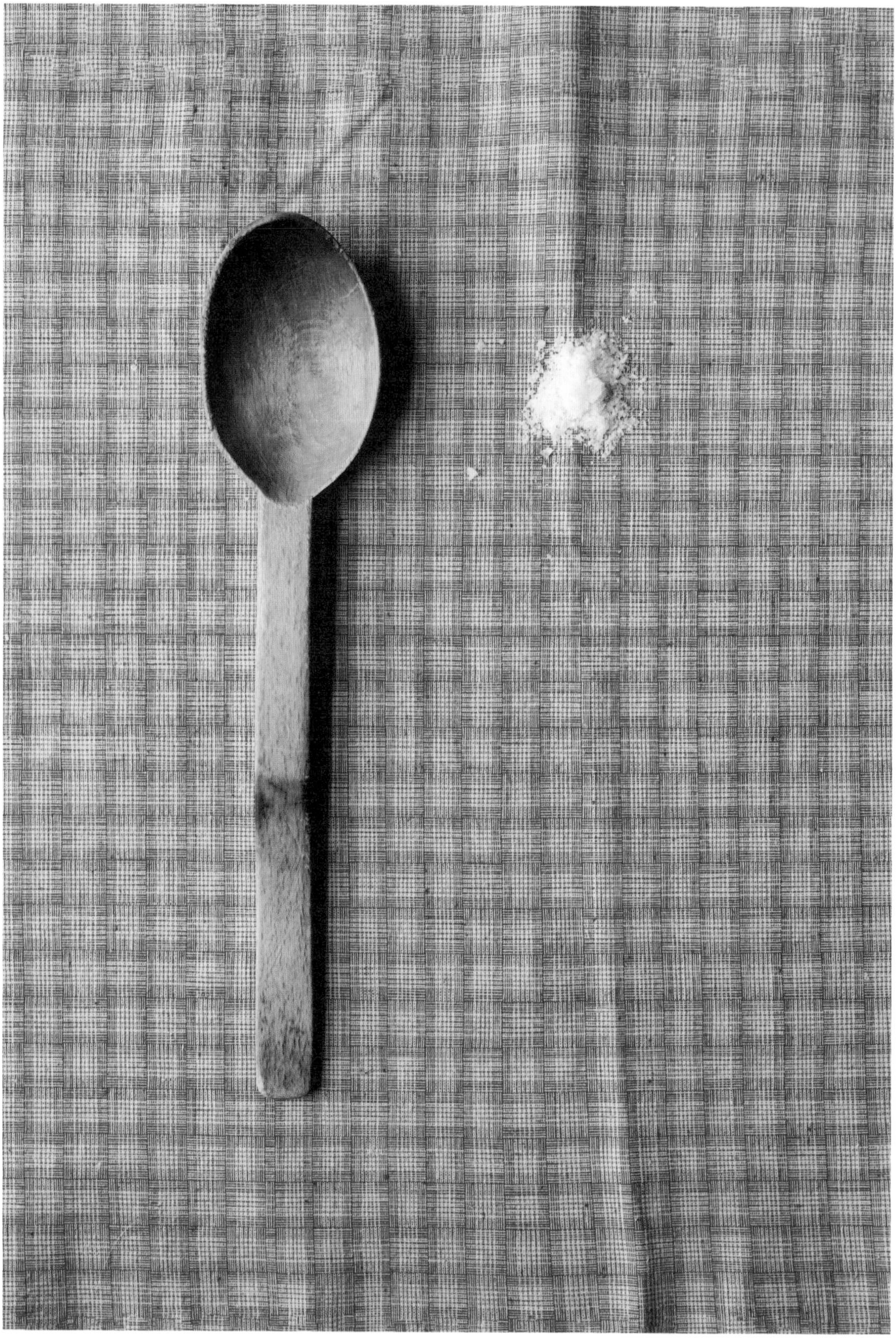

Introduction

"To comfort the heart and take away melancholy.
Take the juice of borage four pounds,
the flowers of borage half a pound:
let these stand infused in hot embers fourteen hours,
then being strained and clarified,
put to good sugar two pounds
and boil it to a syrup."
The Treasurie of Commodious Conceits and Hidden Secrets, 1591

The secret of better home cooking is not to be found in fancy gadgets, chefs' tricks, or hidden ingredients. The secret of cooking is the person who cooks, whoever that person may be. It is the human standing at the stove who brings the words of a recipe to life (or who summons up a meal without any recipe at all, drawing on memories so deep they seem to be instincts). Each of us carries into the kitchen our own particular tastes and values, our passions and blind spots, and our motivations for cooking—or not cooking. Whatever the meal or the occasion, the person who cooks is by far the most important element. Recipes are just "notes on a page, waiting for you to bring them to life," as the Italian food writer Marcella Hazan wrote in one of her cookbooks. If we want to eat a more delicious dinner, we need to look after the cook. That means finding the ways of cooking that work for you, no matter how anyone else does things.

Before there were cookbooks, there were things called *Books of Secrets*. From late medieval times onward, these esoteric volumes became widespread across Europe. Many of these books of secrets presented themselves as works of science, promising to reveal the mysteries of nature, such as the healing powers of herbs or ways to mix up different colors of paint. They were collections of remedies, as much as recipes. In these books, cooking is treated as a kind of everyday magic. By the sixteenth century, a typical book of secrets might offer the reader a mix of practical cooking tips and weird potions with impossible claims. There might be recipes for candied walnuts and melon jam alongside more wishful "remedies" for anything from curing a child's cough to saving someone from the plague or healing the passions of the heart (a recipe involving roses and oil of mace). "To make a tart that is courage to man or woman" is a recipe title from 1591. In these books, cooking is seen as just one secret among many that a person would need to know in order to lead a happier and more comfortable life and to cheat death for as long as possible. To preserve pears. To poach eggs. To soothe sore feet. To provoke sleep. To stop the bleeding of a wound. To make fine cakes.

It's easy to laugh at the absurdity of these secrets. You can't actually cure the passions of the heart with roses (at least, it hasn't worked for me). But is this really any crazier than the idea that if you follow the words of a chef, you can truly make the world's best chocolate cake or that if you drink a particular green juice created by an Instagram guru, you will somehow attain wellness?

The secret of cooking is still a prize that plenty of us wish for. Making meals from scratch, we are told, is the antidote to much that is wrong with modern life. If only we could make fresh home-cooked dishes every day, we would lead healthier, happier, and more sustainable lives. We would support farmers, save money, lose weight, and have better relationships. Cooking is also said to be a salve for anxiety and a way to keep ourselves in the moment. It all sounds amazing. But how on earth do we actually find time to do it?

When I talk about the secret of cooking, I don't mean the secret ingredients that top chefs once guarded so jealously for their signature sauces—an extra pinch of saffron or an undetectable hint of anchovy. The hard part of cooking is almost never the cooking itself (which is one of many reasons why being a home cook is so far removed from being a chef). The truth is, the hard part is all the other stuff that has to happen before you can find your way to the stove ready and able to cook. It's those things that the TV chefs don't talk about as they stand in their pristine kitchens wielding shiny appliances that cost more than a winter coat. It's one thing having the skills to rustle up a perfect plate of lemon linguini. It's another thing deciding what to do when one person at the table thinks lemon zest is too bitter and another won't eat linguini because it is "carbs."

For many of us, everyday cooking has become an annoying chore that we feel we should do more of, like flossing our teeth. What makes cooking hard is not so much technique as all those other things, large and small, that get in the way. I'm not saying that everyone knows how to butterfly a fish or arrange the rhubarb for a pie in a perfect diamond formation. But if you truly wanted to acquire those skills, you could, thanks to the miracle of YouTube (though you should know that rhubarb pie still tastes great without any diamond formations). In this age of online cooking videos, the greatest stumbling block to cooking is seldom the food preparation itself. What trips us up on the way to the kitchen is time, money, guilt, brain space and other people, and yet, for some reason, most cookbooks don't say anything about how to handle these vital ingredients.

"Cooking will be much easier if you have the right tools for the right job," writes Jane Todd in *Cooking is Easy*, a 1978 cookbook aimed at children. Well, yes. But the tools of cooking are not just items such as whisks and high-speed blenders. You also need a generous supply of confidence, and ideas, and a sense of the seasons and of which flavors go best with which—tools that are more powerful than any gadget. There was a time when this store of cooking knowledge was inherited almost automatically in families, passed on from parent to child. Recipes were once like collective memories that kept a culture alive. That time has gone, hence that slightly lost feeling we now have in the kitchen.

What does it take for cooking to be less of a drag and more of a joy? The answer will be different for each of us, depending on our life circumstances. A quick recipe may not be quick if you are disabled. Or maybe you are just slower at peeling vegetables than the chef who wrote the recipe. Before you can cook more, you need to figure out what it is that holds you back from enjoying cooking more right now.

For most of us, the biggest obstacle to cooking is the fact that our poor, overloaded brains seem to lack the headspace required to plan a meal. There is also the cost and complication of buying the exact ingredients a recipe says we require, not to mention the working hours and long commute or overflowing email inbox that may keep you away from your kitchen at the critical moment.

Put someone in a clean kitchen with a wooden spoon, a free day, no pressure, and a fully stocked fridge and most of us become like children again, mixing potions. What could be easier than stirring delicious ingredients in a pan or putting them into an oven and waiting until they smell so good that you can't resist eating them? Imagine how simple cooking could be if you had someone sitting on a kitchen stool by your side handing you each piece of equipment and ingredient one by one, already prepped?

When you are right in the midst of it, cooking is a joyous kind of game, a game you play with all your senses, a game where no one loses. I recently got talking with a man who told me he had taken up cooking in middle age when he realized he was too old for Lego. I liked his thinking and wondered why I didn't fully share it. For many of us, the daily grind of cooking can often feel as frustrating as being asked to construct a Lego house when half the bricks are missing.

As a child, the kitchen was the place I went to cure my worries. From a young age, I spent hours at the kitchen table, reading cookbooks and experimenting with food, whenever my parents would let me. Cooking was almost a compulsion to me. I will never forget the heady moment, as a teenager, that I taught myself to make gougères—cheesy French morsels made from choux pastry. I couldn't see how anything could be more fun. First, there was the mysterious satisfaction of making choux pastry: cracking golden-yolked eggs into the flour and butter mixture and stirring like mad. Then there was the magic of taking the gougères out of the oven and seeing that each flat mound of dough had expanded and crisped into a golden cheese-cloud. At the time, I thought the kitchen would always feel like my own secret hideaway, full of delicious transformations, a place that could soothe me after the worst school day.

So years later, as a middle-aged parent of three children, I was slightly astonished to realize that cooking itself had become a source of daily anxiety. I still loved cooking on the weekends but was finding it harder to feel the same excitement in the kitchen day in and day out. There was a mismatch between the meals I felt I should make (a leisurely feast assembled from in-season farmers' market produce) and the meals I actually did make (a hurried collation made from the disappointing offerings at the only supermarket I could get to on the way home). Many of the meals I produced tasted—to me, anyway—like compromise and disappointment. I almost never felt that I was on top of the ingredients in my fridge. Why did I possess three jars of preserved lemons and no olives? And why—despite claiming to hate food waste—did I throw away so many vegetables every week? I still cooked, almost every day, but it was no longer the unalloyed pleasure it had once been. Family dinner often felt like a race against the clock at the wrong time with the wrong ingredients.

The more I asked around, the more I realized how many others were experiencing similar levels of cooking anxiety. I spoke to people who said they hated the shopping part more than the cooking. Others said that cooking would be OK, if only there were time. I kept meeting people who complained of the amount of mental space they devoted to planning their meals, without much reward. They spoke of cooking as an annoyance, an interruption, a series of daily hurdles to overcome. Some said that they wished they could cook more, but life got in the way and they ended up relying on takeout or ready meals. Some said how hard it was to cook when different people in the family were on different diets or had radically different tastes. I got chatting one evening with a woman who said she would have enjoyed cooking, if only it weren't for her children. They were picky about lots of things, including onions, and this put her off trying new recipes because "what recipe doesn't start with an onion?"

I love cookbooks, but I found that the cookbooks on my shelves only took me so far. If you came to my house you would see that some of the rooms are more cookbook than room. I have books that promise to teach me how to make a flakier pie crust or how to have friends over for dinner without too much fuss. I have cookbooks full of delicious Indian spices and cookbooks that celebrate the authentic cuisines of Spain or Italy. What I don't have is a cookbook that helps me decide which of the many cookbooks to use on a rainy Tuesday evening when my spirits are flagging and various family members are saying they are hungry right now this second.

Most recipes—though fine and delightful if you happen to have all the ingredients on hand—do not solve the problem of cooking because they start too late in the game. They assume that you are already there in the kitchen with a perfectly sharpened knife in one hand and a gleaming-fresh set of ingredients in the other. A so-called thirty-minute recipe might realistically take three hours by the time you have done all the shopping for it, not to mention the extra time you need to spend on washing up afterward.

This book sprang from personal experience. I wanted to crack the code of how to fit cooking into the everyday mess and imperfection of all our lives without it seeming like yet another undoable thing on the to-do list or yet another reason to berate ourselves for falling short.

My own relationship with cooking changed, suddenly, about a year into this project. In June 2020, in the middle of the pandemic, my husband of twenty-three years, the father of my three children, left me for another woman. For much of that year, I resembled Munch's painting *The Scream* (or at least, that is how I felt). I tried anything I could think of to take my mind off the grief of it—watching television, yoga, reading novels, vodka—but almost everything reminded me of him (especially the vodka). With social distancing in place, I couldn't hug friends. My mother, who has dementia, was in a care home where I wasn't allowed to visit. To cap it all, I suddenly had to do all the laundry and all the cooking. This wasn't such a shift; we never divided the cooking 50–50. But there is still a difference between being the person who does the vast majority of the cooking for a household and being the person in charge of all of it.

Yet to my surprise, I found that my new enforced role as sole cook came with benefits. In my lonely state, the kitchen was one of the few places I felt better rather than worse. Cooking anchored me to the person I had been before I met my husband. I could make myself a chicken stew with the sweet scent of parsley and white wine, which reminded me of the stews my mother used to make. No matter how tearful I had been the night before, I still had to get up in the morning and cook breakfast for my son, who was then eleven. The act of cracking eggs into a bowl to make my son's favorite pancakes or waffles felt steadying and gave me back my appetite. I started to take pride in the way I could make a perfectly lacy crêpe almost every time. I was suddenly reminded of a passage in the novel *Heartburn*, by Nora Ephron, in which the main character takes comfort in cooking after discovering her husband is having an affair. Ephron writes that the act of melting butter and adding flour and hot stock and watching it get thick is "a sure thing in a world where nothing is sure." This was how I felt. My legs were like jelly but I found that holding on to the friendly handle of a wooden spoon could keep me upright.

We spend so long in the modern world talking about the stress of cooking that we can miss the ways in which cooking itself can be the greatest of all remedies for stress. Cooking brought me out of my thought loops and back into my senses and into a world of good smells and sounds. If I could pay enough attention to the sizzle of garlic in a pan or the squeaky sound of mushrooms frying, I could forget the darker thoughts.

I also felt good about the fact that I was keeping myself and the children nourished. We seemed to connect more deeply over meals than we had before. My teenage daughter and I have always shared a love of eggs, but in the past we tended to eat them for lunch in a very limited range of ways (boiled, scrambled, shakshuka). Together, we branched out with eggs, taking it in turns to cook them and discovering two new methods for making an omelet especially tender and delicious (see page 178). Even my youngest child started cooking more. He was the first person in the house to test the recipes for the chocolate and hazelnut macaroons (page 350) and for Raymond's butter-poached carrots (page 37), and I have never seen anyone so proud as he was when he lifted the lid and saw that the carrots were perfectly cooked, despite his erratic knife-work. I started to see that the secret kitchen of my childhood still existed.

I am not pretending that *cooking mended my broken heart*. When life sucks, it doesn't stop sucking just because you have cooked the best pavlova of your life (with raspberries and little fragments of toasty hazelnuts, page 389) or finally figured out how to make a vinaigrette that works every time (page 114). But these things also don't hurt.

My rekindled love of cooking made me all the more determined to find ways to make it much easier, both for myself and others. Almost all of us have at least one cooking secret up our sleeve, shortcuts or flourishes that we get so used to doing that we forget how special or unusual they are. I bought a large green notebook with a soft cover and started collecting kitchen tips from friends and books. For a while, every time I met someone new, I pestered them for their cooking secrets and scribbled them down. I've learned ways to speed cooking up and ways to slow it down, depending on the demands of that particular week. I've unearthed tricks that mean I can get dinner on the table even on those days when the spirits are flagging and stocks are low. I've discovered ways to make family meals less of a strain when you are feeding a group of people with radically different tastes. I've found that a meal that is cooked virtually hands-free—on a baking sheet in the oven—can taste more lovingly seasoned than one that has been stirred resentfully on the stovetop by an exhausted person.

I learned so many shortcuts that I wish I had known years ago. I found that, contrary to what almost every recipe says, it is not essential to sauté the vegetables for a soup or stew or sauce—you can just simmer it all together in the pot, which makes the whole process so much less effort on days when you are exhausted. Another discovery was that I could make the most delicious buttery tomato pasta sauce in almost no time at all using a box grater. I started to reprogram many of my assumptions about how to get food on the table (or into a lunchbox, as the case may be). One of the most mindblowing discoveries of all was that it is often not necessary to preheat the oven, even when making a cake or roasting a chicken. Oh, and you *really* don't have to start every recipe with an onion (unless you want to).

Some of these secrets may not be news to you at all. Behind closed doors, home cooks around the world have always been quietly inventing ways to make their lives easier and dinner more delicious, but most of them have not found their way onto the pages of cookbooks.

Making cooking more enjoyable is largely a question of timing. We are often told that we don't have time to cook but the part we miss is that time is not a single thing. Time is not just about how much or how little we have; it's about the quality of those minutes and when in the day they fall. The real secret is that we need the cooking that suits the particular time we have. Sometimes you have acres of headspace to plan a meal but little time for cooking and sometimes it is the other way around. I found that one way to save huge amounts of time during the week without any compromise on taste was to make universal cooking sauces in advance and store them in my freezer, so that I could have the makings of a delicious red or green or yellow curry at short notice without ordering delivery food. Even if you make no other recipes from this book, I promise that these universal sauces are a way of cooking that can help you to eat more deliciously on those rainy Tuesday evenings.

But beyond all these tricks and tips, the secret we all need the most is how to get the spark of cooking back into our lives so that the kitchen becomes a place we actually want to be.

Delicious is not just about the way food tastes; it is a mindset. More than anything, the secret ingredient that makes the difference in the kitchen is enjoyment. And what this means is that we have to learn ways to make food that delights us, because no cook enjoys making a dish when the end results are disappointing. One of the secrets I discovered was that cooking can be a series of remedies that made me feel strangely calmer and more equipped to deal with the rest of what life had to throw at me.

One proviso. I have mentioned that one of the biggest obstacles to cooking is money. This is a tricky subject. Even by the standards of these fractious times, asking a roomful of people—or the online equivalent—whether home cooking can save a person money is one of the quickest ways to ignite an argument and it can never end well. Will home cooking save you money? This depends on what you cook, and how much money you spend on food right now. To put it even more bluntly, it depends on how rich you are, which is one of the unsayable truths that modern cookbooks seldom address. I will also share the things I've learned about how to stop throwing perfectly good food away. But someone who is already eating on a bare-bones budget does not need to be told that homemade minestrone will make all the difference. They need more money, and to live in a world in which people can earn enough to feed themselves. There are huge, and growing, social inequalities around food that are beyond the realm of any food book to address (though a great place to start with truly money-saving cookery is the superb books of Jack Monroe).

A second proviso. This book contains recipes with many origins and many different people behind them. Some of the flavors I've used were inspired by dishes created by cooks from India and Malaysia and Indonesia and South Korea; others by cooks from Argentina, Turkey, France, Italy and Spain, among others. I did not grow up in any of these cultures and you might say that these are not my secrets to tell. I would agree. We are in the middle of a long overdue conversation about who gets the credit for traditional dishes. I have tried to acknowledge, with gratitude, where my ideas come from, but I know I won't always have got it right because sometimes a single dish has many sources.

I can't promise you that following the ideas in this book will change your life, because I have no idea what your life is like at the moment. But I do want to assure you that if, like me, you wish you could cook more and also enjoy it more, it is possible, even when the rest of life is as sad or difficult as the rest of life usually is. If there is something that is preventing your cooking, I hope this book can give you some ways in or ways back. We all need to find pragmatic ways to cook that work for our own lives and our own tastes, not for anyone else's. When you think you are too busy to cook, those are sometimes the very times that we need cooking the most. There is still magic in the kitchen, if you know where to look.

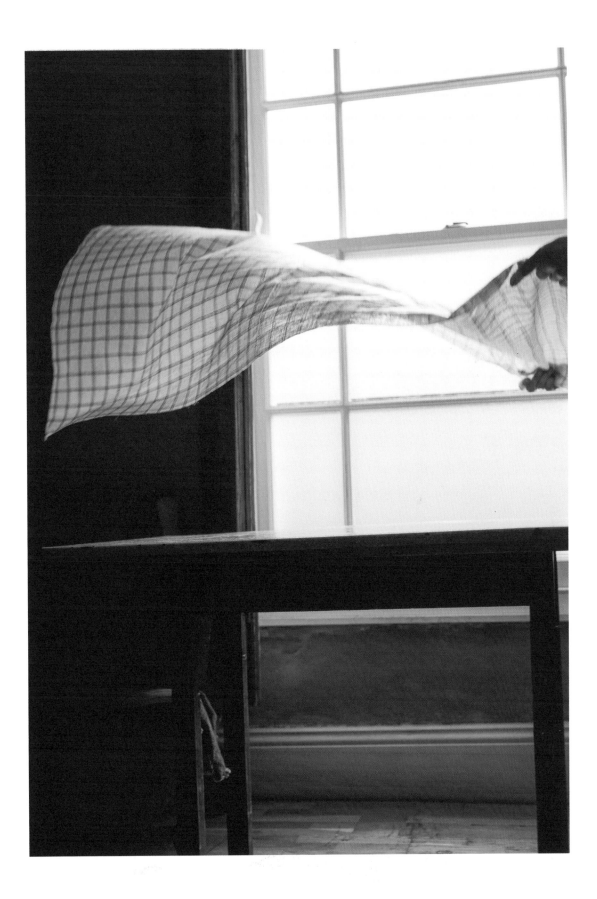

Cut yourself some slack

"No ingredient was spectacular all the time,
and no dish was appealing every day."
  Judy Rodgers, *The Zuni Café Cookbook*

If I could beg you to do one thing and one thing only to improve your cooking life, it would be to cut yourself some slack. If you want to make cooking a regular and enjoyable part of your life—and I'm assuming that you do, or else you wouldn't be reading this—you need to give yourself as much leeway as you can in how you get there. Drown out the voices that say you can't be a good cook if you ever use stock cubes or buy frozen vegetables or if you never make your own oat milk or if your knife skills are not up to scratch. Never feel the need to apologize—to yourself or others—for serving an imperfect meal. The only way to cook, or to live, is imperfectly. It's far better to cook and be prepared to compromise than never to cook at all because you are trying to live up to impossible standards.

Perfection is a terrible idea because it makes us feel bad and stops us from doing so many things that would make our lives better. This is as true in the kitchen as it is anywhere else.

Cooking is so much more fun—both for the eaters and for the cook—when you allow it to be the messy, experimental thing that it really is and give yourself credit just for creating something tasty and hot—even if it's a grilled cheese sandwich—at the end of a long day. If you lower your expectations in the kitchen, there's a good chance you will exceed them, which feels so much better than the nagging sense that you are falling short of something flawless. "Good enough" is a much kinder mantra to live by than perfection, but it is also a more effective one. The less you expect your cooking to be perfect, the more you create an atmosphere in which you can practice it and so become more confident in doing it. The times when cooking counts the most are not in the big production dinner you make for Christmas or Thanksgiving but in the bowl of soup you rustle up on a rainy Tuesday for no particular reason except to satisfy yourself.

I'm not saying that perfect moments or perfect flavors never happen when cooking. In fact, they happen surprisingly often and when they come along, we should celebrate them. Sometimes, miraculously, the cookie doesn't crumble and the pie crust doesn't collapse. It's easy to lament the sauce that doesn't emulsify and the pine nuts that scorch in the pan and to miss the frequent and happy occasions when the nuts *don't* burn and the hollandaise sauce doesn't split. There are evenings when the stars align and you take a bite of omelet and realize that you have finally achieved a perfect one: not too rubbery, not too wet, a tender oval of just-set egg. But the next time you try to make exactly the same omelet recipe with the same pan, it just doesn't work quite as well. Maybe the eggs were different, or maybe you missed the timing by a few seconds or maybe your mood was off. It happens. What I'm saying is that you can't fully plan for perfection. Yes, you can seek out great recipes and take pride in the craft of what you are doing, but the truth is that no one is ever fully in control of ingredients and how they behave because they change in characteristics from day to day and so do we as cooks.

We don't talk anything like enough about how stressful cooking can sometimes be, even for those of us who love it. In September 2020, I put out a request on Twitter for people to tell me what, if anything, they were scared of when they cooked, and received dozens of heartfelt replies. Again and again, the theme of perfection came up as something that terrified people or held them back from cooking. It seems that many of us have an idea of what a good cook should be and that we feel we can't live up to it. In contrast to the cooks we see on Instagram or YouTube, we feel we are not skilled enough or authentic enough; our ingredients are not as pristine or organic as they should be and our knife skills are rubbish. Food photographer Del Sneddon said that for years he was terrified of failure in the kitchen because he was so "mesmerized and in awe" of his grandmother's excellent cooking.

TV cooking shows have a lot to answer for in having planted the notion in our heads that getting dinner on the table is somehow a vicious dog-eat-dog competition in which someone must lose. My respondents on Twitter spoke of their shame at getting things wrong, the fear that dishes would "turn out horrible," the terror of disappointing others, and the daunting sense that cooking was a performance, something at which you could easily fail and be judged for. One person remarked that he hated cooking until he lived alone: "I think what scared me was feeling like if it wasn't perfect I'd be messing up a shared kitchen and feeding people something gross." Another common theme was that cooking felt so laborious and time-consuming to so many people. People described being terrified of the work involved in prepping vegetables. "I honestly felt like cooking anything without a jar would be SO HARD," said one person.

Before it is anything else, cooking needs to be doable and that means it needs to be tailored to the life of the person who is doing it. What is doable for any of us will vary from day to day or week to week. There have been times—after my children were born, after my husband left—when I wasn't able to do much more than shove a sheet of something in the oven and hope for the best. Sometimes, that something was fish sticks. That isn't culinary failure—it's life.

There's a curious idea afoot that anything other than cooking from scratch is somehow cheating. As food writer Ella Risbridger writes in *Midnight Chicken (& Other Recipes Worth Living For)*, "cooking is not a contest or a virtue test, and it is not only for those with plenty of time." If there are easier or quicker ways to do something—and there usually are—we should not berate ourselves for choosing them over lengthier or more traditional techniques, assuming you like the end results. A jar of pre-chopped garlic; a package of puff pastry; a can of cooked beans; a tub of curry paste; any or all of these may be the shortcut that makes you feel able to cook tonight without tearing your hair out. Such items are sanity-giving and there is no shame in using them.

What does "from scratch" really mean, anyway? It is all relative. We do not tell ourselves we are cheating when we buy packages of pre-churned butter and bags of pre-ground sugar and flour, even though to cooks of earlier generations these would have seemed like unimaginable luxuries. If a Victorian cook wished to make a dish involving sugar, he or she would first have to chisel off a lump of hard sugar from a larger loaf and then grind this into a powder before finally pushing it through a series of sieves until it was fine enough to use.

Any time you come across an ingredient or tool that makes it easier for you to fit cooking into your life, welcome it as you would a lucky penny by the side of the road. Take frozen peas. In the West, these have been in our lives for so long that we can be almost blasé about what an astonishing boon they are. When chef Asma Khan arrived in Britain from India in 1991, she had only ever known peas as a fresh and very laborious vegetable eaten in winter. Khan recalled that before a feast, all the children in the house would "be rounded up to pop the pea pods to make the pulao." The first time she saw her husband pouring frozen peas from a bag, she was surprised: "I was imagining an army of children popping pea pods to fill those bags."

There are no prizes for making cooking harder than it needs to be. Sometimes, you may feel like luxuriating in a satisfyingly slow cooking project. But, for most of us, daily cooking needs to be much, much easier and more streamlined or it won't happen at all. One of the biggest secrets of cooking is that it doesn't have to be as complicated as we often make it.

Take the easy way out

Learning how to cut corners can make the difference between feeling willing and able to cook, and wanting to curl up on the sofa with a takeout (fun as that can be). The key is knowing which corners you can cut and which will ruin the dish. "A pot-saver is a self-hampering cook," writes the great Julia Child. Loath as I am to contradict Julia, I can't say I agree. A pot-saver is often a smart cook who understands that sometimes you need to cook dinner fast and in a single pan or not at all. We speak of taking the easy way out as if it were a bad thing, but the real question is why anyone would take the difficult way when an easier and equally delicious option presents itself. I think of this as win-win cookery. Here are a few examples straight off the bat.

—Rice noodles are quicker to cook than any other kind of noodle and as an added bonus you can serve them to your gluten-free friends.
—Fresh ginger doesn't need to be peeled before it is grated. I spent ages searching for the best method of peeling these knobbly rhizomes—a small spoon, a swivel peeler, a tiny knife—only to discover that it doesn't need to be peeled at all. Just rinse and grate.
—Instead of topping a fish pie with mashed potato (that takes ages to make) you can just cube some bread, toss it in melted butter and possibly some finely chopped rosemary and top with that instead. Whoever you serve this to will think this is an original new take on fish pie rather than any kind of compromise.
—You don't need to pre-salt eggplant slices before you cook them. Old cookbooks tell you to do this because eggplants used to be more bitter than they are now, but with modern varieties there is no need.
—Don't fret if you don't have any stock for a soup. Many excellent chefs, including Rowley Leigh, prefer the clean, clear flavor given to a soup by water and salt alone.
—When you want vegetables but you are tired, there are always frozen peas. Also frozen spinach, frozen corn, frozen artichokes and frozen baby okra (so good in stews).

It's also important to recognize that not all forms of cooking lend themselves to the easy midweek dinner. There are a few kitchen tasks that can't easily be simplified, especially in the realm of pâtisserie. If you set out to make a Gâteau St Honoré, an amazing French dessert that calls for four different kinds of pastry plus caramelized sugar and pastry cream, you know you are in for the long haul. But when it comes to everyday meals, there are usually far more workarounds than we realize. If you can find a way to make something wonderful in a much easier way, that means you will get to eat wonderful stuff more often.

One of the ways we torment ourselves in the kitchen is with the idea that "traditional" or "authentic" cooks would never take shortcuts. This is nonsense. Traditional cooks didn't suffer for their art because they thought it was noble but because they had no choice.

All over the world, traditional cooks are embracing electrical devices that help them to make the same delicious food in a fraction of the time. It would be unusual now to meet a South Korean cook who didn't use an electric rice cooker, and electric blenders have been adopted everywhere from India to Lebanon.

Long before the advent of electric gadgetry, cooks were inventing ways to make food prep simpler because—contrary to popular opinion—people (people here usually means: women) have always been busy with plenty of tasks around the house other than cooking. These shortcuts have not often been recorded in cookbooks, which have tended to be written by elite male chefs. They are not recipes so much as ways of life. I have a friend who speaks of "survivalist cooking:" the kind you need when just getting something on the table is an achievement. When my children were small, almost all my cooking fell into this survivalist category.

When I am feeling truly low but need to cook, one of the things that suddenly seems too effortful is the instruction to chop and sauté the vegetables for the soffritto that seems to form the start of almost every soup, stew, or sauce. Sautéing vegetables is enjoyable when you are in a leisurely mood; not so much when you feel rushed. So I was elated to discover from Lynne Rossetto Kasper (in *The Italian Country Table*) that there is a whole category of Italian vegetable soups involving no sauté at all. As Kasper instructs, "You put everything in the pot and simmer until the flavors melt into each other. Do this in water or broth." It sounds too easy to be true but trust me, it works. The first time I did this, I thought that somehow the soup would be flavorless or thin, but actually, all the vegetables seem to end up tasting deliciously of each other. You don't even have to chop them small if you are planning to blitz the soup at the end, which is what I usually do (although another option if you are not a fan of smooth soup is to chop the vegetables smaller and keep the soup untouched and chunky at the end).

Mellow soup for frayed nerves

It's one of the small disappointments of life that the times when you most need and crave a wholesome bowl of homemade vegetable soup tend to be when you feel too wiped out to make it for yourself. I remember the bone-crushing loneliness I felt during my first term as a university student, away from home for the first time, when I came down with flu and realized in a self-pitying way that no one would feed me a nourishing soup to hasten my recovery unless I did it myself.

This is the answer: a no-sauté (and virtually no-chop) soup that contains medicinal quantities of vegetables yet is so easy-going that you can spend most of the cooking time lying in bed. Don't worry too much about the particular mix of vegetables. The whole point of this soup is that it should be adaptable to anything you have or can easily obtain. The main proviso is not to use too many bitter-tasting roots such as rutabaga or turnip because they will bully the other flavors into submission. I also wouldn't add spices because they end up tasting a bit flat when you haven't sautéed them. If you want it spicy, fry spices in butter and add them at the end. Kasper recommends a fifty-fifty split of mild vegetables or legumes such as squashes, potatoes, and beans and aromatic ingredients such as tomatoes, onions, carrot, and celery. The basic formula I've come up with is 1¾ pounds/800g prepared weight of vegetables to 3⅓ cups/800ml of water or stock (you can always add more water at the end if it's too thick), but this is almost infinitely adaptable. Sometimes I add a tin of beans or chickpeas, sometimes not. I used to make this with stock cubes but now I find that the vegetables themselves impart plenty of flavor after simmering for 45 minutes.

This green version on the next page—my favorite—reminds me of my mother's watercress soup. My friend Deirdre, who tested it for me, said "it has some of the richness of leek and potato but is much more interesting and balanced." The quantities and ratios of vegetables can all be adjusted, as long as you keep the water, salt, and butter the same. If your spring greens come in a 10½-ounce/300g bunch rather than 7-ounce/200g, that's perfectly fine.

Serves 4–6

12¼ oz/350g potatoes, peeled and roughly chopped

1 large or 2 small zucchini, trimmed and roughly chopped

1 leek, trimmed and roughly chopped

A few fat green onions, trimmed and roughly chopped

7 oz/200g spring greens (or cavolo nero), roughly chopped

3 tablespoons butter

At the end: 1 tablespoon of lemon juice or rice vinegar and a big handful of green
  herbs such as parsley, cilantro, or sorrel

Milk or cream to thin it out

Put all the vegetables into a large pot. Add the butter, 1 teaspoon of salt, and
3⅓ cups/800ml of water. Put the pan over high heat, bring to a boil, then turn
the heat down and simmer for 45 minutes with the lid on or until the vegetables
are totally tender. You don't have to watch it much or do anything for this 45
minutes—just rest your weary bones and notice as the kitchen starts to fill with a
cozy steaminess. When it is done, add the handful of herbs and the lemon juice or
vinegar, blitz with an immersion blender, and check the seasoning. Don't overblitz
or the potatoes will go gluey. Thin it to your desired consistency with milk or cream.
Top with anything you like: a dollop of sour cream, a pinch of chile flakes, a handful
of chopped herbs, or grated cheese. Eat with buttered toast and feel better.

Instant Pot version: since I have an Instant Pot, this is actually the way I most
often make it. Put everything except for the lemon or vinegar and the final herbs
into the Instant Pot and cook on high pressure for 8 minutes. Allow to slow-release.
Add the lemon or vinegar and herbs, blitz (or not), adjust the seasoning, and eat.

VARIATIONS

Cream of pumpkin soup (vegan)

This version has the sweet restorative comfort of canned soup, only it tastes so much
better. The squash or pumpkin makes it taste creamy, even though it contains no
cream. I make this for myself when feeling under the weather and there's a chill in
the air.

1 lb 2 oz/500g of squash or pumpkin (peeled weight) cut into chunks, 2–3 carrots,
peeled and cut into chunks, 3½ oz/100g of fennel (or celery), 1 onion, peeled and cut

into chunks, 1 teaspoon of salt, 3 tablespoons of olive oil, 3⅓ cups/800ml of water. At the end, after blitzing, check for seasoning and add lemon juice to taste. As Ruth Reichl observes, this kind of smooth pumpkin soup is very good with a contrasting "crisp dice" of either apple or pickled walnuts in the bowl.

Chickpea, tomato, and bay soup (vegan)

I think of this one as a kind of all-purpose vegetable soup, but with a little added protein from the chickpeas. 2 large tomatoes, rinsed and quartered, 4 carrots, peeled and cut into large chunks, 2 stalks of celery, trimmed and cut into large chunks, 2 leeks, rinsed and cut into large chunks, 1 × 15-oz/425g can of chickpeas (drained), 2 cloves of garlic, peeled and grated, 2 fresh bay leaves (if you have them), 3 tablespoons of olive oil, 1 teaspoon of salt, 3⅓ cups/800ml of water. At the end, before you blitz it, remove the bay leaves, add the zest and juice of a lemon, and check for seasoning.

Whole white bean broth

As mentioned above, if you feel energetic enough for some more knifework, you can chop all the vegetables and herbs finely at the start, which will mean that you don't need to bother blitzing at the end. 2 teaspoons of lemon zest, 2 tablespoons of flat-leaf parsley, 4 carrots, peeled and diced, 1 fat bulb of fennel (or 2 stalks of celery), diced, 2 leeks (or 1 bunch of green onions), rinsed and diced, 1 × 15-oz/425g can of white beans (liquid and all), 2 cloves of garlic, peeled and grated, 3 tablespoons of olive oil, 1 teaspoon of salt, 2½ cups/600ml of water. At the end, check the seasoning, add a squeeze of lemon and serve with torn basil or mint leaves or more chopped parsley. This version is more minestrone-like and benefits from lots of parmesan added to the bowl.

All-in-one tomato sauce

The same all-in-one zero-effort method can be applied to tomato sauce for pasta. Lynne Rossetto Kasper calls this "Tomato Sauce Mellowed by Simmering." She points out that it tastes "softer, more tomatoey and mellow" than sauté-based tomato sauce. The best-known version of this sauce is Marcella Hazan's tomato sauce with onion and butter, whose cult following is surely due as much to its incredible ease as to its rich buttery taste. To make a version of this, you simply simmer a 14-oz/400g can of whole, peeled tomatoes with 5 tablespoons/75g of unsalted butter, a medium onion, peeled and cut in half, and a pinch of salt for 45 minutes before discarding the onion and mashing the tomatoes with a wooden spoon. Much as I love this sauce, which I have made dozens of times, it always used to upset me to discard the onion, so I started blitzing the onion and tomato together at the end with an immersion blender.

But then I wondered if the method wouldn't work even better with garlic, olive oil, and bay leaves and this is now my preferred way: 3 cloves of garlic, peeled and bashed with the flat side of a knife, 2 tablespoons of your best olive oil, 2 × 14-oz/400g cans of whole, peeled tomatoes, 2 fresh bay leaves (sometimes I leave these out or add a sprig of rosemary instead), and a pinch each of salt and sugar, simmer for 30 minutes, stirring every so often, remove the bay or rosemary, and blitz. This is now my house tomato sauce for anything from pizza to many variations of tomatoey pasta. It's so easy that when you have made it once you will never again consider buying a jar of sauce. This makes 4–6 servings. And it's adaptable—see below.

SOME WAYS TO USE TOMATO SAUCE

—Pour it over slices of roasted eggplant (roasted in a hot oven with olive oil for 20–25 minutes), top with panko breadcrumbs mixed with parmesan, lemon zest, and olive oil, and bake in a hot oven for 15 minutes to make a quick almost-Parmigiana.
—Add a glug of heavy cream to the sauce to soften the flavor before tossing with a rich egg pasta such as tagliatelle or pappardelle.
—Mix with a drained can of borlotti beans, plus some chopped rosemary, a couple of teaspoons of molasses, a diced zucchini, and a small spoonful of Dijon mustard, and simmer for 10–15 minutes to make homemade baked beans.
—Before tossing it with pasta, warm the base sauce with a couple of cans of tuna, some capers, and basil leaves.

Roaste,d vegetables every which way

I wish that all things in life were as forgiving as a sheet of roasted vegetables. Not a week goes by that I don't put at least one sheet of vegetables into the oven. Any time you have vegetables lying around and can't think what to do with them, roast them, particularly if you already have the oven on for something else. I often roast a couple of sheets of vegetables on a Sunday night, and keep them for a few days in bowls in the fridge ready to add to salads or rice bowls or risottos or to devour with green tahini sauce or turn into a meze plate with some hummus and chile sauce and flatbreads. In the dry heat of the oven, everything from cabbage to bell pepper to broccoli seems to intensify in flavor and sweeten.

Try not to get too hung up on a recipe, and have faith that it's very hard to make any roasted vegetable taste bad. They can be happily slotted into an oven alongside pretty much anything else, from cake to lasagne. Whichever vegetable you pick—and you can pick anything except for very tender greens such as lettuce, spinach, or bok choy—toss with a spoonful or two of oil and some salt and put on a baking sheet. Other things you could add at this stage include a spoonful of miso, a spoonful of chopped thyme or rosemary, and the juice and zest of a lemon. But the more often you roast vegetables, the more you start to notice that they don't need much seasoning because they get their flavor from the heat of the oven plus their own sweetness. There is an Italian word, *insaporire*, which Anna Del Conte says means "to enhance the flavor of an ingredient during the preparation of a dish." I think of this when I roast vegetables because it is the cooking itself that seasons them. If you roast vegetables with nothing but oil and salt (sometimes I even skip the salt), you can always add extra flavor at the end in the form of chopped herbs.

Here are some timings for various roasted vegetables, on the assumption that you have preheated the oven to 425°F. But actually, as with the slow-start roasted chicken (see page 75), it's perfectly possible to roast vegetables from a cold start and at lower temperatures. Just increase the cooking time accordingly and check the vegetables every 10 minutes or so until they are done the way you like them. It's also lovely to roast a mixture of vegetables. Just use the timings on the next page and add the quicker-cooking vegetables such as tomatoes toward the end.

15 minutes
Whole asparagus, trimmed
Broccoli, cut into small florets
Strips of red or yellow bell peppers
Cherry tomatoes or sliced big
    tomatoes

20 minutes
Thin rounds of eggplant
Chunks of zucchini
Whole or quartered portobello
    mushrooms

30 minutes
Slices of cabbage (this is unbelievably
    delicious and often overlooked)
Unpeeled cloves of garlic
Wedges of onion
New potatoes, halved
Pieces of butternut squash, either peeled
    or unpeeled
Fat slices of fennel
Small beets, peeled and quartered
    (large ones can take as much as
    1 hour)

Have a backup plan

When cooking, it's easy to get fixated on plan A: the perfect and elaborate versions of things that we make when time is no object and the fridge is well-stocked. But more often, the thing you need is a plan B: a form of standby cooking that will have your back when life is complicated (which it is, after all, most of the time). If plan A is quiche, plan B might be a frittata cooked in the oven. If plan A is apple pie, plan B is a berry cobbler or crumble made from berries stashed in the freezer (that take almost zero prep compared to apples). Plan C is berry croissant cobbler: take the best croissants you can buy, slice them, arrange them over the sugared frozen berries, sprinkle with more sugar, and bake until crisp.

A backup plan in the kitchen can take many forms. It might mean keeping a few sauces in the freezer that you can turn into dinner on short notice by adding some vegetables, with or without meat. Or maybe it means memorizing a few quick recipes you can make almost instantly using tins of beans (see page 262) or fish from the pantry. Or it could be an even quicker way to make pasta that can be adapted to pretty much any ingredients you have on hand, assuming you have a package or two of dried pasta in the pantry.

Magic pasta

When I first saw references to this all-in-one method of making pasta, I was sceptical. Surely it couldn't be possible to cook the sauce and the pasta all at once in the same pan? It seemed to violate every rule in Italian cooking. But then I realized that the method is not really so far from a risotto. The bonus of this technique—aside from incredible speed and ease and minimal washing up—is that the pasta is seasoned by the sauce as it cooks and becomes deeply flavored with wine, aromatics, stock—whatever you choose to add. It works with any shape of pasta—but a good quality brand makes a big difference here—and almost any combination of vegetables and other flavorings such as anchovies or cured meats. You just have to be careful to measure the ratio of pasta to water accurately, use a wide shallow frying pan or sauté pan (it won't work in a tall narrow saucepan) and be generous with your seasoning.

This will never be my first-choice way to cook pasta. On leisurely evenings, I still prefer the time-honored process of cooking the noodles and the sauce separately (a method that my youngest son now calls "Muggle Pasta" to distinguish it from "Magic Pasta"). And yet, I can't urge you strongly enough to learn this technique and have it in your head for when you are in a pinch and you need a hot meal right now.

On those days when time and/or energy are scarce, you can rely on this formula to pull you through. It's a dish that is very kind on the cook and you feel you are somehow pulling off a miracle. I made a version of it with cauliflower and chorizo for a late lunch the day of my father-in-law's socially distanced funeral. Because of the pandemic, there was no food after the funeral. Family members stood in a cold and empty parking lot trying to make gestures of love and sorrow to one another from behind our masks. When the children and I finally arrived home, we felt flat, grief-stricken, and insatiably hungry. Fifteen minutes later, we were sitting down to a warming and savory tangle of linguini with chorizo and flecks of saffron-yellow cauliflower. We were still sad but at least we didn't feel quite so empty inside.

Actually, my favorite version of this pasta isn't the cauliflower one but a variant made with mushrooms and garlic and cream and wine that tastes the way I remember Italian restaurant food tasting in Britain in the 1980s. It's also a bit like the canned mushroom soup my father was once so fond of; don't let that put you off. It has a deep umami quality that comforts me to my core. But do try the cauliflower version too—it's good.

Magic pasta with mushrooms, garlic, cream, and wine

Serves 1

4 oz/120g mushrooms (I usually make it with brown button but any kind will do, even plain old white button)

3½ oz/100g pasta, any kind that says on the package that it will cook in 10 minutes (I favor linguini here but penne also works)

1–2 fat cloves of garlic, peeled and grated

A knob of unsalted butter

1½ cups/30g flat-leaf parsley, chopped

2 tablespoons white wine or vermouth

2 tablespoons heavy cream

A squeeze of lemon

Parmesan, to serve

Take the mushrooms and grate them coarsely on a box grater (or blitz them in a food processor). Put all the ingredients up to and including the white wine into a wide frying pan or sauté pan (keeping back a handful of the parsley) and add ⅓ teaspoon of salt and 1⅔ cups/400ml of water from a freshly boiled kettle. It will look wrong putting wet and dry ingredients together so haphazardly but have faith—it will all come together. Put over high heat and bring to a boil with the lid on. Continue to simmer with the lid on for 5 minutes, checking and stirring every 1 minute. Now remove the lid and cook for 3–5 minutes more with the lid off, stirring frequently with tongs or a wooden spoon. If it looks dry or if the pasta isn't cooked, add another splash of water but you don't want it to go too soupy. Creamy, yes; soupy, no. Continue to cook, testing pieces of pasta, until it is done to your liking. Add the cream and squeeze of lemon. Test for seasoning. Serve with the reserved parsley and parmesan on top. Devour.

Once you get the basic concept of this pasta, you soon see you can adapt it to almost any flavors that you like. Here are a few more ideas for 3–4 people:

Cauliflower, saffron, and chorizo

7 oz/200g of chorizo (any kind), cut into coins, 1 tablespoon of olive oil, 12¼ oz/350g of dried pasta, a large cauliflower (about 1 lb 2 oz/500g), chopped very small, 3½–7 oz/100–200g of cherry tomatoes, halved, 2 fat cloves of garlic, peeled and grated, 5¼ cups/1.25 liters of water, 1 teaspoon of salt, a pinch of saffron strands, 1 teaspoon of smoked paprika. At the end: a squeeze of lemon and some toasted sliced almonds plus chopped parsley.

Leek, seaweed, and ginger

12¼ oz/350g of dried pasta, a few sliced leeks, 3 tablespoons of olive oil, a quarter of a cabbage, sliced, 1 large spoonful of miso paste, a thumb of ginger, grated, ¾ teaspoon of salt, 2 cloves of garlic, grated, 5¼ cups/1.25 liters of water. A minute before the end: 1 cup/150g of frozen peas. At the end: lime juice and zest, black sesame seeds, torn nori seaweed.

Backup dessert

When I am in backup cooking mode, I don't often bother with dessert. Ripe fresh fruit will do. More than do. But sometimes, it's nice to have something sweeter and more ceremonial to round off a meal. My stumbling block with desserts when I am feeling stressed is pastry. Pastry is one of the most satisfying things to make when you are in a leisurely mood—the crumbly feeling of the butter and flour under your fingers, the smooth texture of the dough as it comes together. But homemade shortcrust is one thing that you can't hurry (it is never as good when you don't rest it). One excellent solution is to buy pre-rolled puff pastry—I usually have a block or two of the all-butter kind in the freezer. You can make the most heavenly simple fruit tarts from a few halved or sliced stone fruits (such as plums, apricots or peaches), arranged on circles of puff pastry spread with jam and topped with a little sugar before baking in a hot oven for 10–15 minutes, or until puffed and golden. Or you can make desserts involving no pastry at all (see the four-ingredient chocolate mousse on page 118).

A more forgiving sweet tart: Orange and cardamom shortbread squares

Citrus-flavored tarts are one of my favorite things to eat but not my favorite thing to make when under pressure. The filling is no trouble; it's the fragile pastry that can be temperamental, especially when I am making it for guests. This is my solution (based on a Claire Ptak recipe for lemon bars): little shortbread squares with a cheeringly bright and tangy orange and cardamom curd topping. I think of these as a citrus equivalent of brownies and everyone seems to love them—including the cook. Instead of rolling out a fragile sweet pastry, you simply use your hands to pat a sweet shortbread into a baking pan. Low stress, high pleasure.

Makes 20-30 squares, enough to serve 8-10

For the shortbread base
⅔ cup/80g confectioners' sugar
2¼ cups/280g all-purpose flour
1 cup/220g unsalted butter, softened (I put it in the microwave on high for 20 seconds)

For the filling
4 large eggs
1¼ cups plus 2 tablespoons/280g granulated sugar
Zest of 1 large unwaxed orange
Juice of 2 lemons plus the juice of half of the orange to make ½ cup/120ml in total (add the second half of the orange if there isn't enough)
14 cardamom pods, seeds removed and ground in a mortar (or ½ teaspoon ground cardamom)
3 tablespoons/20g all-purpose flour
2 tablespoons/15g cornstarch
1 teaspoon baking powder
Ground cardamom, orange zest, and confectioners' sugar for dusting

Set the oven to 400°F. Line a baking pan (9 × 13 inches/23 × 33 cm, give or take) with parchment paper. For the shortbread, put the sugar, flour, and ½ teaspoon salt in a mixing bowl and whisk to combine. Add the softened butter and rub everything together with your hands until there are no big lumps of butter. Now start squeezing it more assertively until it comes together as a dough. If the butter is soft enough, the whole mixing process should take no more than 5 minutes. Alternatively, just put everything in a food processor and whiz until it comes together. Now pat the dough into the lined pan until it covers the bottom. Bake for 20–25 minutes or until golden.

Meanwhile, whisk together the eggs, sugar, zest, juice, cardamom, flour, cornstarch, and baking powder. Carefully pour the mixture over the shortbread and return it to the oven for 15–20 minutes or until just set but still jiggly. If in doubt, take it out—the joy of these squares is in the contrast between squidgy curd and crisp shortbread. Ideally allow it to cool for at least 1 hour or longer before cutting into squares: the shortbread will crisp up as it cools and the curd will firm up. If you like, dust with a little confectioners' sugar plus more cardamom and orange zest but this is by no means essential.

Teach yourself to cook with a carrot

"Those that do teach young babes
Do it with gentle means and easy tasks."
     Desdemona in *Othello*

When I asked my then eleven-year-old what scared him about cooking he said, "Not knowing how to do it." He's not alone. Lack of skills—or words to that effect—was the most common answer given on Twitter when I asked what it was that people feared about cooking.

The best way to learn to cook any given dish is simply by doing it, failing a bunch of times, and then doing it some more until your hands and eyes are so grooved to the process that it becomes second nature. Or at least this would be the best way to learn to cook in a world where people didn't care about failure or about wasting food.

When money is tight, you don't actually want to fail a bunch of times with expensive ingredients. You don't want to fail even one time, because aside from the expense, a failed recipe means a disappointing meal: something that I have still not trained myself to be brave about. It's a horrible feeling to go to all the effort of shopping for an elaborate dinner, only to realize that you have screwed up and that your pricey ingredients are ruined.

There are a few ways to feel less crushed by kitchen disasters. One approach is to tell yourself that no meal is truly ever a failure when it is shared with those you love. No, I don't buy that one either, or at least not while I am staring at the unappetizing wreckage of my own expensive screw-up. But honestly, your culinary fiasco is almost never as bad as you imagine and the odds are that those you are cooking for don't mind it as much as you do. It's also worth remembering that something delicious can usually be pulled from the ruins if you adjust your expectations.

A more lasting way to shore yourself up against the fear of kitchen failures is to ease yourself into getting more cooking experience using ingredients that are inexpensive, familiar, and accessible. This way, the whole enterprise feels lower stakes and with the pressure off, your confidence and success rate as a cook will also go up. I suggest practicing with a bag of carrots. This idea is not original to me. In 2019, no fewer than two delightful short cookbooks came out with the same theme, namely that carrot cooking can be a handy apprenticeship for cooking in general. The first

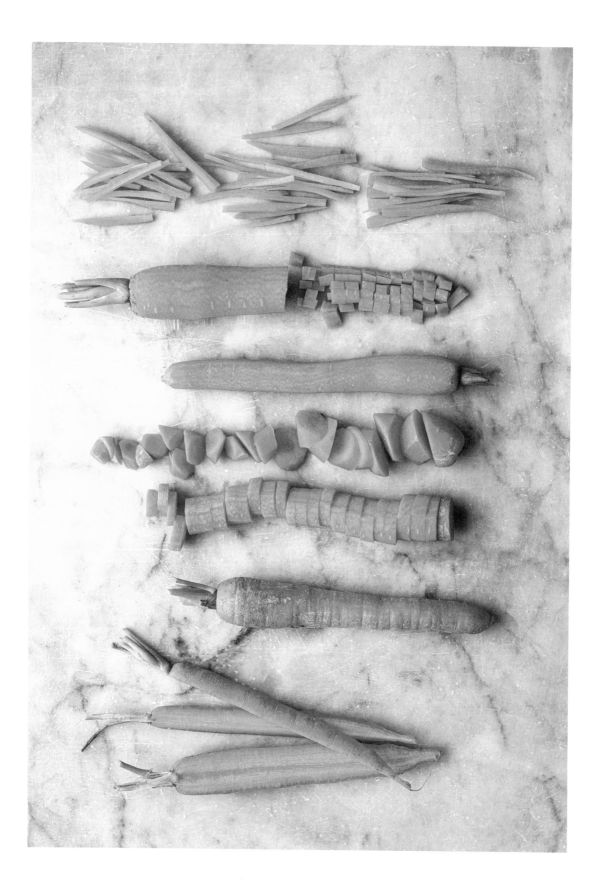

book is *Organic Carrot Cookbook* by Kerstin Rodgers, a wonderful food blogger who goes by the name Ms Marmite Lover, and the second is *50 Ways to Cook a Carrot* by Peter Hertzmann. Reading these books confirmed my hunch that cooking a range of different carrot dishes is a great way to expand cooking confidence in general. Anyone who can roast a chicken can roast a carrot. The difference is one of scale, not skill.

Or consider knife skills. A carrot, a board, and a sharp knife are all you need to master the basic principles of cutting just about any vegetable into slices, batons, julienne, dice, or roll-cut angles. A carrot is an approachable thing with which to get some knife skills under your belt. I'll cover some of these techniques in this chapter, but also bear in mind that no matter which knife skill you wish to master, there will be an internet video to demonstrate it more clearly than my words ever could. You may also wish to improvise your own carrot-cutting techniques, following the anatomy of the carrot itself. The most obvious way to cut these orange cylinders is into round coins that look like tree trunks with rings inside. Once you've gotten comfortable doing this, you could see what happens if you make the cuts at an angle instead of straight down, to yield flattened carrot ovals. You can get a mini power rush from seeing what a huge difference you can make to the shape of a carrot simply by making a tiny adjustment with your knife. Show the carrot who's boss.

Why carrots in particular? They are cheap, versatile, readily available, healthy, and most of us have a favorite way of eating them. "Eat them with ginger! Lots of ginger!" said the woman at the organic vegetable market where I bought almost seven pounds of carrots one day while testing some of these recipes. By focusing on this one ingredient, you can start to pay attention to the way that not all carrots are alike, from the tiny cone-shaped Chantenay carrots to long bunches of glamorous purple carrots at the farmers' market. Carrots offer simple lessons in how seasonal variation plays out through changes in flavor and texture and how to adjust your cooking to reflect this. A sweet snappy baby carrot in the spring is a very different proposition from a fat earthy winter carrot. I have a friend who adds tarragon to spring carrots but never to winter ones, which she feels call for deeper earthier flavors such as cumin. Spring carrots are usually best unpeeled because there is so much flavor near to the skin, whereas winter carrots can be too bitter if you *don't* peel them (I also worry about pesticide residues in the skin of non-organic carrots).

What follows are a few of my favorite carrot recipes, reflecting my own preferences. Each one is designed to showcase a particular cutting technique and cooking method and I hope you will take them out into the world and play with them because, after all, the best way to learn to cook is simply by doing it. If you try all eight, you will be a master carrot cook. And if any of them should go wrong, the consolation is that all you will have wasted is a few carrots.

Grated carrot salad (with variations)

CUTTING TECHNIQUE: PEELING AND GRATING
COOKING TECHNIQUE: NONE

Serves 4

When deciding how to cook any given thing, especially if that thing is a vegetable, it's worth remembering that sometimes the best option is *not* to cook it. The purpose of cooking is to make food more edible and delicious, but a raw carrot—with its bright crunch and herbal sweetness—may be unimprovable, depending on your mood and the quality of the carrot. As the food writer Constance Spry recognized as long ago as 1956, very few cooking methods can match the "intrinsic fresh and delicate flavor" that a carrot brings without any help from the cook, right out of the ground.

Forgive me if this is insulting your intelligence, but if you want carrot sticks, you need to know how to peel them. Technically, peeling is the wrong word, because a carrot doesn't have a separate peel in the same way that a pumpkin does, or an apple. The stripy outer part of a carrot is something called the periderm, which is simply the outer part of the carrot. Old cookbooks speak of paring carrots rather than peeling them. Whether you pare or you peel, here is how I do it. First, get a good peeler, by which I mean a swivel-blade peeler with a thick and comfortable handle. I favor an OXO Good Grips one. If the carrots are the unwashed kind, first rinse them in cold water. Hold the peeler in your dominant hand and hold the carrot horizontally in your non-dominant hand. Sweep the peeler from top to root, then rotate the carrot in your hand and repeat, until all the skin is off. I know that some people prefer to hold the carrot vertically against a board and peel from middle to bottom, before flipping and peeling again from middle to bottom, but I always found my way quicker. Find whichever way feels right to your hands and try peeling many carrots until you can do it as fast as unzipping a dress.

If you want to take raw carrots a step further, grate them into a salad. I think of French *carottes râpées* as the Platonic ideal of carrot salad and an example of how salads don't always need to taste of anything much except the central vegetable from which they are made. Ideally, this French carrot salad is made in a food processor with a grater attachment, which transforms the carrots into fine threads, so juicy

in their sweetness that the salad needs little additional dressing. After you have fed the peeled carrot through the fine disk of the food processor, decant it into a bowl, removing and eating the end pieces that fail to go through the disk (cook's perk). Add a squeeze of lemon, a nip of oil (walnut for preference, but olive is more than fine), and a large pinch each of salt and sugar. That's it, except for a second final glug of oil on top and maybe a sprinkling of herbs. This simple carrot salad makes a perfect lunch with black olives, a huge platter of hard-boiled eggs, and thick wobbly homemade mayonnaise with bread (baguette for preference). Assuming you like mayonnaise and eggs, this lunch is the epitome of cheap luxury and somehow the carrot salad is an essential element in giving it overtones of French chic.

A simpler and quicker way to make a carrot salad is with an ordinary box grater (see page 139). The strands come out coarser than in a food processor but they are just as tasty in their different way.

Carrot salads, I find, are even more adaptable than the classic salad of green leaves. You can dress them up with pumpkin seeds, slices of orange, feta, and mint for a healthy lunchbox. Or take batons, steam them, drizzle with oil and red wine vinegar, add parsley and a smidge of crushed garlic, wait a few hours, and you have an Italian carrot salad. Should you possess a swivel peeler, you can "peel" off long ribbons of carrot and give them a Japanese tinge with ginger, soy, and lime.

CARROT SALAD IDEAS (FOR 4½ CUPS/500G OF GRATED CARROT)

—Burmese-style: 1 tablespoon of lime juice, 1 teaspoon of fish sauce, a handful of salted peanuts, a pinch of salt, 1 fresh chile, seeded and chopped, 2 tablespoons of chopped mint, and a handful of fried shallots at the end.
—Moroccan: 1 clove of garlic, peeled and crushed to a paste, 2 tablespoons of olive oil, a big pinch each of salt and sugar, 2 oranges, peeled and sliced, 2 teaspoons of toasted cumin seeds, 1 tablespoon of lemon juice.
—Poppy seed and lemon coleslaw: add a quarter of a red cabbage, grated, 5 tablespoons/70g of mayonnaise, a big pinch of salt, 1 tablespoon of lemon juice (or more, to taste) plus the zest of a lemon, 1 tablespoon of finely chopped or scissored chives, and 1 tablespoon of poppy seeds. This is especially good with a baked ham.

Raymond's butter-poached carrots

Of all the recipes in the book, this might be the one that excites me the most. It is a way to make a daily side dish of vegetables that is transcendently quicker than any other method you might choose (even microwaving), yet it results in some of the best-tasting vegetables you will ever cook. If you swap to this method from your usual boiling or steaming, not only will you save yourself a lot of trouble but you will be able to prep your vegetables hours in advance when that helps. And you can do all this using a technology that is low tech, energy efficient, and more than 10,000 years old: the cooking pot.

This way of cooking vegetables is not my invention but that of the great French chef Raymond Blanc. In his 2011 book *Kitchen Secrets* he mentions quite casually that he has a "great little secret for cooking vegetables; one that has served me well for many years." You place the prepared vegetables in a covered pot with a small amount of butter and water and a pinch of salt (Raymond adds pepper too, but I don't). When you are ready to eat, you simply heat the covered pot over very high heat for 5 minutes (other vegetables may be done in as little as 1 minute). I thought long and hard about what to call this method. It's somewhere between poaching (simmering in water) and stewing (cooking in an enclosed pot). In the end, I felt that butter-poaching captured it best although it also works with oil.

CUTTING TECHNIQUE: COINS

COOKING TECHNIQUE: BUTTER-POACHING

These quantities serve 2 but you can scale it up
9 oz/250g carrots, peeled, trimmed, and cut into ½-inch/1cm coins
1 tablespoon unsalted butter

Place the carrots and butter in a smallish pot with a lid (I use my smallest Le Creuset) and add ¼ cup/60ml of water and 2 pinches of salt. When you are nearly ready to eat, put the pot over your highest heat, still with the lid on, and time it for 5 minutes. On lifting the lid, you will see that the butter and water have formed a silky emulsion and, because of the quick cooking time, the carrots retain their orange color and sweet flavor in their buttery bath.

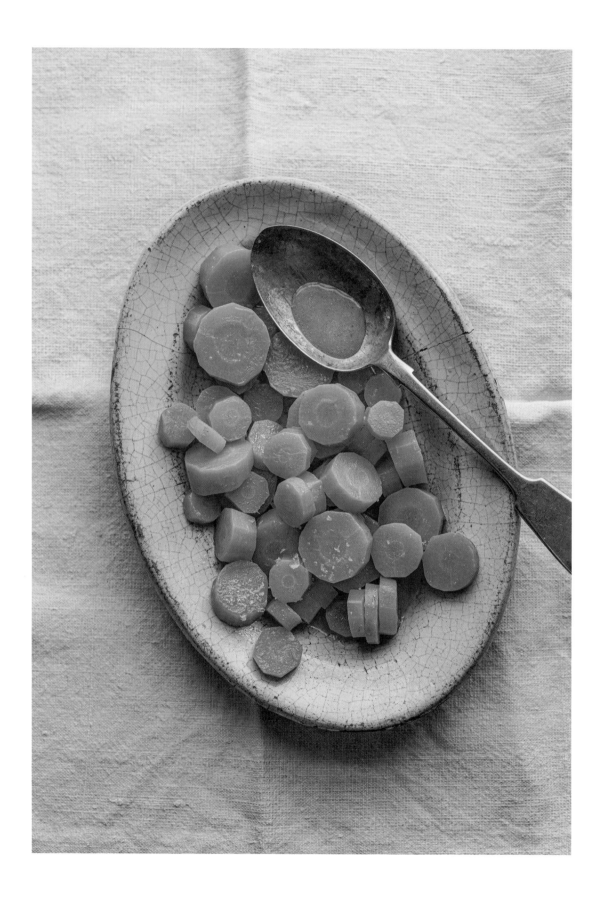

VARIATIONS

— Use 1 tablespoon of olive oil instead of the butter and add any herb you like at the end. Tarragon or basil would be nice. For once, I don't add lemon.

This technique will work with almost any vegetables you are serving as long as they are prepared and sliced fairly small (though it wouldn't be the ideal method for tough root vegetables). Raymond says that the cooking time varies from 30 seconds to 5 minutes. I experimented and these were:

7 oz/200g trimmed green beans—2–4 minutes depending on thickness
7 oz/200g bok choy, sliced—1 minute
7 oz/200g asparagus, cut into 1½-inch/4cm segments with the woody ends
    discarded –2 minutes for skinny asparagus and 4 minutes for thick asparagus

Carrot and panch pooran pickle

There are many ways to pickle a carrot and I seem to have tried most of them. But of all the ones I tried, my favorite was this simple Punjabi carrot dish, which is really more of a fresh relish than a true fermented pickle. It will keep nicely in the fridge for up to one week and seems to enhance everything, from scrambled eggs to curries to a grilled cheese sandwich. The recipe is adapted from Vicky Bhogal's book *Cooking Like Mummyji*. The panch pooran spice mix is readily available at South Asian grocery stores but if you can't find it, substitute ½ teaspoon each of cumin seeds, nigella seeds, fennel seeds, and mustard seeds, or any combination of these that you happen to have.

CUTTING TECHNIQUE: JULIENNE
COOKING TECHNIQUE: STIR-FRY

Serves 4
1 lb 2 oz/500g carrots
2½ tablespoons olive oil
2 teaspoons panch pooran spices
¼ teaspoon ground turmeric
2 teaspoons sugar
Juice of 1 lemon

Take your time peeling, trimming and cutting the carrots into the thinnest batons, "matchsticks," or julienne that you can manage. This is how I personally would do it, but you might have your own way: Halve each peeled carrot lengthwise. Then place the halved carrot flat side down on your chopping board and grasp your knife in your right hand, with your left hand holding the carrot. Rest the blade of the knife against your left forefinger and make fine cuts into the carrot. Then pick these slices up, stack two or three of them and again cut thinly lengthwise. Continue with all the carrots until you have a pile of fine strands. Technically, these are not a true French julienne cut, which would start by "blocking off" the rounded carrots into neat cuboids before making the cuts. This leaves you with much more satisfyingly uniform shapes but the downside is it also leaves a lot of offcuts (that you could use in soup or a stock). If you have a Japanese mandoline with a julienne attachment, you might want to use that instead.

Once you have cut the carrots, the pickle itself is a matter of moments. First, heat the oil over high heat in a large frying pan. Add the panch pooran, turmeric, sugar, and 1 teaspoon of flaky salt and stir, inhaling the fragrance from the spices as they hit the oil. Add the carrots and stir them fairly constantly for 3 minutes. Notice how quickly the rigid orange carrots soften and turn yellow. Turn off the heat, stir in the lemon juice, and let cool. Store in a covered bowl or jar in the fridge for up to 1 week. This deepens in flavor, tasting most delicious on the third day.

Gochujang carrots with fried green onions and silken tofu

This is proof that you can make a meal that tastes deep, fiery, and satisfying even when it seems you have little in the house but a bag of carrots. During lockdown, I would often make it for an ad hoc lunch for my daughter and me, to eat with noodles. Sometimes, she would take her bowl and sit in front of Zoom school and I would eat mine at the kitchen table, but we were still somehow connected by the food. The key ingredient here is gochujang, the divinely rich and savory Korean chile paste. My recipe is based on one in the *New York Times* by Eric Kim for Gochujang-Glazed Eggplant with Fried Scallions, which is one of the best eggplant dishes I've ever tasted. But I've now come to love it just as much with carrots, which take on a fudgy, toothsome texture when they are braised like this. To save time, I've streamlined Kim's process for frying the green onions. The whole dish is a cheap miracle.

The cooking technique here is braising, which means first frying something and then cooking it in liquid over low heat in an enclosed pot. If you can braise a carrot, you can in theory also braise beef short ribs in red wine or cubes of pork shoulder to make a Hungarian goulash. Unless you are vegetarian, in which case braising a carrot may be as far as you wish to go.

This recipe is also an introduction to the joy of roll cutting, which is one of the most underrated ways to prep a carrot for almost any dish involving roasting or braising. I swear, once you learn how to roll-cut a carrot you will never look back.

CUTTING TECHNIQUE: ROLL CUT

COOKING TECHNIQUE: BRAISING

Serves 2 with noodles or rice as a main course or 4 as a side dish

1 lb 2 oz/500g carrots, preferably large and organic

4 green onions

2 tablespoons neutral oil or olive oil

1 tablespoon soy sauce

2 teaspoons sugar

1 teaspoon sesame oil

2 cloves of garlic, peeled and grated

2 tablespoons gochujang (or 1 tablespoon Chinese chile bean paste or garlic chile paste mixed with 1 tablespoon miso)

9-10½ oz/200–300g silken tofu, to serve

Limes, to serve (optional)

Peel the carrots and trim the ends. To roll-cut a carrot, you make the first cut, but instead of cutting straight through it vertically to make a coin shape, you angle your knife at a 45-degree angle. Next, roll the carrot forward by a quarter turn (90 degrees) and make another cut at 45 degrees. Keep on rolling forward in quarter turns and cutting until you reach the end of the carrot. The beauty of this method is that you end up with carrot pieces that are pleasingly irregular in shape yet because they are roughly the same size, they will all cook in the same time.

Confession: here I am telling you how easy it is to roll-cut a carrot. But geometry was never my forte in math and the first time I read about this technique, it did my head in. I just couldn't visualize what 90 degrees meant. And so I invented my own eccentric way of roll cutting without the rolling, which I call zig-zag chopping. To do this, hold the peeled carrot lengthwise on the board and simply turn your knife at angles left then right as you cut, zig then zag, the whole length of the carrot. I find this a very satisfying process. A zig-zagged carrot would win no prizes at culinary school. No matter. The prize is that you get a pile of nicely angled carrot pieces in almost no time.

Trim the green onions and cut them into 3¼-inch/8cm pieces. Then cut each of the pieces lengthwise into thin strands (or as thin as you can muster).

Heat the oil in a large frying pan, add the green onions, and fry until crispy and brown in places—3–4 minutes. While this is happening—stir every 1 minute—get a small bowl and mix the soy sauce, sugar, sesame oil, garlic and gochujang with ¼ cup/60ml of water. This will become the braising sauce for the carrots.

Remove the green onions from the oil using a spider or tongs and set aside on a plate.

Now add the carrots to the same oil and cook over high heat until they are deep brown in places. Cover with a lid and continue to cook for 2 minutes or until nearly tender and brown all over. Add the sauce, clamp the lid back on, and lower the heat to cook for another 2–3 minutes. Remove the lid and continue to simmer until the sauce is reduced and evenly coating the carrots. If it seems to have dried out too much, add a splash of water. Serve with a big scoop of silken tofu per person, if you like (the bland whiteness of the cold tofu is good against the fiery red sauce), followed by the fried green onions and lime wedges on the side. We usually have this over rice noodles but it's also great with plain steamed white rice or as a side with something not too rich, such as white fish or poached chicken, in which case you might like to leave out the tofu.

Seared carrots

For years, pan-searing has been one of my default ways to cook almost any vegetable (it's especially good with Brussels sprouts). It's a cinch, and the process of tossing something in a burning-hot pan with oil will deepen and sweeten the flavor profile of any vegetable by creating the Maillard reaction. The effect is similar to roasting but without the wasted energy of switching on the oven for a single portion of vegetables.

CUTTING TECHNIQUE: COINS
COOKING TECHNIQUE: SEARING

Serves 4 as a side dish
1 lb 2 oz/500g carrots
2 tablespoons olive oil
Optional extras: toasted pine nuts or any nuts, basil, currants, thyme leaves,
    a splash of red wine vinegar

Peel the carrots and cut them into coins around ½-inch/1cm in diameter (but don't worry too much about being exact). Heat the oil in a large shallow pan until very hot, then add the carrots in one layer and a big pinch of salt. Cook them without moving for 1 minute, then flip and cook for 1 minute more. Cook over high heat for around 4 minutes in total, or until the carrots are charred in places and mostly tender but with a bit of crunch. Add another pinch of salt and serve, adding any of the optional extras. Sometimes I do this half and half with carrots and zucchini. Seared carrots are good as a starter with a ball of milky burrata or mozzarella cheese plus more olive oil, toasted pine nuts, basil, a few currants, and a splash of red wine vinegar. Or you could make it the basis of a hearty warm salad with any kind of canned beans plus fried pumpkin seeds.

VARIATIONS

—Seared-steamed carrots (or any vegetables). If your seared vegetables are slow to soften, add a couple of tablespoons of water, cover with a lid, and let them steam for 2 or 3 minutes, until tender. For extra punch, I add sliced garlic and chiles before the water and a splash of vinegar at the end. This is good with Broccolini.

Kerstin's carrots baked like potatoes

Though I have sliced and roasted carrots many times, I never thought to bake one like a potato until I read *Organic Carrot Cookbook* by Kerstin Rodgers. It is an inspired idea, as long as you have the large, thick organic carrots you get in the winter (it wouldn't work with the spindly spring carrots). There is something deeply reassuring about whole baked carrots, split down the middle and liberally filled with butter. They taste familiar and yet new at the same time and are a good thing to serve to a friend on a low-carb diet in lieu of potatoes. I particularly like these as an accompaniment to roasted pork but they are also good with chicken or just by themselves, showered with grated cheese and green chile. A revelation.

CUTTING TECHNIQUE: NONE
COOKING TECHNIQUE: BAKING

Serves 3–4 as a side dish
8 large organic carrots, the fattest you can find and ideally all roughly the same
   size
Unsalted butter

Preheat the oven to 425°F. Rinse the carrots under cold water and dry them in a clean kitchen towel. As Kerstin notes, this is important to help them form an approximation of a skin in the oven. Put them on a baking sheet and sprinkle with a little flaky salt. Bake for 30–40 minutes, or until the outsides are crispy and dark and the insides are soft and almost fluffy. Slit lengthwise down the middle and serve with butter and salt or anything else you might add to a baked potato, such as sour cream or chimichurri sauce.

Garlicky carrot mash

This is based on a celery root recipe from *Honey & Co: Food from the Middle East* by Sarit Packer and Itamar Srulovich, which is one of my all-time favorite cookbooks. You could eat it as a side dish or as a dip alongside other meze. It is also amazingly good if you combine the carrot half and half with celery root.

CUTTING TECHNIQUE: DICE
COOKING TECHNIQUE: PURÉE

Serves 3–4 as a side dish
1 lb 2 oz/500g carrots, peeled and diced
1 teaspoon rosemary needles, finely chopped
2 tablespoons olive oil
6 cloves of garlic, peeled
1 teaspoon butter
A squeeze of lemon or 1 teaspoon vinegar

Place the carrots, rosemary, oil, garlic, and ½ teaspoon of salt in a lidded saucepan with 7 tablespoons/100ml of water. Cook over high heat for 5 minutes, then put the lid on and continue to cook for 10 minutes or until the carrot is super-soft. Meanwhile, melt the butter in another pan and keep melting until it is nutty and brown. It's a tiny quantity of butter but it is here for the flavor. Add the butter to the carrot pan with an extra 7 tablespoons/100ml of water and the lemon or vinegar and blitz with an immersion blender. Check the seasoning. Keep it fairly chunky for a dip or smoother for a purée to have as a side dish. To make it extra-creamy, add a spoonful or two of full-fat yogurt, crème fraîche, or cream at the end. You could even thin this out and eat it as a soup. Without the salt, this would make a sublime baby food.

Roasted carrots with lemon and coriander

As a child in 1980s Britain, I remember eating carrots that were boiled to flavorless oblivion, carrots that were steamed (still flavorless but marginally less soggy), and, just occasionally, for a huge treat, carrots that were glazed by simmering in a pan with water, butter, and sugar. But back then no one in my family ever thought to put a carrot in the oven, even though our oven was in constant use for other things, from roasted meat and roasted potatoes to cakes, breads, and cookies.

Western cooks of forty years or more ago had everything they needed to make a gloriously sweet dish of roasted carrots—an oven, a baking sheet, some carrots, oil, and salt—yet they somehow never discovered the secret of doing so. I find this a reassuring thought. Who knows how many other delicious things remain to be discovered without stepping further than the threshold of our own kitchen?

If you are new to roasted vegetables and wondering what to roast first, you can't go wrong with a carrot. As Kristen Miglore has written, "roasted carrots seem like a perfect realization of everything a carrot should be: their blunt crunch softened, their sweetness concentrated, their smooth façade pleasantly crinkled." I especially love spiced roasted carrots. This recipe is based on one from Claudia Roden in her wonderful book *Med*. But you can also roast them plain or any which way you like. If they are spring carrots or Chantenay carrots, you don't even have to peel them.

CUTTING TECHNIQUE: QUARTERING
COOKING TECHNIQUE: ROASTING

Serves 4

2 lb 2 oz/1kg carrots, peeled and cut lengthwise into quarters if they are large or halved if they are small spring carrots; or you can use Chantenay carrots and leave them whole

1 teaspoon cumin seeds

1 teaspoon ground coriander

½ teaspoon ground cinnamon

A pinch of ground cardamom

3 tablespoons olive oil

Juice of ½ a lemon

1 tablespoon honey or maple syrup

To serve: a handful of chopped cilantro leaves, a handful of toasted sliced almonds, and the zest of the ½ lemon

Preheat the oven to 425°F. Put the carrots into a large roasting dish. Add the cumin, coriander, cinnamon, cardamom, oil, and lemon juice plus a few pinches of salt and toss everything together until the carrots are thoroughly coated with the spicy mixture. Bake in the oven for 30 minutes. Turn the carrots, add the maple syrup or honey, and bake for 15 minutes or until very tender. Let cool. Serve at room temperature with the cilantro, sliced almonds, lemon zest, and a little more oil. These are wonderful as part of a meal of meze, alongside the burned finger lentils on page 102 and the beet dip on page 270, for example.

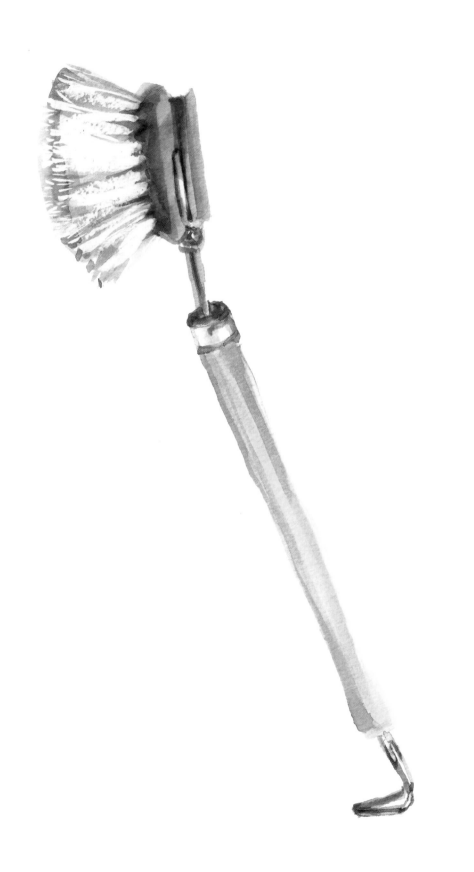

What no one tells you about cooking

"You need to learn what kind of cook you are
in order to be truly happy in the kitchen."
    Letitia Clark, *La Vita è Dolce*, 2021

When I was a child, I thought that cooking was all about making a mess: throwing things in a pan and stirring them up, like a potion. This was what I saw chefs doing on TV. They set fire to stuff and chopped ingredients incredibly fast and tossed whole pans of food with a casual flick of the wrist and sometimes got drunk while they were doing it. It looked like so much fun. It was disillusioning to grow up and discover that, when you are in charge of the whole shebang, a huge amount of cooking is really just tidying and most of the rest is vegetable prep. Cooking is half mess, half order. Before you can get to the fun bits, there are so many surfaces to clean, so many packages to put away, so many plates to scrub and stack. And even when you do get to do the creative hands-on activities, it doesn't work out quite like on TV. Try as you might, your hands won't chop as fast and when you set fire to food, all that usually happens is it tastes burned.

There are many important things that never seem to get mentioned about cooking, things that you have to figure out for yourself along the way. One of these is that when we do it at home, cooking is not the only reason a person walks into the kitchen. For many of us, the home kitchen is not just a room where we cook but a place where we wash and dry clothes, eat meals, listen to the radio, play card games, feed pets, have intense conversations with friends over strong coffee. Sometimes cooking has to wait its turn.

What matters most is whether you can make your own kitchen into a place where you feel at home. I don't mean that you need to do an expensive redesign with granite countertops and special steam ovens. What I'm talking about is arranging things the way you like them so that you actually want to spend time there. Some of the details in my kitchen might seem eccentric to another person. I store the filters for my Aeropress coffee-maker on top of a sugar bowl and for some reason, I use a second sugar bowl as a garlic holder. This may not make any sense but it works for me.

Does your kitchen smell and sound good to you? If in doubt about where to start with cooking, start with good smells. In *A Handbook of Cookery*, published in 1923, Jessie Conrad wrote that "The bane of life in a small house is the smell of cooking." She observes that in nine cases out of ten, bad smells result from careless cooking. This is a subject that most modern cookbooks are extraordinarily coy about—maybe because there's a mistaken belief that vent hoods take all the smells away—but good smells still make a huge difference, as anyone trying to sell a house understands. Freshly ground coffee; cinnamon waffles; toasted cumin seeds; a pile of chopped green herbs. Any of these can fill the kitchen with the uplifting scent of home. I keep pots of mint and basil next to my kitchen radio and sometimes tear a few leaves for no reason except to lift my mood. Before you can welcome anyone else into your kitchen, you need to know how to make yourself feel at ease.

Good sounds can also make a huge difference when you are cooking. I have started timing many elements of my cooking by songs rather than by the clock. It makes the time pass so much more easily. For simple kitchen tasks, I might play a short, snappy Beatles song, whereas for more laborious cooking, I use something like "As" by Stevie Wonder, which lasts for a full seven minutes (but doesn't feel like it). When I am not in the mood for cooking at all, I put on anything by Django Reinhardt and feel instantly cheerier. Having said this, some people prefer to cook with no music at all except for the sounds of the cooking itself: the gentle bubbling of soup in a pot, the hiss of onions as they fry, the rhythm of a knife chopping herbs. Try it both ways and see which you prefer.

Another thing you need to decide on before you start is whether you are a recipe follower or a recipe rebel. I recently met a man at a party who told me that whenever he cooks anything he follows it "to the inch." He feels scared to change a single element in a recipe. But his partner would get angry about this pedantry, he said, because she preferred to ignore many of the details in a recipe. She could not feel that she was fully in charge of the cooking unless she had put her own mark on a recipe. Neither approach is right or wrong. You just need to know which you are and choose your cookbooks accordingly, because if you are a "to the inch" kind of cook you may be distressed by recipes that deal in handfuls and pinches and drizzles. Maybe in time you will accept that there is no such thing as following a recipe to the inch because even the best recipe only takes you so far.

All recipes are incomplete

"Sometimes, I felt there was a lot missing."
Delia Smith on learning to cook from cookbooks

The biggest problem with recipes is not what they tell you but what they don't tell you.

No matter how good they are, all recipes have giant gaps in them: assumptions that are made and things that go unsaid. To make it even worse, the things that are not mentioned are often the very things that you most need to know. This isn't the fault of recipe writers (or not usually). It's a problem that is baked into the enterprise of recipe writing, which is an attempt to translate doing into writing and back into doing again. Words on the page can only ever be a very partial reflection of the deeply physical and sensory series of actions that go into cooking a meal.

Every recipe—even a great one—is like an instruction manual with half of the steps missing. I'm not talking about outright mistakes, though these are deeply annoying if you don't spot them in time, such as the fish recipe that tells you to chop an onion but never tells you what to do with it, so you are left with an annoying pile of raw onion sitting on your chopping board at the end; or the curry that blows your head off because the recipe asked you to add one tablespoon of dried chile when it meant half a teaspoon.

But even when a recipe is free from errors, it will still contain moments of bafflement and confusion where you ask yourself, "What on earth do they mean by that?" There is no solution to this problem because what is self-evident to one cook is mystifying to another. In a cookbook, the reader and the writer are always speaking two slightly different languages. They are the languages of before and after or unknowing and knowing. The recipe writer can never fully re-create the state of confusion they were in before they knew how to cook something, because now their confusion is gone. They may not have noticed that what they are saying is gobbledygook to the uninitiated. The novelist Julian Barnes has described being flummoxed by a recipe that asked him to "melt the tomatoes," which made no sense to him because tomatoes simply don't melt. What the author meant was to cook them gently in fat until they were melting in texture. But never having melted a tomato, Barnes could not be sure.

All recipes make assumptions, large and small. Some recipes assume you are rich, either in money or time. Most of them assume you are able-bodied. And many of them, strangest of all, assume you don't really need a recipe. One of the biggest traps for a recipe writer is the idea that there are certain recipes that everyone already knows and that therefore need no explaining. "Do not think for a moment that I would be so pretentious as to tell you how to make meatballs. This is a dish that everyone knows how to make, beginning with the jackass," wrote the Italian Pellegrino Artusi in his best-selling *Science in the Kitchen and the Art of Eating Well* (1891). Well, call me a jackass, because I didn't have a clue how to make meatballs until I first learned how to do it following a Marcella Hazan recipe and even then it took me a few attempts to get it right.

The problem with recipes is that nothing about cooking is obvious until you have done it at least once. The writer John Lanchester (who as well as being a novelist was for a time the restaurant reviewer for the *Observer*) told me over the phone one morning in June that he realized some time ago that "recipes all have this point where they break down." It is Lanchester's theory that all recipes contain at least one "aporia," meaning a logical impasse (the word *aporia* comes from the Greek for difficulty and perplexity). Lanchester made this realization the first time he came across the word *fold* in a recipe. "I just very straightforwardly didn't know what it meant," he told me. To fold—as he subsequently learned—means to stir something by cutting down vertically into it with a large metal spoon or spatula. The motion has been described as "down-across-up-and-over," which is easier to do than it is to say. Folding is quite different from the usual circular agitating motion that most of us do with wooden spoons in a pan. Its purpose is to combine an airy mixture such as a soufflé without losing too much of the air. Lanchester knows all this now and therefore the word *fold* holds no fear. But when he first saw the word, it made him freeze and he realized that all recipes have moments a bit like that because the writer "can't know what you know and what you don't know."

Fold is far from the only bewildering word in recipes. Depending on your point of view, other problem words include blanch, baste, brown, simmer, whiz, deglaze, refresh, scald, julienne, truss, and parboil. "I won't cook any recipe that asks me to reduce stuff," said my friend Sophie one day when we were walking our dogs one late summer afternoon. She then went on to describe a particularly good puttanesca pasta sauce she had made the previous night for her family involving canned tomatoes and garlic and anchovies and capers and olives, which all bubbled away to form a delicious concentrated sauce. "But what you were doing was reducing it," I said. "Yes, but I don't call it that," Sophie replied.

"A recipe is only ever scaffolding, not the building," Lanchester told me.

"A recipe can show you what the structure is but the inside of it is partly dependent on knowledge that you get from elsewhere." I think that what he meant was that the most important thing you need to cook from a recipe is not the recipe itself but all the other experience about food that you have accumulated along the way. There are dozens of things that recipes don't tell us, which will trip us up if we don't already know about them.

The greatest recipe writers are the ones who try to catch us before we fall, by allowing for our moments of bafflement in advance. The writers I trust the most are the ones who highlight little areas of doubt or jeopardy: who kindly warn me not to freak out when a vast bag of spinach cooks down to almost nothing or who tell me I might need two spatulas instead of one to lift a fragile piece of fish from a pan. But no recipe writer can possibly anticipate every question you might have, or if they did, the recipe would become so long and wordy as to be unusable.

We do ourselves no favors when we talk about foolproof recipes (let alone best or ultimate or perfect recipes). If you find a recipe difficult to use, even a supposedly easy one, it doesn't mean that you are a fool. It means that you have a different set of experiences in the kitchen from the person who wrote it. I have learned this many times over while writing this book. Quite a few times, I would ask my eighteen-year-old daughter, Tash, to test one of the recipes in the book for me and it would bring home how difficult it is for a reader to second-guess what the writer actually wants—and vice versa—even when they are living and eating together. When I used ambiguous phrases such as "a little oil" I would find that Tash's idea of little was much smaller than mine. I realized that sometimes I had written "a little oil" in a recipe in a slightly dishonest way to disguise the true amount of oil that I was sloshing in a pan. Tash also found it hard to interpret terminology such as "brown" or "golden brown" or "translucent." "This tastes great but why didn't you brown the cauliflower?" I asked when she tested the red cauliflower and shrimp curry on page 250. "But I did," she said. She is studying art and is more alert to subtle changes in color than I am. Her idea of browning cauliflower florets was cooking them until they took on the faintest beige hue but were still crunchy. My idea of browning a cauliflower is getting it a dark chestnutty brown all over, the kind of browning that also suggests a change in flavor and texture to sweeter and softer. I've adjusted the recipes in this book with Tash in mind but I know that won't mean—can't mean—that it will cover all the questions you might wish a recipe to answer. Please accept my apologies in advance and know that my intention was never to annoy you.

"I don't talk about recipes, I talk about systems," said Kimberley Bell, an extraordinary baker (and the founder of Small Food Bakery in Nottingham) when I took her sourdough workshop one day. The point Bell was making was that every

THE SECRET OF COOKING

tiny variable in baking affects every other variable. Change one thing and you change everything. If it's a hot day, then the dough will take less time to rise than the recipe says. If you change the flour that you use, then you also need to change the way that you knead it. What matters in each case is knowing what you are looking for and adjusting accordingly, no matter what the recipe says. Bell has made so many

60

thousands of loaves that she can read the dough just by feeling it with her fingers.

Much unnecessary anxiety in the kitchen is caused by the idea that recipes can teach us to cook. Recipes can *help* us to cook, for sure. If you take a good methodical recipe and follow it as faithfully as you can a few times, you will learn a huge amount about ingredients, and how they respond to heat. But the real teacher will always be your own experience because cooking doesn't happen on the page but in the kitchen. The more you cook, the better you will get at filling in the gaps.

To give an example, there are two vital objects that you need almost every time you cook a meal and yet they are virtually never mentioned by recipe writers. The first thing is a trivet (or trivets) and the second is a discard bowl. Without them, the whole business of cooking is so much trickier than it needs to be. Yet these objects are surrounded by a conspiracy of silence in cookbooks. The good news is that you will already have versions of them in your kitchen even if you are not yet using them.

What's a trivet? It's a utensil that is placed between a hot pan and a surface such as a table or a countertop to prevent heat damage. Old-fashioned trivets are made from fancy wrought cast iron and stand on three little legs. But you don't need to get this kind if you don't want to. Another way to go is a thick cork pot stand: like a giant drink coaster in a range of shapes from round to square to fish-shaped. My own current trivets are made in Denmark from silicone formed in a hexagonal pattern. But if you don't have any of these, you can still make a perfectly functional trivet for most purposes from a folded thick kitchen towel. Or you can rest hot pans on a switched-off stovetop if you are not using it for anything else (this is what I do with a pan that is searingly hot). The point is simply to find something—anything—that will help you to take a hot pan of food off the heat without ending up with scorched counters (I speak from experience).

I learned my lesson on trivets early in my cooking life in my twenties. I was in the first kitchen I ever cooked in that wasn't either my family home or a student kitchen and I had decided to make tempura vegetables, my first adventure in deep-frying. The tempura came out beautifully crisp and golden but then there was the question of what to do with the pot of boiling-hot oil. I put it straight down on the white Formica countertop, figuring that it was a tough-looking surface. It made a horrible singeing smell and left a deep brown ring that no amount of scrubbing could remove. Afterward, I felt so stupid. A childhood of reading cookbooks had not prepared me for this. I did not know the word *trivet* but went out and bought one the very next day.

Another thing I had to learn on my own through trial and lots of error was the need for a discard bowl for the vegetable peelings and preferably a few other bowls for the prepped vegetables. There doesn't need to be anything remotely special about these bowls. They could be small mixing bowls. I use shallow soup bowls. The point is just that you need a system for keeping the unwanted peelings away from the neatly prepped ingredients, otherwise you will have a sense of mild chaos that haunts you each time you cook. Without a discard bowl, your chopping board will never feel orderly. When I am cooking a big, elaborate meal, I might get through several discard bowls' worth of trimmings. Each time it fills up, I empty it into the compost bin. But for a simple family meal, a single bowl is usually enough. These bowls are part of the essential choreography of cooking. Get your apron on (if you use one), wash your hands, get out a chopping board and find a discard bowl. Then you are ready to cook. When I mentioned discard bowls to John Lanchester he agreed that they are a "game-changer" but that he was fifty before he started to use one, because no recipe writer had ever mentioned that he would need it.

Why do cookbooks not divulge these secrets? It isn't because their authors are trying to make your life difficult. It's partly that they don't want to waste your time or patronize you. If every recipe started by telling you to get your trivet and discard bowl ready, it could get lengthy and tedious. The other reason for the silence is because these things are considered so obvious as not to be worth mentioning.

To take another example of a thing that is not mentioned, most recipes for pasta tell you to "drain the pasta" and do not say how. The assumption is that you will drain the pasta in a colander in the sink. This is a deeply flawed way to go about it. For one thing, if you are clumsy like me the journey to the sink carrying the hot heavy pan with oven mitts on is fraught with danger. For another thing, when you drain the pasta in a colander, you lose all the starchy pasta water, which is a crucial last-minute addition to the sauce to make it smooth and lovely. Most recipes compensate for this by asking you to drain off a cup or so of the pasta water to save and add at the end. But there is another simpler and better way, which would save you all the bother. Instead of using a colander, you could simply lift the cooked pasta from the water into the pan of sauce in batches using a spider. It's far easier, and the other good thing is that some of the pasta water clings onto the pasta, so you get just the right amount of water in the sauce without really trying. When I am cooking long pasta such as spaghetti or tagliatelle, I do the same thing but using long tongs instead of a spider because the long strands can get slippery.

A spider is the most brilliant and essential utensil and yet hardly anyone seems to know about it, except for cooks from China and Korea and other Asian countries—which is yet another sign that much of the home cooking of Asia is more evolved than that of the West. A spider—sometimes referred to as a skimmer—is like a small sieve attached to a long handle. It is generally seen as a retrieval device for

deep-fried foods, but it works every bit as well for retrieving foods from hot water. I am constantly using mine to scoop up vegetables or boiled eggs. The strange thing is that they are usually nowhere to be seen in those 5-piece utensil sets you see in kitchenware stores. These tend to include a slotted spoon, which is like a spider only much, much more ineffective. But you can pick one up for a song from a Chinese grocery store and I strongly urge you to do so. I have two spiders. One

is Italian with a fairly fine wire mesh and one is Chinese with a coarser sieve. I love them both.

The good thing is that once you have a spider and a trivet and a discard bowl, you are ready for almost anything in the kitchen. These are your secret weapons, which will help make you feel more equipped for any recipe. They are the first step to kicking away the scaffolding and starting to cook for real.

There is always another way of doing something

"Try new things . . . Since you're not going to be able to make dishes taste the way they do in the restaurant, make them taste right for you."
  Daniel Patterson, *Coi*

One of the many stumbling blocks to cooking is the sense that there is a single proper way of doing things that you must follow—or else. But the truth of the matter is that there is always another way of preparing something in the kitchen. You should find the one that works for you and gives you the most pleasure as you go without worrying too much about correctness or authenticity.

If one form of cooking freaks you out, simply find another way. If using knives to chop a red pepper makes you shudder, use scissors instead. If handling raw meat makes you worry about bacteria, cook vegetarian meals (which is probably something we should all be doing a lot more of anyway). If intense heat alarms you, focus your cooking around learning how to compose delicious salads. If you fear pressure cookers, you never have to use one (though be assured that the new electric ones are not at all fearsome). None of these things makes you a terrible cook. It just makes you human. There is always another way of doing things that you might find more enjoyable. There are enough things to be scared of in this world without making the kitchen one of them.

Sometimes we trap ourselves in certain dogmas in the kitchen only to find that another way works just as well or better and is easier. For years, every recipe involving dried beans would warn of dire consequences if you added the salt too soon. Recipe writers cautioned that the beans would harden and they would never cook properly! It turns out this is total nonsense. Adding salt to the water doesn't harden the beans as they cook; it only makes them tastier. By the same token, yeasted bread dough doesn't have to be kneaded, which is one of the most extraordinary discoveries of modern baking.

Another unquestioned mantra is the phrase "preheat the oven," which appears at the start of almost every recipe. Often, the instruction is added far too early, the result being that an empty oven is left blasting out heat while you are occupied with doing vegetable prep. It's an understandable convention. Most readers want to know how hot the oven will be before they start a recipe, so the writer decides to get the information out of the way early on, but this doesn't mean that you need to do it immediately. I find that it's a good idea to make a note of how long it takes your particular oven to reach standard temperatures and factor this in when following recipes. I also discovered to my amazement that more often than not, an oven doesn't need to be preheated at all. Roasted chicken and pound cake are actually better when you start them in a cold oven; recipes for both are given below. Most kinds of roasted vegetables also work fine from a cold start (though not classic roasted potatoes, which need to go into a pan of sizzling-hot oil).

The best way to cook anything is the one that works best for you and your life right now. When my children were younger and tugging at my ankles to make me sit on the floor and play, I was a big fan of putting things in the oven where they were safely out of the way and no one could get burned. But now that they are older, I am returning to cooking things on the stove much of the time, which is not only more energy-efficient but gives me the pleasure of some meditative stirring and good cooking smells at the end of a long day.

Sometimes the best way to cook something is not to cook it at all. Don't apply heat to what is better served raw. There is nothing you can do to a perfectly ripe peach or fig or to a pod of young crunchy peas that will improve it, so you may as well spare yourself the trouble.

Perhaps the strongest reason to experiment with different ways of cooking is that you might discover new ways of cooking favorite ingredients that please you more. It's easy to get in the groove of cooking something in a particular way, maybe to please your partner or other family members, without ever considering whether it is the way that you like best. A friend from Romania says that when her father died, her mother finally felt free to cook polenta the way she actually enjoyed it, without the potatoes that her husband always insisted on.

It can take trial and error to find the approach to cooking something that will excite you the most, both in the eating and the cooking. Asparagus is my favorite vegetable—I think of it as one of the great luxuries of spring and summer—but for years, I felt it would be almost taboo to cook it in any way except boiled. I was not alone in being so unimaginative about asparagus. There are nineteen asparagus recipes in *Haute Cuisine* by Jean Conil, first published in 1953, and except for one recipe for green asparagus soufflé, they all consist of boiling it and serving it hot or cold with a sauce.

The recipe that changed how I think about asparagus was River Café penne with asparagus carbonara, which I first read about in the year 2000. This was a carbonara, but with spears of asparagus cut on the diagonal in place of the pancetta. The thing that startled me was the wondrous economy of the method. While the pasta boiled until al dente for nine minutes, you cooked the asparagus in a separate pan. The stalks were added first, then, after two minutes, the tips, which cooked for four minutes. The blanched asparagus was tossed with pasta, yolks, parmesan, butter and thyme to make a richly springlike dish: green and golden. The first time I made it, I couldn't believe that the asparagus had come out so perfectly with so little effort. I never used my asparagus boiler again, realizing that I could boil the spears unbundled in a big pan for 5 minutes, with none of the fuss and better results.

And then I realized—finally!—that asparagus didn't have to be boiled, after all. It was Yotam Ottolenghi who convinced me that broiled or grilled asparagus could make a welcome change from plain-boiled. Freshly harvested asparagus contains a lot of natural sugar, and charring it accentuates both its sweetness and its umami flavors. Ottolenghi's first cookbook contained a recipe for grilled asparagus, zucchini, and halloumi cheese salad. The asparagus was blanched before it was charred with thin slices of zucchini and anointed with garlicky basil oil. The firm bright spears took on a savory depth that was a revelation. I have since discovered that I like charred asparagus even more if it is sliced up, tossed with salt and oil, and browned for 5–10 minutes under a very hot broiler, with lemon zest added at the end.

The best way to cook asparagus, I am now convinced, is neither boiled nor grilled but butter-braised (braising being a French term that originally meant cooking in an enclosed pot with a charcoal fire above and below). By braising, I mean browning the asparagus in a single layer in a large frying pan before cooking with butter and a splash of water or stock until the liquid emulsifies to a glossy sauce, which takes less than 10 minutes. Braised asparagus offers both the browned intensity of charred asparagus and the delicacy of boiled. My introduction to braised asparagus was J. Kenji López-Alt's excellent recipe on the Serious Eats website. As López-Alt writes, during its brief season, we should embrace asparagus "in all its forms from raw and crunchy to braised, olive-green and totally tender." If you don't try things a different way once in a while, you will never know what you are missing.

Butter-braised asparagus

Serves 4 as a side dish, or 2 if you want to turn it into a meal with a couple of poached eggs each
1 tablespoon olive oil
1 lb/450g asparagus, trimmed
1½ tablespoons unsalted butter
A small squeeze of lemon

Heat the oil over high heat in a shallow pan large enough to fit all the asparagus in one layer. Add the asparagus, season with salt, and cook until browned on the bottom and starting to smell sweet (a couple of minutes). Turn it and cook for another couple of minutes. Add 1 cup/240ml of water and the butter to the pan, then cover it and cook until the asparagus is completely tender. Check after 5 minutes, but it might take up to 10 minutes depending on the thickness of the asparagus. You are not aiming for grass-green crunch but sage-green softness. The water and butter should have reduced and thickened to a shiny sauce. If it has all bubbled away, add a splash of water. If it isn't thick enough, transfer the asparagus to a serving plate and bubble it by itself for another 1 minute before pouring over the asparagus. Either way, check for seasoning and add a tiny squeeze of lemon.

No-knead herb garden focaccia

This bread recipe goes against everything my mother ever told me about dough. But to try it is to believe it.

If you have heard of no-knead bread, it is probably because of Jim Lahey's superb recipe that appeared in the *New York Times* in 2006 (in an article by Mark Bittman) and quickly became one of the great cult recipes of the internet age. Lahey started selling no-knead bread from his Sullivan Street Bakery in 1994. But great minds think alike, and the idea of no-knead bread was not unique to Lahey as he has acknowledged, telling the Eater website that his no-knead method was similar to bread-making techniques dating back thousands of years.

A year before the Sullivan Street Bakery opened, in 1993, a baker named Suzanne Dunaway was already selling her own no-knead focaccia at a market stall in Los Angeles, which later became a bakery called Buona Forchetta. Dunaway first discovered that she could break the rules of bread-making when she accidentally left a batch of focaccia dough longer than planned because she got distracted gardening. When she came back, having missed the moment when she should have knocked the dough down and kneaded it, she found that it had already begun fermenting "with me or without me" and was already beautifully light and risen. "It dawned on me that if I did not knock it around too much, if I gently poured it out on to a baking sheet, the wonderful lightness of the texture might be preserved and it would need no second rise."

It was Dunaway's recipe that first converted me to the astonishing ease of no-knead bread. I have many friends who believe they have no aptitude for bread-making, but trust me when I say that if you can stir flour and water with a spoon, you can make this. It partly works because the mixture is very wet, which helps it to rise itself without kneading. It needs a few hours at room temperature for the flavor to develop—you can do it overnight or over the course of half a day—but once you get into the swing of it, this is less trouble than you think it will be.

I've tweaked the original formula quite a bit by changing the ratio of flour to water and adding more oil and some honey, to help the rise. In summer, I also like to cover the unbaked focaccia with a garden of herbs and edible petals—this is a lovely project to do with a child. But most of the time, I just bake it plain with or without a sprinkling of flaky sea salt. This loaf is as good toasted with marmalade for breakfast as it is in a basket on the table with dinner.

The only potential downside of no-knead bread, as Dunaway notes, is that if you are someone who likes to punch dough as a way of taking out your aggression this won't do it for you. She advises kick-boxing instead.

For 1 large focaccia
4 cups/500g white bread flour (or swap half of the strng white flour for more nutritious flours such as spelt or rye or whole wheat)
1 x ¼-oz/7g (1 envelope) instant dried yeast
1 tablespoon honey (or agave syrup, for vegans)
4 tablespoons/60ml olive oil

For the herb garden topping
Flaky salt or 1 tablespoon of caper brine or olive brine, plus a mix of any leaves and edible petals that you can grow or forage, such as sage, marjoram, rosemary, marigolds, rose petals, pansies, fig leaves

Measure the flour into your biggest mixing bowl. Using a big wooden spoon or spatula, stir in 2–3 teaspoons/10–15g salt, the yeast, honey, and 1⅔ cups/400ml lukewarm water. Stir well until it comes together and there are no unmixed bits. Add up to 2½ tablespoons/40ml more water and keep stirring until you have a wet, shaggy dough. Cover with a plate and let rise at room temperature for at least 4 hours or up to 8. It should be very bubbly and will have doubled or tripled in volume (hence the need for your biggest bowl). Take a big heavy pan—I use a 12-inch/30cm iron pan but if you don't have something similar, it will also work fine on a lined baking sheet. Line it with parchment paper if it's a pan that sticks. Pour 2 tablespoons of the olive oil into the bottom of the pan or sheet and gently pour in the bubbly dough. Using your fingers, make deep holes in the dough, like craters on the moon. Spread the final 2 tablespoons of oil over the top. Let rise at room temperature for another 2 hours or so until it is even more risen and bubbly. When you are nearly ready to bake, preheat the oven to 450°F. Decorate the focaccia with a range of leaves and petals (bear in mind that they shrink in the oven so use more than you think you need) and sprinkle with a little flaky salt or drizzle 1 tablespoon of brine from a jar of capers, which adds a delicious tang. Bake for 20–30 minutes, or until the color of autumn leaves. Cool on a wire rack.

This focaccia makes the most amazing sandwiches. My favorite consists of slices of eggplant (sliced lengthwise), roasted in the oven for 20 minutes or a bit longer with oil and balsamic vinegar (put them into the oven at the same time as the bread to save on oven heat), plus a generous handful of arugula and/or basil and cool milky slices of fresh mozzarella cheese and some olives or capers.

Slow-start roasted chicken

I have roasted a chicken many different ways in my life and none were bad, but this is my current favorite. It is buttery and tender. When I started writing this book, I was going to urge you to roast chicken by Barbara Kafka's brilliantly simply high heat and no baste method (for a 3⅓-pound/1.5kg chicken, you give it 40 minutes at 500°F, having first sprinkled it with salt and stuffed it with a lemon cut in half). But then I started reading up on how high-temperature roasting is one of the most energy-hungry ways to cook. Meanwhile, I picked up *The Complete Robuchon* by French chef Joël Robuchon and saw that he recommends starting roasted chicken in a cold oven to make it more tender. It works. In this recipe, the chicken gets flipped three times in the oven, which (to me) makes it noticeably more succulent, but feel free to ignore that part if you consider it an annoyance.

Serves 4
1 free-range chicken, preferably organic, about 3⅓ lb/1.5kg
3 tablespoons butter, melted
2 or 3 sprigs of marjoram or thyme
A few cloves of garlic

In an ideal world—the kind where you rise each morning at five to write your novel—you will have salted the chicken the day before you cook it. Sprinkle it lightly but evenly all over with salt, cover it loosely, and keep it in the fridge. When you are ready to cook it, put the chicken in a roasting dish and coat it with the butter. (If you didn't salt it the day before, salt it now). Stuff the cavity with the herbs and garlic. Turn it on its side and put it into the oven. Set the heat to 400°F and set the timer for 25 minutes. Take it out, turn it onto its other side (I used tongs or a large fork, but be careful not to pierce the skin if you can avoid it), and baste the chicken with the fat before pouring 3 tablespoons of water into the dish. Return it to the oven for another 25 minutes. Again baste with the fat and add a little more water to the dish. Turn it breast up, and return it to the oven for a final 15 minutes or until it is bronzed and crisp. Check the thickest point of one of the thigh joints with a skewer to make sure that the juices run clear with no blood. Rest on a board for 20 minutes or so.

To make a very simple thin gravy, spoon off most of the butter, which will have combined deliciously with the chicken fat (save it to cook vegetables, such as the braised asparagus on page 70). Add ¾ cup plus 2 tablespoons/200ml of water (or a small glass of Marsala) and set the roasting dish on the stovetop to bubble, stirring occasionally with a wooden spoon to scrape up the meaty bits until it reduces down.

In summer, I might eat the chicken with a pot of plain bulgur wheat or quinoa (one cup of bulgur or quinoa to one and a half cups of water, season generously with salt, add a bay leaf and oil, bring to a simmer and cook with the lid on for 12 minutes before letting rest off the heat for 10 minutes) in winter, with butter-poached carrots plus a bowl of garlicky yogurt (see page 96). Or for a heartier dinner, after the chicken has gone in the oven, I prep a baking sheet of vegetables to roast (such as a whole Savoy cabbage, cut up and drizzled with oil) and another of peeled potatoes (quartered if large) with oil, salt, and rosemary, and perhaps a couple of peeled, sliced onions. As soon as the sheets are prepped, put them in the oven. The potatoes should be ready when the chicken is; the vegetables might need to come out a bit sooner.

Lime and spice pound cake

I used to think it was a law of nature that you had to preheat the oven before putting a cake in. But it turns out that pound cake, with its dense, pebbly texture, actually works better from a cold start because you don't want it to rise too dramatically. It took me a long time to find a pound cake I really loved, but this is it. The technique was inspired by an orange cake in *The Modern Pantry* by Anna Hansen and the flavor was inspired by Niki Segnit writing (in *The Flavor Thesaurus*) that lime and cinnamon are two of the cornerstone flavors of Coca-Cola. The crumb has the warmth of nutmeg and the bright hit of lime, and then it has a sugary crust, like a lemon drizzle cake, which makes you wince with sharp pleasure from the lime juice, a hit of acid that disguises just how sweet this cake is. It looks plain but it isn't, and it keeps very well for a few days.

Serves 8–10
1 cup plus 2 tablespoons/250g unsalted butter, softened, plus more for the pan
1¼ cups/250g granulated sugar
3 large eggs
3 tablespoons whole milk or yogurt (full fat or Greek)
1 teaspoon ground ginger
2 teaspoons ground cinnamon
Grated nutmeg: about 20 strokes on a grater or ¼ teaspoon
¼ teaspoon ground cloves
2 limes, preferably unwaxed
1½ cups/200g all-purpose flour (or white spelt flour)
1½ teaspoons baking powder

For the topping
2 limes (preferably unwaxed)
½ cup/100g sugar

This works just as well made in a homely 9 × 5-inch/900g loaf pan or in a bundt, if you have one. Butter or oil the pan and then line with parchment paper (no need to line if using a bundt).

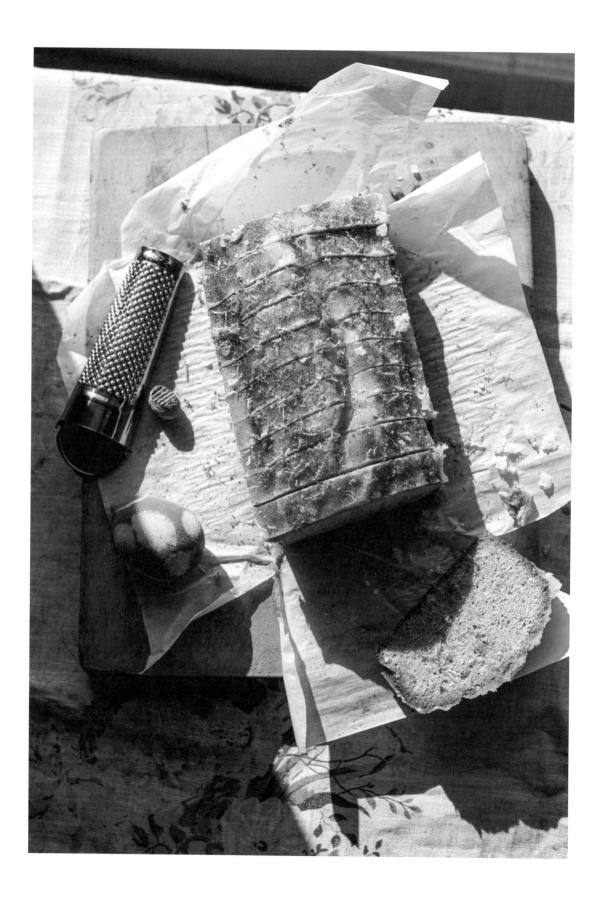

In a mixing bowl, using electric beaters (or in a stand mixer if you have one), combine the butter and sugar until they are whippy and light. Whisk in the eggs, one by one, followed by the milk or yogurt, all the spices, and the zest of the 2 limes.

In another bowl, whisk together the flour and baking powder, then fold this into the mixture gently but thoroughly, using a large metal spoon or a silicone spatula. Spoon into the prepared loaf pan or bundt. Put into the oven, turn the heat to 350°F, and bake for 1 hour or until a skewer inserted into the deepest part comes out clean. Check after 45 minutes. It will take a little longer in a loaf pan compared to a bundt (so much also depends on the oven).

While the cake is in the oven, zest and juice the limes for the topping. You want about ¼ cup/60ml of lime juice. If the limes are not very juicy ones (they vary so much), add the juice of one of the limes you zested for the cake mixture. Mix this zest and juice with the ½ cup/100g of sugar.

When the cake is out of the oven, let it cool in its pan for 5 minutes. Then jab it all over with a skewer to help the syrup sink in and spoon the sugar-lime mixture all over it. Allow it to continue to cool. This keeps well for a few days in an airtight container at room temperature and is as good with a cup of tea in the afternoon as it is for dessert after dinner with clouds of whipped cream.

Cooking is mostly about washing dishes

"A life, the major part of which is spent in sweeping,
that the dust may re-settle; in washing, that clothes
may be again worn and soiled; in cooking, that the
food prepared may be consumed; in cleansing plates
and dishes, to put back upon the table that they
may return, in grease and stickiness, to the
hardly-dried pan and towel."
    Marion Harland, *Breakfast, Luncheon and Tea*, 1886

For years, I used to say that I loved cooking and hated washing dishes. Now, I think this was crazy talk. Washing dishes—and more generally, keeping the kitchen clean enough that you feel good about being there—is a fundamental part of cooking. If you want to enjoy cooking more, you also need to find ways to help yourself enjoy washing up, or at least not to hate it quite so much. Washing up is the finale of every meal and the precursor of the next. It's how we restore calm to the kitchen after the necessary mess and heat of cooking. To argue against washing up is like arguing with the moon and the sun.

One of my friends and heroes when I was in my twenties was a man named Alan Davidson, the author of the greatest food reference book ever written (*The Oxford Companion to Food*). Alan was kind to young people and took me under his wing. He lived in Chelsea with his wife, Jane, in a house stuffed to the rafters with books. Sometimes I went to lunch there and I would marvel at Alan's deep knowledge of food but also his eccentricities. Alan—who first developed a passion for food when he was a diplomat posted to Laos, where he enjoyed exploring the local fish markets—was fond of wearing Hawaiian shirts and watching screwball comedies of the 1930s (he adored the beautiful female film stars of that era such as Carole Lombard and Barbara Stanwyck). He liked eating marmalade on toast, fish soup, and trifle. He didn't touch a drop of alcohol and claimed he loved washing the dishes. At the time, I thought that he was joking about this—he had an impish sense of humor and you couldn't always tell whether he was being serious—but in the years since he died (in 2003), I have come to realize that he really meant it, and that he was right.

When we put on our rubber gloves, it's easy to see ourselves as drudges and start feeling martyrish. Alan Davidson thought this was a huge mistake. He wrote an essay in *The Oxford Companion to Food* about how the person who cleaned the dishes at the end of the meal was in a position of "privilege" and "honor" because they alone were the ones who could bring the meal to a close.

I will probably never love washing up as deeply as Alan Davidson did. But I have learned not to be as annoyed by it as I once was and even to find it soothing. My ex-husband was the one who did most of the washing up—something I appreciated. During the first shaky weeks after he left, it felt like an affront that I was suddenly the one who needed to empty the dishwasher every morning and scrape the food debris from every cooking pot in the evenings, especially in my grief-stricken state. But then I realized that if the job was all mine, I might as well do it in a way that didn't make me feel resentful or helpless. I started getting up earlier and found a mild sense of accomplishment in spending ten minutes emptying the dishwasher and clearing the drying rack with a cup of tea and the radio before anyone else had woken up. In the evenings, I roped my children in to help and we made washing the dishes at the end of dinner into a kind of game, dividing up the washing and the drying and taking it in turns to pick songs on my phone and dance around the kitchen as we cleaned. Before we knew it, our tolerance for washing up increased, and so did our standards. My younger son discovered a hitherto unimagined yen for rubbing stainless-steel pots with steel wool.

The secret of washing up—as with cooking in general—is to find a method that works for you, regardless of whether it works for anyone else. If you have the space and the money, I would implore you to get a dishwasher. Apart from being the most energy-saving way to wash dishes—assuming you fill it up and put it on the eco setting—it also saves hugely on human energy. A dishwasher will not only get your glasses sparkling but keep them out of your sight and mind when they are less than sparkling. I think of it as a storage device for dirty dishes as much as a device for washing plates and bowls and spoons. The older I get, the harder I find it to relax in a kitchen piled high with unwashed crockery.

Whether you have a dishwasher or not, you can never escape a certain amount of washing by hand. The question of how to wash dishes is divisive because everyone believes their own method to be the most logical. Some rinse the dishes, then scrub them in hot soapy water, then rinse them again. Some simply scrub them with a soapy sponge in an empty bowl and then dunk them in a bowl of plain water to rinse before drying. Some have a beloved system in which they work methodically from the smallest dishes to the largest and some have an equally perfect system in which they work from largest to smallest. Some believe that pre-soaking is essential to soften the worst of the debris and others believe that the person who suggests soaking the dishes overnight is just trying to avoid the job of washing up.

The single best way to do less washing up is to get fewer pans dirty. This is one reason—but far from the only one—that one-pot dishes are so appealing. Try to notice when recipes tell you to use an unnecessary number of pans and bowls—and ignore them.

Do you use a sponge or a brush to clean dishes? Lately, I've started using both, with steel wool for backup. I am a brush person by inclination and still have a sense that a sponge scourer is something you use to wipe down counters rather than wash dishes, but when my sister visits, she looks at me oddly for using a dish brush. I think a sponge is better for knives and forks and for pans but I prefer the brush for dishes. I like the gentleness of the bristles and the fact that the handle keeps my hand at a slight distance from the grubby plates but my sister—rightly—points out that it is a feeble tool for cleaning baking sheets that are deeply encrusted with food. To which I reply: "that's what steel wool is for."

Washing up aside, there is also far more cleaning to do in the midst of cooking than most cookbooks ever acknowledge. One of the ways in which most restaurant kitchens have an advantage over home kitchens is that they have a clearly worked-out system of hygiene. It helps to have *lots* of cloths in the kitchen and to wash them often. You ideally need separate cloths for wiping up spills, for drying plates, and for wiping your hands and you need to feel confident that they are clean enough that you are not just spreading germs around. My mother could keep a manky old kitchen towel on the go for several weeks but I've gone the other way. Every clean cloth feels like a fresh start.

Even if you are a messy cook—or what my math teacher Mrs. Jones used to call "a mucky pup"—you will have to do a fair bit of cleaning as you go when cooking. To take just one example, you will probably need to wash up your chopping board a few times when preparing an average meal. Chopping boards are one of the main ways that food poisoning happens in the kitchen if they are not washed frequently. Any time you handle raw meat, you will need to wash the board—and your hands—straight away. This is one reason I like washing-up brushes, because I can do this kind of quick mid-cooking cleaning without putting gloves on (a brush keeps your hands at more of a distance than a sponge). Even if you are not a meat eater, you have to wash your chopping boards a surprising amount. If you cut onion or garlic on a board and don't rinse it, the next thing you chop will taste oniony. If you want to make a clean wooden chopping board extra clean, rub it all over with lemon juice.

We all have a different comfort level when it comes to cleanliness in the kitchen.

The Oxford writer and literature professor John Bayley (husband of the novelist Iris Murdoch) kept his kitchen in such a state of disarray, piled high with papers, unwashed plates, books, and medicine, that he once put down a large pork pie somewhere never to find it again in all the mess. The chaos does not seem to have made Professor Bayley enjoy cooking any less. My son Tom, a student, is similar in his kitchen attitudes. "Did you know that these capers have something orange floating in the jar?" asked his friend one evening when I was at his place eating pizza. He shrugged and ate the capers anyway. At the opposite extreme, you have someone like the character Monica Geller in the sitcom *Friends*, who puts numbers on the bottom of every coffee mug so that she can keep them organized to her satisfaction. Most of us are somewhere between these two extremes in the kitchen hygiene stakes. What matters is knowing what your own standards are and trying to meet those standards and no one else's.

No matter how relaxed you may think you are about mess, it's hard to do your best cooking in a state of nausea. The emotion of disgust is one of the many important things about food that cookbooks don't mention. Think of how it feels to drink water from a sparkling-clean glass compared to how it feels to drink from one that is smeary.

If you look at Western recipes from hundreds of years ago—especially those involving dairy—there was much talk of keeping vessels and ingredients "scrupulously clean." Salads must be rinsed clean. Broths must be strained clean. Modern cookbooks don't talk about cleanliness so much, as if it were something uncool or boring. Who would focus on the dull process of getting grit from a leek when you could be talking about creating amazing new flavors. But to forget hygiene in the kitchen is a mistake, because a clean kitchen is the springboard from which everything delicious emerges. This is something that becomes even more pressing when you cook for friends who are celiac or who have nut allergies and you need to keep things extra orderly to avoid cross-contamination.

A clean kitchen is not the same as a sterile one. Some of the best cooks I know are also the untidiest. It doesn't do to get so obsessive about cleaning things up that you can't allow yourself to enjoy the messier joys of cooking: the clouds of flour that fill the kitchen when you are rolling pasta or the squidgy feeling of meatball mixture as you form it with your hands. But for this delightful chaos to happen, you need a bit of space and structure and some surfaces that you feel confident about placing food on. The kitchen floor doesn't need to be clean enough to eat your proverbial dinner off. But anything you actually want to eat your dinner off really should be.

Find the missing element
(a chapter on seasoning)

"What is this art of tasting?"
  Jean Conil, *Haute Cuisine*, 1953

Everyone knows that the secret of good cooking—or a large part of it—is in the right seasoning. But despite what you may read on the internet, the key to seasoning is not to be found in a top-secret patented spice blend that will supposedly give you the wizardry of a top chef. Seasoning is mostly about *noticing*. It is about recognizing that some foods such as celery are already salty, while some, such as tomatoes, positively drink salt and others, such as mushrooms, seem to get most of their seasoning not from salt but from the heat of a pan.

Seasoning is not just about learning how to add things but also about learning how to hold yourself back from adding things. It is about responding to the food in front of you and bringing it into balance with your own taste. "Vote early and vote often" is the old joke made about corrupt elections. The same is true of seasoning. Early salting tastes different from late salting. I taste food constantly during the cooking process, the only proviso being that I don't taste raw meat. There is a depth of flavor that you get from confident early salting that can never fully be recovered later on, particularly when cooking something such as pasta. An unseasoned pot of pasta can never be made salty enough at the end. But you should also continue to taste and season as you go along. Never forget to test the seasoning right at the end, just before you eat.

Seasoning does not even have to mean adding salt. This chapter is about three simple tricks to improve your seasoning game that have nothing to do with salt. The tricks are lemon, crunch, and water. The word *season* comes from the Old French *saisonnier*, meaning to render something palatable by the influence of the seasons or to ripen fruit. When we season food what we are trying to do is bring the flavors into the same state of fullness and balance that ripe fruit has all by itself. Seasoning might mean adding sweetness or sharpness instead of salt or it might mean adding nothing at all if you feel that a certain ingredient tastes fabulous just as it is.

This needs lemon

"Sourness brings contrast, balance, variety, zing—pleasure."
Mark Diacono, *Sour*

If you feel your cooking lacks zing, there is a very simple solution that will make everything you cook taste instantly more delicious. No matter what you are cooking, right at the end, when you are happy that the salt levels are right but you still feel it could be a touch more exciting, add a little lemon juice, starting with a small spoonful and working up from there. If you still feel it lacks something, add some of the lemon's zest too, which will enhance the sour effect of the juice in an upliftingly perfumed way. That's it. That's the whole tip. Apologies if it seems crashingly obvious, but I am frequently surprised to meet people who don't know that you can season food with lemon as well as salt. Instead of salt and pepper, we should talk of salt and lemon as the two universal seasonings. Obviously there are dozens of other flavorings you might want to add in addition to the salt and lemon, from fresh tarragon to ras el hanout. But salt and lemon (or some other form of acid such as vinegar) provide the basic structure: a sturdy coathanger on which to hang any outfit that takes your fancy.

What of pepper? Years of cooking for children who recoil at the bite of anything hot has convinced me that it's better for all kinds of reasons to keep the pepper grinder on the table along with a dish of chile flakes rather than in the kitchen. Personally, I adore the pungency and perfume of coarsely ground black pepper, a pungency that actually helps digestion because the active ingredient in pepper—piperine—encourages saliva and gastric juices to flow. But I feel that black pepper is a flavoring so heady and particular that it should be saved for those occasions when its heat and perfume can really make an impact, such as on soft-boiled eggs or over a plate of spaghetti carbonara. I love black pepper too much to follow the convention of adding it thoughtlessly to every single dish.

When you season with pepper, the food ends up tasting of pepper, which drowns out whatever flavorings you were intending the food to taste of. When you season with salt and lemon, assuming you are not heavy-handed, the food ends up tasting more fully of itself.

The need to season with acid as well as salt is something that I suspect many of us know instinctively, even if we do not do it consciously. When I started reading cookbooks and recipe columns as a child in the early 1980s, a small detail started to bug me. No matter what the dish, British recipe writers would suggest serving it "with a green salad" or sometimes, "with a green salad and some crusty bread." What was the purpose of all these green leaves? I love salad as much as the next person. Apart from tasting and looking fresh, a simple salad is a quick way to get vitamins and fiber on the table without needing to cook any vegetables. But is an automatic green salad really called for with every single meal?

It was only much later, after reading *Salt, Fat, Acid, Heat* by Samin Nosrat, that I developed a theory about this whole "serve with a green salad" business. Nosrat made me see for the first time what a truly essential element acidity is in all cooking, in bringing flavors into focus and giving a jolt of much-needed brightness to rich or heavy or starchy ingredients. To Nosrat, a plate of food without acidity is a plate of food with something missing: like pasta that has been cooked in unsalted water. She has talked about the fact that cranberry sauce is a crucial element in the traditional Thanksgiving meal because without it, there would be nothing acidic on the table to offset the richness of the turkey and gravy and mashed potatoes and stuffing.

"Serve with a green salad" is another way of saying this recipe will be a bit bland unless you have something sharp and tangy alongside. "Serve with crusty bread" is saying the same thing but about texture: it's like an admission that a given recipe lacks crunch (a subject I will return to in a moment). The default instruction to "serve with a green salad" comes from a hidden instinct on the part of the recipe writers that, as written, their recipes lack the final touch of zinginess that most eaters crave. The reason for the salad—other than imbuing dinner with overtones of healthiness—is to bring the tang of vinaigrette to season the rest of the meal. The instruction would be redundant in a food culture such as India's, where tangy bowls of pickle or chutney or fresh relishes are incorporated into every meal.

Nothing is quite as powerful in correcting the seasoning of a dish as a small late squeeze of lemon just before you serve it. It needs to be added late because unlike salt, sharp flavors lose their potency if you cook them too much. This is as true of risotto or a platter of roasted vegetables as it is of a rich meaty casserole or fish and chips. Samin Nosrat calls this final squeeze of lemon a "garnishing acid" and notes that while "no amount of salt at the table will make up for underseasoning food from within, a hit of acid at the very last second often improves food." The only time that lemon may not add much is when you are cooking something that is already heavily sour, such as a Filipino chicken adobo cooked in vinegar or anything containing a lot of tomatoes, which are already acidic.

Salt at the start, lemon and herbs at the end. You won't go far wrong with these two rules of seasoning, except that sometimes, you might want to use lime or vinegar instead of the lemon and sometimes you want a little extra salt at the end too. To me, a squeeze of lemon is like a squeeze of sunshine on the plate. It makes me feel more alive. When I visited China a couple of years ago, I felt at home when I realized that there was vinegar on the table in every restaurant and I knew I was among eaters who prized sourness as much as I do.

Imagine how different cooking must have been in Europe before citrus fruit became commonplace. If you look at British cookbooks from Renaissance times, they make heavy use of verjuice (a highly acidic grape juice) and of barberries (tiny sharp berries that are still popular in the cooking of the Middle East). This shows that the thirst for sourness was a human constant, even before the lemon entered our lives.

As a good rule of thumb, when a recipe tells you to "check your seasoning" at the end, assume that this means "check your acid" as well as "check your salt." When you feel that your seasoning is a bit off, you have options. The most obvious move is to add more salt, but go easy at this final stage because while salty food tastes of life, oversalted food is deadening. Sometimes, the answer is fat. A final spoonful of good olive oil or a generous slice of unsalted butter can work wonders in rounding flavors out and marrying them up with each other. Occasionally, the answer may be sugar— just half a small spoonful to take the bite out of a tomato sauce, for example. Depending on your palate, the food may also be calling out for the bite of pepper or chile but as I'll explain in more detail later on in the section on cooking for children (see page 351), I feel that seasoning with heat is a personal affair, often best left to the eater on the plate than the cook in the kitchen.

Of all the basic tastes—sweet, sour, salty, bitter, and umami—sourness is the most overlooked and, I would argue, the most important secret weapon in a cook's arsenal. Good cooks have always known this. In *What Mrs. Fisher Knows About Old Southern Cooking*, the first cookbook by an African-American cook, published in 1881, Abby Fisher recommends basting broiled venison with currant jelly "should you like your venison tart or a little acid." Mrs. Fisher also has a recipe for something she calls "meat dressing," which she adds to all her meat entrées and soups. It's a kind of sour seasoning made from grated carrot, onion, and cauliflower boiled with vinegar and brown sugar and then strained and cooked some more. She says that it's nice to add one tablespoon of this to every quart of stew. By the same token, I quite often add just a small spoonful of vinegar to a stew or soup at the very end but as Mark Diacono remarks in his wonderful book *Sour*, less is more. "A thimble of vinegar" will transform a plain leek and potato soup "into a delight" but if you are too bold with the vinegar you end up with "leek and potato and vinegar soup," which probably isn't what you wanted.

Other than lemon, there are many ways to add a final hit of sourness to a dish. Tamarind or pomegranate molasses are good if you want some dark characterful sweetness along with the sour hit. Sour powders such as amchur (dried mango

powder) and sumac (a tangy red spice used a lot in Arab cuisine) can give a bracing lift to salads and meze. A dash of rice vinegar lends a soft and unobtrusive acidity and it's what I turn to on those sad occasions when there are no lemons in the house. Another source of gentle sourness is yogurt (and other fermented dairy such as kefir or sour cream). My most regular condiment is a bowl of thick yogurt seasoned quite highly with salt and whisked together with half a grated clove of garlic. Sometimes, I sprinkle either nigella seeds or a dusting of sumac or paprika over it. I am happy to eat this yogurt sauce with almost any meal. I prefer it to ketchup for dipping fries. I am paranoid about serving a meal that is too dry, and a bowl of this on the table ensures that even a slightly overcooked chicken breast is luscious again. It's incredibly good drizzled with my other favorite condiment, the crispy chile oil that you can buy from Chinese supermarkets. The red chile oil marbles in patterns.

But when it comes to souring agents, nothing has quite the versatility or impact of a simple squeeze of lemon. In their book *The Art of Flavor*, Daniel Patterson and Mandy Aftel explain why lemon is so good at making food taste more balanced. Patterson and Aftel note that in contrast to the "piercing acidity" of some wine vinegars, citrus juice contains sweetness as well as sourness and its brightness has the power to "knit other flavors together."

With lemon, as with anything, it's possible to have too much of a good thing. Patterson and Aftel note that while a little lemon or lime can punctuate a salad, too much can overwhelm it and "diminish the savory qualities you have worked so hard to build." Unless you are making lemonade, the juice of half a lemon is often better than the juice of a whole lemon. Acidity dials down umami, so you don't want to add so much to a dish that you dilute the overall flavor.

You know you have got the amount of "garnishing acid" right when you taste something and instead of thinking: "This tastes lemony," you simply think: "This doesn't need anything more."

Manjula's preserved lemons

Preserved lemon is a lovely way to add the sharpness of lemon in a more complex form than juice alone. Just a tiny piece of preserved lemon, finely chopped and added at the last minute, does wonders for rice dishes, sandwiches, and salads. I was first given a recipe for preserved lemons by Manjula Rajan, the mother of Ranjita, who is one of my oldest and dearest school friends, and so now I always think of them both when I eat preserved lemons. Manjula's classic recipe is great—it's nothing but whole unwaxed lemons cut lengthwise and packed with lots of salt in a sterilized jar—but each jar takes 6–8 weeks to be ready. When I am feeling impatient, I use this much quicker method to get the flavor of Manjula's pickle by using sliced lemons, adapted from *Honey & Co: Food from the Middle East* by Sarit Packer and Itamar Srulovich. You can eat the lemons just a day after they are made, although they continue to mature in the fridge.

Makes 1 x 1½-cup/360ml jar
4 unwaxed lemons
3 tablespoons flaky salt
Extra-virgin olive oil

Sterilize a 1½-cup/360ml jar (run it through the hot cycle of a dishwasher). Halve the lemons lengthwise and slice as thinly as you possibly can—I do this using the slicer attachment in the food processor but use a mandoline if you are brave, using a safety glove. It's very important that the lemons are paper thin. Remove any visible seeds. Mix the lemons with the salt in a bowl. After 30 minutes, pack them into the sterilized jar, cover with oil, and seal the jar. You can start eating them after 24 hours. Store in the fridge and use within a couple of months. You can use these in any way that you would use any other preserved lemon.

WAYS TO USE PRESERVED LEMONS

—Add some to a vegetable risotto at the end to give sharpness (this is especially good with pea or asparagus risotto).
—My friend Ranjita sometimes adds fine strips of preserved lemon to avocado toast for breakfast, which gives the buttery blandness of the avocado an energizing

tang that wakes you up, with or without a double espresso alongside.

—Sprinkle preserved lemons over hummus or in a hummus and falafel sandwich to add brightness.

—Make a piquant sauce by chopping some preserved lemons very finely and mixing them with a chopped red chile, chopped cucumber, green onions, and mint.

—Finely chop 1 tablespoon of preserved lemon, mix it with olive oil, and use this sharp lemony oil to anoint a ball of buffalo mozzarella.

SOME MORE WAYS TO GIVE YOUR FOOD LAST-MINUTE BRIGHTNESS

—Top with some grated cheese. Hard cheeses are acidic. This is why parmesan is in some ways the perfect seasoning, because it adds not just salt and umami but also acid.

—Add a tiny slosh of sherry to a soup just before eating. Eliza Acton, a brilliant nineteenth-century cookbook author, finishes some of her soups with a glass or two of sherry or "port wine."

—Pickle juice. The dill vinegar left over from a jar of pickled cucumbers is a lovely thing to splash over smoked fish or to fold into a potato salad.

—Dried barberries—as used in Iranian cuisine—can add intense bursts of sourness to salads.

—Pickled chiles. A couple of fresh chiles, seeded and finely chopped and mixed in a small bowl with apple cider vinegar. This is good for cutting the sweetness of pumpkins or roasted root vegetables.

—Garlicky yogurt. Grate a clove of peeled garlic into a bowl of plain yogurt, season with salt, and sprinkle with toasted nigella or cumin seeds.

—Fig and pistachio sauce (an Ottolenghi idea). You can use any dried fruit and any nut. Chop some soft dried figs, mix with the same amount of chopped toasted pistachios, and season to taste with lemon juice and chopped green herbs. This offers a sweet sourness, perfect with roasted meat.

Crunch!

"There is also the biting touch. If biting an apple,
no matter how strong your teeth are, they are
nevertheless alive with sensitive nerves."
  Jean Conil, *Haute Cuisine*, 1953

One of the most neglected aspects of eating—and therefore cooking—is texture. When you ask a child why they like or dislike a certain food, nine times out of ten the reason will be texture. Maybe they hate mushrooms because they are so slimy or they love cherry tomatoes because every time they pop one in their mouth, they get a tiny explosion of juice and seeds. Adults, too, are hugely driven by texture when it comes to food. Whether someone loves polenta or porridge, for example, is very little to do with the starchy flavors and a great deal to do with that creamy gelatinous texture that some of us adore and others can't abide. Yet Western cookbooks are often strangely silent on the question of texture in contrast to flavor.

There aren't many universals when it comes to human taste—other than the fact that all babies are born with a love of sweetness and an aversion to bitterness—but one thing that practically everyone seems to relish in one form or another are foods that are crunchy (assuming that you have a robust set of teeth).

The single most frequently used word for texture in the US is "crisp," according to scientists Ole G. Mouritsen and Klavs Styrbaek in their book *Mouthfeel: How Texture Makes Taste*. But crispness can actually mean many different things. The crispness that you get when you bite into a juicy apple is different from the crackling crunch of a good piece of bread fresh from the oven, which is different again from the fatty crispness of a piece of roasted chicken skin or the shattering crispness of a sheet of peanut or sesame brittle. What all these forms of crispness have in common is that they make a loud sound when your jaws bite into them and that they are deeply appealing. The loudness of the crunch is a big part of the appeal because it keeps things interesting with each mouthful.

I'm not claiming that crunch is always the answer. Sometimes, you are feeling low and want a meal that is nothing but silent softness. When I have a sore throat or a toothache or am just feeling in need of cosseting, I find myself gravitating toward foods with the unchallenging textures of baby food. Vegetable purées.

Bananas covered in custard. Squishy raspberries and cream. A pillowy piece of brioche dipped in a mug of milky coffee. Chicken noodle soup. Irish colcannon potatoes drenched in melted butter. A bowl of soothing congee. Fish pie so soft you can eat it with a spoon.

But in most moods, the quickest way to make any meal more exciting is to give it a bit of crunch. When you add crispiness to softness, your mouth is constantly wondering what will come next. What makes Persian rice so dreamy is the crispy bottom—or *tahdig*—formed at the bottom of the pot. Equally, the thrill of a good Caesar salad is largely in the staccato crunch of the croutons that amplify the quieter crispness of the romaine lettuce. A handful of granola offers crunchy delight to a bowl of soft Greek yogurt and berries. If you have no granola, you could try popping some quinoa for an instant form of crunch that is good both on yogurt and in salads. This surprised me at first, because I didn't know you could eat toasted quinoa without boiling it first. Simply heat a spoonful of quinoa in a small frying pan over medium heat until it pops, then quickly scatter it over the yogurt and top with a chopped apple or pear, a drizzle of maple syrup, and a handful of chopped Brazil nuts or almonds with a tiny grating of orange zest.

Or consider what crunch can bring to macaroni and cheese. This is lovely enough by itself: the soothing dairy richness of cheese combining with the soporific carbs of the pasta. But you can take macaroni and cheese to a whole other level simply by adding breadcrumbs or cracker crumbs to the top before you bake it. When I say breadcrumbs, this doesn't need to be any more complicated than cutting or tearing up a couple of slices of good bread such as sourdough that is old but not positively stale.

As with acidity, crunch is something that most experienced cooks consider automatically, without necessarily advertising the fact. I recently went through one of my favorite cookbooks by Diana Henry—*From the Oven to the Table*—and noticed that the whole book was full of little grace notes involving crunch. A dish of chile-roasted tomatoes with feta and dill is topped with pistachio nuts. Roasted cabbage wedges are sprinkled with rye breadcrumbs. A salad of chicken and bitter leaves are cheered up with the waxy crunch of pine nuts plus the heftier crunch of torn sourdough.

How can you get more crunch in your meals? Let me count the ways. Crispy bacon is one: crumbled over a spinach salad or alongside soft scrambled eggs for weekend breakfast. Raw vegetables are another. There's something to be said for the old French tradition of eating crudités at the start of a meal to satisfy your thirst for crunch. Radishes are an obvious choice but raw sugarsnaps are sweet and satisfying in the summer, like little green boats. When you are serving vegetables in a cooked form that makes them very soft, consider holding back a little of the vegetable to add raw, finely shredded, over the top, perhaps tossed in oil and lemon. Example: a bit of raw crunchy fennel thinly sliced is the one of the best things to add to slow-cooked roasted fennel. By the same token, cauliflower florets sliced paper-thin look like crisp little flowers on top of a cream of cauliflower soup.

Croutons of all kinds are another source of crunch. The laziest way is simply to make a few slices of toast in the toaster and then cut them into cubes. Sometimes, I rub the slices with garlic and sprinkle them with oil and a little salt before I cut them. These simplified croutons are good tossed in any kind of salad. It is hardly more trouble to fry croutons in butter. To ¼ cup/50g of butter melted in a shallow pan, add one cup or so of torn bread and cook until both butter and bread smell toasty but not burned—around 4 minutes. The ideal crouton is crisp and crunchy on the outside but still with a little softness on the inside.

You can create a crunchier and finer crumb with a handful of Japanese panko breadcrumbs, which are a great pantry standby. I think of panko as electric breadcrumbs because the bread they are baked from is made using an electric current rather than a conventional oven. They were invented during the Second World War as a way to conserve energy. The word panko comes from the Japanese for bread (pan) and small pieces (*ko*).

When frying breadcrumbs, you might also like to add some spice to the butter, such as cumin seeds, smoked paprika, or a little finely chopped rosemary plus chile flakes. On the theme of croutons, don't overlook tortilla chips and potato chips. Carla Lalli Music writes in *Where Cooking Begins* that "everyone should be topping more things with potato chips" given that they are naturally gluten-free and "zero-effort." Music sprinkles plain salted potato chips over a salad of charred leeks. If this sounds off, remember that long before the potato chip was a commercial snack food, it was something called a game chip, served on aristocratic tables in England: an ethereal morsel designed to go with roasted game birds such as pheasant and grouse. Another idea along the same lines is the Indian use of sev—or deep-fried noodles made from chickpea flour—to give exciting crunch to vegetable dishes such as aloo chana chat: potatoes with chickpeas. The crunchy sev are what make you keep going back for mouthful after mouthful.

Why do we love to crunch on things so much? It has been suggested that the human love of crispy foods such as potato chips goes back all the way to our hunter-gatherer ancestors, for whom crunchy insects were an important source of protein. But these days, I suspect that most of us would rather crunch on an almond than a beetle.

Crunchy nuts

When I feel something needs crunch, my default move is to add some kind of nuts or seeds. To get the best out of a nut—both taste-wise and texture-wise—you should toast them, a process that crisps up the nut's waxiness and makes its flavor toasty and warm.

If toasted in the oven, most nuts take 15 minutes on a parchment-lined baking sheet at 350°F, except for pine nuts and walnuts, which should be done after 10 (check pine nuts after 5 because they notoriously go from raw to burned in almost no time). But my preferred way to deal with most nuts and seeds is to pan-toast them with or without a little oil. It's much more energy efficient, they are ready in a minute, you can make them in small batches, and the presence of the oil means that you can add extra flavors such as spices. And because they take such a short time to cook, it's much easier to give them your full attention for long enough to avoid burning them.

Here are a couple of ways to get started, one savory, one sweet, enough for 2 people.

Pumpkin seeds fried with salt

A joy to make and to eat. I add them to every kind of salad. In a small frying pan, combine ⅓ cup/50g of pumpkin seeds, a small spoonful of olive oil, and a big pinch of salt. Within seconds, the seeds will start to pop and disgorge their insides, like popcorn. The moment they have popped and smell toasty, tip them into a bowl to arrest the cooking. You can add all sorts of flavorings to the oil such as a small spoonful of soy sauce, a big pinch of cumin seeds, a sour pinch of sumac, chopped rosemary, smoked paprika.

Instant praline

Any kind of nut can be turned into a near-instant praline to eat for dessert. This is almost absurdly easy and deeply craveable.

In a small pan, heat ½ cup/50g of sliced almonds (or any other nut, chopped if large) with 2 teaspoons of confectioners' sugar, stirring constantly. As it melts, the sugar will seem to vanish before your eyes. A moment later, the nuts and the sugar will have stuck together and formed an instant praline. Tip it into a bowl and allow to cool and harden. This is divine over plain vanilla ice cream or thick Greek yogurt, or added for last-minute sweetness and crunch to almost any fruit-based dessert.

Burned finger lentils

This is a Syrian dish, popular for Ramadan in Damascus. According to Itab Azzam and Dina Mousawi (in their book *Syria: Recipes from Home*), the reason it is called burned finger is because it is so delicious that supposedly no one can wait for it to cool down before tucking in. The brown lentils are addictively sweet and sour from a combination of tamarind and date or pomegranate molasses. A friend, who is vegetarian tried it and said: "So often, lentils are either boring or too salty and this is neither."

It's become one of my all-time favorite vegetarian dishes, not least because it has three forms of crunch on top to counter-balance the soft lentils: the gentle green crunch of cilantro, the oily crunch of fried onions, and a chewy pasta-like crunch from little round deep-fried croutons.

These croutons were what made me first notice the dish on the page because they are cut out using a wedding ring. I took my wedding ring off a couple of months after my husband left but wasn't sure what to do with it. It gave me a spooky-sad feeling to see it there on top of the chest of drawers in my bedroom. But then I made this dish and even though it was very laborious to cut out the dough, I felt better. The ring was no longer the sad ring of a rejected person. Instead, it had become a very tiny pastry cutter.

If you don't have time for cutting out teeny-tiny shapes with a ring, a much quicker way is to cut pieces of flatbread into tiny squares using scissors, toss them in oil, and bake them on a sheet in the oven until crisp (10–15 minutes).

Serves 4–6, depending on what else you are having

For the croutons
½ cup plus 1 tablespoon/70g all-purpose flour
¼ teaspoon baking powder
OR 1 large flatbread, cut into tiny squares with scissors and 2 tablespoons olive oil

For the lentils

1¼ cups/250g brown lentils, rinsed (I mean the biggish flat lentils that are
sometimes called "green lentils" and sometimes "brown lentils," but do use Le
Puy instead if that's what you have)

1 zucchini, very finely diced

2 cloves of garlic, peeled and grated

1 tablespoon tamarind paste

2 tablespoons date molasses (or pomegranate molasses)

Light oil for deep-frying

2 medium-large onions, thinely sliced

A large bunch of cilantro, chopped

Start with the croutons. If making the dough-based croutons, mix together the flour and baking powder with a pinch of salt and add enough water to bring it together as a dough. Knead for a couple of minutes and let it rest in a bowl covered with a plate while you get on with the lentils.

Put the lentils in a saucepan with 3⅓ cups/800ml of water, bring to a boil, and simmer for about 20 minutes, stirring now and then. While this is happening, roll out the dough about ⅛ inch/3mm thick and cut out tiny circles using a ring or use a pizza cutter to cut it into tiny squares.

Or, if you are going the easier flatbread route, toss the pieces of flatbread with the oil and put on a baking sheet in the oven at 425°F for 10–15 minutes, or until golden and crisp.

When the lentils are tender, add the zucchini, garlic, tamarind, and date molasses and continue to simmer for 5 minutes, by which time most of the water should be absorbed.

Heat about 2 inches/5cm of oil in a wok or deep saucepan and fry the onions until very crispy and brown but stop before they burn. Drain on paper towels.

Now deep-fry the dough circles in batches until golden brown—they only take about 1 minute per side. Drain them on paper towels. Make sure you set the pan of hot oil very carefully to one side, somewhere safe. I usually put it outside in the garden. Season the lentils with salt and add a small handful of the cilantro plus a handful of the onions. Arrange the lentils in a big serving bowl and top with stripes of dark-brown onions, lush green cilantro, and golden croutons.

Crisp spiced apple strudel

In my family, we always have to call this "crisp apple strudel," because of *The Sound of Music*, even if it turns out soggy (which it doesn't). It reminds me that there is satisfaction just in saying the words *crisp* or *crunchy*. This recipe is based on one in *Supper Club* by Kerstin Rodgers, but I've changed the flavors a bit. Usually, when people say "as easy as apple pie," it is some kind of sick joke, because a classic apple pie with a double crust is tricky and time-consuming (though completely worth it when you do have lots of time). This strudel, though, is properly a cinch. Because of the filo pastry, you don't need a pie dish, a rolling pin, or any baking skills. If you are the sort of person who thinks you can't make pie, make this and prove yourself wrong. The most time-consuming part here is prepping the apples.

Serves 4
900g tart-sweet apples (I use something like Honeycrisp or Braeburn)
7 tablespoons/90g brown sugar
1 teaspoon ground cinnamon
1 tablespoon all-purpose flour
Juice and zest of 1 unwaxed lemon
Zest of 1 unwaxed orange
¼ cup/50g butter
6 large sheets of filo pastry
Confectioners' sugar, to serve
Whipped cream, to serve

Peel and core the apples and cut them into little dice. In a mixing bowl, combine them with the sugar, cinnamon, flour, zest, and juice.

Melt the butter and find a pastry brush. Tear off a large piece of parchment paper, about twice as long as your baking sheet. Preheat the oven to 400°F. Lay out a sheet of filo on the parchment. Brush with melted butter and join another piece of filo onto it with the shortest edge overlapping by 1 inch/2.5cm. Brush this with butter too. Lay 2 more sheets of filo on top and brush with butter again. Lay the final 2 sheets on top.

Spread the apple mixture over the filo, distributing it as evenly as you can but not worrying too much about the odd gap. Now roll it up from one short end to the other into a fat sausage. Use melted butter to stick the pastry at the end. Brush it all over with melted butter. Using the parchment, lift the strudel onto the baking sheet. Tear or cut off the excess parchment. Bake in the oven for 30 minutes, or until crisp and brown (check after 25 minutes, but it might need as long as 35). Dust with confectioners' sugar and serve with whipped cream. It's best eaten warm.

MORE WAYS TO SEASON WITH CRUNCH

—Crunchy citrus. Using a vegetable peeler, pare the peel from any kind of unwaxed citrus fruit. Place on a baking sheet and dry out in an oven on low heat for 40 minutes or so until hard and crackly. When cool, break into little pieces.
—Crispy chickpeas. A can of chickpeas, drained, tossed with olive oil and salt, and roasted on a baking sheet at 425°F for 20–30 minutes.
—Frizzled ginger. I got this idea from *In Praise of Veg* by Alice Zaslavsky. Take a big chunk of ginger, peel it, and cut it into very fine strips. Shallow-fry in a generous amount of hot vegetable oil until very crisp, and drain on paper towels. Wonderful on top of stir-fried green vegetables.
—Thinly sliced radishes add both crunch and heat plus cheering pinkness to a bowl of noodles.
—Toasted oats—one of the ingredients in the Scottish dessert cranachan—are surprisingly delicious and very thrifty. Take a handful of oats and toast in a dry pan, shaking constantly, until golden.
—Prawn crackers or poppadoms: either crumble them over a salad or serve them on the side of a salad and use as edible spoons to scoop up mouthfuls.

Just add water

"People who habitually drink water become just as
good gourmets about water as wine drinkers about wine."
  Alexandre Dumas, *Dumas on Food*

What is the single most overlooked element in cooking? I'd argue it is neither heat nor salt but water. No other ingredient can do so much, while costing so little. Water is the surprise component that can transform textures and lighten flavors like nothing else, once you know how. "Our culture frowns on cooking in water," states the food writer Tamar Adler, lamenting the tendency to sneer at boiled vegetables, which can be perfectly delicious. She's right. But it's also true that water is so much more than just a cooking medium. The real secret of water is all the other things it can do, including—most surprising of all—making food taste better. There is a traditional Tuscan soup called acquacotta: cooked water. It is a bread-based peasant soup in which stale bread, tomatoes, onions, and olive oil are turned into a frugal feast thanks to the addition of water.

Water is what turns unpromising burned pan drippings into a rich gravy; it can make radishes crunchier and raisins plumper. Warm water is what stops a pasta sauce from turning claggy and what smooths the sharpness in a vinaigrette. A bath of cold water can revive drooping greens and prevent hard-boiled eggs from over-cooking; a dash of ice water can add silkiness to hummus and help prevent pastry from becoming greasy, among countless other uses. When you worry that you have overseasoned a sauce, just a few drops of water can bring it back into balance again, lightening both the texture and the seasoning. Yet most of the time, we treat water as if it were nothing: a mere blank.

One of the daunting things about cooking is the sense that once you have messed something up, there is no way back. But if anything can give you a second chance to make a dish wonderful, water can. There have been times—more than I care to remember—when I've undercalculated the ratio of water to rice when using the absorption method, leaving me with a pan of crunchy and undercooked grains. Then, one evening, instead of berating myself for the failure, I looked at the pot of rice with curiosity: what would happen, I wondered, if I sprinkled on a few drops of water and put the pan back on low heat for a few minutes before letting it stand for a few minutes more? Perfectly good rice, that's what happened.

Water, I've come to realize, is often all you need to pull a dish back from the brink of disappointment. When the tomato sauce for your pasta has reduced so far that the tomatoes stick to the edge of the pan like jam, do not despair. Simply add half a cup of water or so and the sauce will ease itself back to the right texture. Two teaspoons of warm water can save you from the panic of a broken mayonnaise or hollandaise (which is one of those things that only seems to happen when you are trying to make the mayonnaise or hollandaise for a special occasion and therefore really mind about it). You stare at the greasy mess of broken mayonnaise thinking "nothing will fix this" only to see it make a mockery of your pessimism by recombining into a creamy mass as you slowly whisk in the warm water. The crucial thing here is not to overdo it. Add too much water and your mayonnaise will be, well, watery.

Perhaps we should not be surprised that water has such a range of culinary powers given that raw ingredients—like the human body—are mostly water. There are certain ingredients such as cucumber and melon that consist of more than 90 per cent water and whose refreshing wateriness is obvious but even something like an egg or a chicken breast is more than 70 per cent water. Cheese, I was surprised to learn, is around 37 per cent water (depending on the type of cheese). Even a paackage of pasta, which seems as dry as a bone, is still 12 per cent water. If you want to find a food devoid of water, your best chance is to look to oil, water's arch enemy. Olive oil—which is a hygrophobic or water-repelling substance—is one of the few commonly used ingredients that contains not so much as a drop of water.

Cooking, in a sense, is the art of getting food to the perfect degree of moisture. Sometimes, as when roasting meat or sautéing mushrooms, it is a case of concentrating flavor by allowing heat to drive off some of the ingredient's water. But there are other times when you want to use water to moisten or remoisten something. In old French haute cuisine, there was a term *mouiller*, which meant to moisten ingredients with water or stock prior to cooking. In Judy Rodgers's legendary chicken and bread salad from *The Zuni Café Cookbook*, the croutons in the salad are dribbled with chicken stock or lightly salted water just before serving. That salty water not only seasons the croutons but gives them a crucial element of sogginess around the edge.

Giving food a water bath before you cook or eat it can surprisingly improve both flavor and texture. I have made oven fries many times but was never quite satisfied until I came across a very niche cookbook called *Veggie Burgers Every Which Way* by Lukas Volger. He notes that oven fries have a tendency to be "over-cooked on the outside and dry and starchy like cotton on the inside." His answer is to soak the peeled and cut potatoes in cold water for half an hour before drying, tossing with oil and salt, and baking on a sheet in a hot oven for 40 minutes. This quick water bath removes some of the starch from the potatoes and as a result they taste much more like the true deep-fried fries you get in restaurants. If it helps, you can soak the cut potatoes in the water in the fridge for up to 12 hours. By the way, a second trick when making oven fries that has nothing to do with water but is worth knowing anyway is to sprinkle the potatoes with a handful of polenta before baking. This amplifies the crunch in a delightful way, like Nigella's tip of adding semolina to roasted potatoes.

Water baths can work to boost flavor as well as texture if you add salt and other seasonings to the water. As Nik Sharma notes in *The Flavor Equation*, "water is called a universal solvent because more ingredients can dissolve in it than any other liquid, by far." Most obviously, you can dissolve salt in water and use this simple brine to pre-season most kinds of meat or vegetables before they are roasted or pan-cooked or barbecued. The most famous example of this is using a wet brine on a Thanksgiving or Christmas turkey, but actually this is one of the few times I avoid using a brine because, although it makes the meat wonderfully juicy, I find it makes the gravy too salty and serving the people I love bad gravy, I am embarrassed to admit, is one of the things that can reduce me to tears. I would rather save the brine for less high-pressure meals and use it on smaller cuts of meat such as pork chops and chicken thighs, in which case a good brine mix is 6 cups/1.4 liters of water to 3 tablespoons of salt, plus a big sprig of rosemary if you like, and perhaps some bay leaves and juniper berries for the pork. Stir until the salt is dissolved. Brine the meat in a bowl in the fridge for 12 hours or more before you roast it in the oven or pan-sear it in a frying pan. The same brine works well with thick slices of red peppers, onions, and zucchini, which need a much quicker soaking. After 15 minutes, you can remove the vegetables from the brine, brush them with olive oil, and cook them for a few minutes over a hot griddle or barbecue. It sounds like an odd thing to do to vegetables but when I can be bothered to do it, this brine-bath seems to make them cook quicker as well as making them seasoned, through and through.

Another quality that water has is to revive foods Lazarus-like that seem long past saving. If you have a loaf or baguette in your bread bin that is rock hard, assuming it isn't actually moldy, you can run it under the tap and stick it in an oven preheated to 425°F, direct on the oven rack, for about 10 minutes. Don't be scared to get the bread good and wet. You may fear for a moment that you have turned the loaf into a wet sponge yet it will emerge almost as good and crusty as the day you bought it. The water turns to steam in the oven, which makes the crumb moist again, while the heat of the oven gives the crust a second chance at crustiness.

Water—in the form of a cold water bath—can also give new life to raw vegetables, making crisp vegetables crisper and un-drooping droopy leaves. This kitchen practice seems to be more common among Japanese cooks than in the West. The original rationale for the water bath was to freshen up withered greens at a time

when no one had fridges, as well as washing off any stray insects and pieces of soil. But the trick still works. If you have a sad head of lettuce that is almost too saggy to enjoy, it will become dramatically crisper after just half an hour of soaking in cold water. Then spin well in a salad spinner because for all water's virtues, you don't want wet salad leaves, which will repel the dressing.

Water is often treated as a problem in the kitchen: something to be removed or evaporated away. We press water out of tofu before we fry it and wring the moisture out of a panful of wilted spinach before adding cream. We toss berries in cornstarch before adding them to a crisp or crumble so that their juices are not too watery. We remove the water-logged seeds from a cucumber with a spoon and toss the diced pieces in salt to concentrate the flavor.

But sometimes, as surprising as it may seem, water is the only ingredient that will do. "Just add water," as it says on packages of dried soup mix. Writing about texture, food scientists Ole G. Mouritsen and Klavs Styrbaek note that "The unique properties of water have an indirect but extremely vital role in shaping the mouthfeel of food." Water is your best bet when you want to bring something down a notch, whether in flavor or texture.

There are moments in life—whether working, or cooking, or doing yoga, or trying to meet your one true love—when you are straining to achieve more and more when what you actually need is to breathe, stop, and do less. A case in point is vinaigrette, which, even when you have good oil, can easily get too intense: too intensely thick and oily on the tongue and so salty and sharp in flavor that it makes you wince. For years I felt dissatisfied with my vinaigrette, which I felt could never measure up to that of my mother-in-law. The more unhappy I was with my salads, the worse they became. I was forcing things. I tried adding more mustard, more salt, more vinegar, more everything. I made vinaigrettes that were intensely garlicky and others that were so salty they almost blew my head off. I watched my mother-in-law make her dressing by eye one day and saw that she added a bit of sugar. For a while after that, my vinaigrettes became so sugary and cloying that you could eat them for dessert. Then, one day, I don't know why, I stopped trying to make the dressing more intense and instead tried adding a dash of water. The effect was extraordinary and immediate. It was as if all the harsh lines had been softly blurred and replaced with calming Impressionist brush strokes. The emulsified vinaigrette was now both velvety in texture and balanced in taste. A few years later, I was thrilled to read in the *New York Times* in 2019 that Samin Nosrat does the same thing, following a recipe from the West Village restaurant Via Carota, where the chef Jody Williams taught her to soften the harshness of vinegar with a little warm water.

Samin Nosrat explains that she had always thought of water as "the enemy of vinaigrette—why would I want to dilute flavor?" Yet she discovered that just a spoonful of warm water was the missing element that could make a dressing so smooth you will want to drink it.

Green salad with drinkable vinaigrette

Apart from the added water, the key here, in my view, is to use rice vinegar, which is so much softer and less harsh than other vinegars, without being sickly like balsamic can be. If you don't have any rice vinegar, you can achieve a different (but equally lovely) softness by using cider vinegar and mixing it fifty-fifty with apple juice.

This is a masterclass in water because you need water both for the dressing and for rinsing the leaves. Double or triple the recipe and put it in a screwtop jar if you are the sort of person who likes to store vinaigrette in the fridge for impromptu salads. I prefer to make it fresh each time but this is a question of temperament rather than culinary correctness.

Serves 4–6

For the salad
7–9 oz/200–250g mixed lettuces or green leaves such as watercress, whole romaine, endive, arugula, little gems, whole soft lettuces

For the vinaigrette
3 tablespoons of your best extra-virgin olive oil
1 tablespoon rice vinegar
1 teaspoon Dijon mustard
½ clove of garlic, grated or crushed to a paste
A pinch of sugar (optional)

Trim the whole lettuces at the root, separate out the leaves, and tear the larger leaves in half. Put all the leaves into the basket of a salad spinner and soak them in water, swishing the leaves with your hand. Then spin the leaves very dry (the water that clings to the leaves is not the kind of moisture you want here). If you have no salad spinner, soak the leaves in a large mixing bowl instead (first in tepid water, then in cold water) before draining in a colander. Then put them into a clean kitchen towel, form into a bundle, and spin it around as if shaking a rattle at a football game. What this method lacks in finesse, it makes up for in fun.

For the vinaigrette, put the oil and vinegar in a jar, put on the lid, and shake well until the vinegar disperses in the golden oil like glitter in a snowglobe. At this point

the vinaigrette is already nearly perfect and sometimes I feel tempted to stop here. But usually I resist this urge and add the mustard, garlic, and a pinch of salt plus half a large spoonful of water and shake again. Test a bit on a leaf. You might want more salt, a pinch of sugar, a tiny squeeze of lemon.

Put the leaves into a nice big bowl and toss with the dressing until they are all lightly coated. Some swear by tossing salad with their hands. I usually use a serving spoon and fork.

VARIATION

An even quicker way to a delicious green salad that you probably already know is simply to put the rinsed leaves in a bowl, squeeze some lemon juice over the top, and add salt and olive oil to taste. Here, I don't add water (the lemon is juicy enough).

NICE ADDITIONS TO A GREEN SALAD

—Spears of steamed asparagus.
—Toasted seeds or nuts.
—A bunch of trimmed, sliced, sautéed green onion.
—Paper-thin slices of radish or fennel or celery.
—Herb leaves, such as basil, mint, or tarragon, stemmed and rinsed.

Tahini sauce

This is hardly a recipe, more a reminder of the astonishing alchemy that comes about when you add water to tahini. I make this when I am feeling sad and hopeless and want to be reminded that sometimes, things have to get worse before they get better because nothing looks as messy and hopeless as a tahini sauce just before it comes together.

Tahini is nothing but sesame paste, and has all the rich nutty flavor of toasted sesame seeds but, as Kenny Shopsin observes, "Sesame paste has a texture problem. It is dry and pasty, and it sticks to the roof of your mouth for eternity." But the secret to overcoming that texture problem is simply water, which transforms this claggy, oily paste into a fluid cream. I go through phases of adding garlic and cumin to my tahini sauce but mostly add nothing but water, salt, and lemon juice, which I feel makes it more versatile. There is almost no savory dish for which I wouldn't consider this a fine condiment.

I love it with every kind of kofta or meatball; over roasted vegetables (especially cauliflower) with added chile flakes; with a pilaf instead of yogurt; to make a plain piece of grilled fish less plain; or to add moisture and relish to almost any sandwich instead of mayonnaise.

Makes about 1 cup/240ml
½ cup/120ml tahini (try to get the Lebanese kind, which has a much silkier
    mouthfeel than some supermarket brands)
Juice of ½–1 lemon

Put the tahini into a bowl. Add 7–10 tablespoons/100–150ml of ice-cold water gradually, stirring with a whisk. At first, it will look as lumpy and unappealing as wet concrete. You may curse me for suggesting the very idea. Keep going. Add a bit more water and whisk again, and it will stop looking quite as dreadfully lumpy and start to look like very thick mayonnaise. Add the final bit of water (you may not need it all) until the mixture is white and glossy and smooth like heavy cream. Pour in the juice of half a lemon, whisk again, and taste to see if you want more. Add salt and taste again until it delights you. That's it! Store in the fridge in a bowl or squeezy bottle for up to 4 days, which means 4 days of happy, tahini-filled meals lie ahead.

Green tahini sauce

I would be remiss if I didn't also mention Yotam Ottolenghi's green tahini at this point, which I sometimes think is the most delicious condiment ever invented and which also relies on water for its creaminess. In a blender, whiz together: ⅔ cup/160ml of tahini, ⅓ cup/80ml of cold water, 2 cloves of garlic, grated, ½ teaspoon of salt, ¼ cup/60ml of lemon juice, and two large handfuls of flat-leaf parsley. Adjust with more lemon/salt/parsley/water as needed and whiz again.

Four-ingredient chocolate mousse

Water used to be seen as the worst thing you can add to chocolate. I remember fierce warnings from TV chefs that so much as a drop of water in melting chocolate could make it seize up. But this was proved completely wrong in 2008 when a French food scientist called Hervé This published a recipe for something he called Chocolate Chantilly. He figured out that if the water and chocolate could be combined in a ratio that gave the mixture the same fat content as heavy cream, the fat molecules could actually become suspended in the water in an emulsion or mousse, rather than seizing up. If you want to try this two-ingredient chocolate mousse, you can google it. But in all honesty, I much prefer a more traditional mousse made with added eggs and sugar, but which still relies on water to bestow lightness.

For 4 modest portions (I recommend doubling the recipe if in doubt, because having extra chocolate mousse in the fridge is never a bad idea)
2 large eggs
3 tablespoons sugar
3½ oz/100g dark chocolate (minimum 70 percent cocoa solids), broken into small pieces
Heavy cream, to serve

First, separate the eggs. Put the yolks into a small bowl and put the whites into a large mixing bowl. Using electric beaters, whisk the whites with the sugar until they are snowy and stiff.

In a saucepan over medium heat, melt the chocolate with ¼ cup/60ml of water. The moment that the chocolate looks half-melted, switch off the heat and allow it to stand. It will continue to melt in the residual heat of the pan. This method saves you the bother of melting the chocolate in a bowl suspended over hot water but you do have to watch it constantly and switch it off before it overcooks. Mix the yolks into the melted chocolate. Fold the whites into the chocolate mixture: use a large metal spoon or silicone spatula to make cutting motions into the chocolate, lifting and cutting over and over again. You are trying to stir it while losing as little air as possible. A few streaks of egg white don't matter (or I don't think they do). Spoon the mousse into 4 individual ramekins or little tea cups or drinking glasses and chill in the fridge for at least one hour and preferably two. Pour a layer of heavy cream over each mousse before you eat, like the white head on a dark pint of Guinness. If you want a flavored mousse, add ½ teaspoon of vanilla extract or the zest of half an orange or a little ground cardamom to the water. Or you could replace the water with coffee but my twelve-year-old would kill me if I did this.

SOME MORE WAYS WITH WATER

—When stir-fried vegetables are slow to get tender, add a large spoonful of water and clamp on a lid for 1 minute so that they cook in the steam.

—Hydrate your bread dough! Try adding just 10 percent more water to your favorite bread recipe and see how it yields a moister, more delicious crumb. A friend named Josh (who happens to be an expert on cooking insects but that's irrelevant to this story) once arrived at my house with one of the best loaves of sourdough I've ever tasted. "How do you make this so good?" I asked. "Hydration," was his reply.

—Soak sliced raw onions in cold water for 15 minutes to soften their acrid tang before adding them to a salad.

—Add tepid water to meatballs for a lighter texture (see page 368).

—Sprinkle a few drops of cold water over leftover lasagne (or any kind of baked pasta) before reheating it.

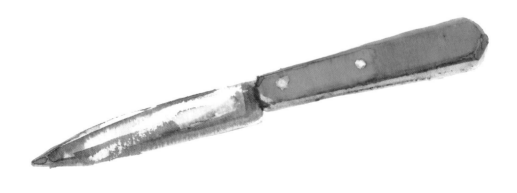

Use the tools you have and get the tools you need

"A good cooking stove . . . is one at which it
is possible to cook without crying."
    Carl Friedrich von Rumohr, 1822

Out of all the kitchen tools for sale, how do you choose the ones that will actually help you when you need them? "Have nothing in your house that you do not know to be useful or believe to be beautiful," said the great Victorian designer William Morris in 1880. It's still great advice, after all these years. But when it comes to cookware, I would add that you should have nothing in your kitchen that you find a pain to use or that you can't bear to wash up or that gives you twinges of guilt (electric juicers, I am looking at you on all three counts). I used to have a deluxe castle-shaped pan for making bundt cake. It would have passed the Morris test. I can't deny that it was both beautiful and useful. This cake pan looked like the sandcastle of my childhood dreams, cast in heavy aluminum. It was useful, too: when I poured in the cake batter, it baked evenly and efficiently and the cakes it produced made my children gasp in wonder. But how I hated washing that thing up. Crumbs would cling to every crevice and turret. It has now left my kitchen and is languishing with some roller-skates in a cabinet near the water heater until I decide its ultimate fate.

The most important thing about any given kitchen tool is that it should make you enjoy everyday eating and cooking more rather than less. I feel that the cooking guru Baron von Rumohr had it right in 1822 when he wrote that a good cooking stove was one at which it was possible to cook without crying. He was referring to the smokiness that bedevilled the coal-fired cookstoves of the time. But the no-crying rule has more general application. Cooking is a deeply personal business and one person's garlic press is another person's potato ricer. It doesn't matter how highly recommended a gadget may be, or how much it cost. Unless it makes *your* life easier, it is as good as useless. Someone who is left-handed or someone with arthritis may benefit from very different tools than other cooks. A tool needs to feel right in your own hand, you need to be able to decipher the instruction manual, and you also need to be certain that there is space for it on your countertop or in your drawers.

Go through every item in your kitchen and ask yourself six questions:

1. Do I find it beautiful?
2. Is it useful?
3. Do I like the way it makes me feel when I use it?
4. Can I bear to wash it up?
5. Does it do anything I can't do better with a knife and my own hands?
6. Do I have room for it?

Anything that gets all or mostly "Nos" needs to go. Yes, even if it was given to you as a wedding present. The person who gave it to you would honestly never need to know. If they come over and are cheeky enough to ask what you did with it, say it was so great that you lent it to a friend.

Next, go through duplicates and consider how many you really need of a given item such as lemon squeezers or pastry brushes or even wooden spoons. There are only so many spoons a person needs. Give away the ones that you never reach for and the ones that are left will suddenly seem extra special: like the chosen ones. There are few things more satisfying than a kitchen clear-out because what you are left with at the end is something more precious than any labor-saving gadget: cabinets that actually shut.

The choice of the "best" kitchen tools is not always a logical business. For years, I had a futile running argument with my mother about vegetable peelers. In my view, one of the greatest tools ever invented is the ergonomic swivel-bladed vegetable peeler because it makes the task of peeling fruits and vegetables—something I do every single day, give or take—both more pleasurable and much quicker. But my mother—who learned to peel potatoes with a blunt paring knife—never saw the point of peelers. It used to drive me crazy to watch the way she peeled the pear for her breakfast, which she ate every morning in a ritualistic fashion, after her coffee and toast. She would take an ordinary blunt butter knife—or sometimes an equally blunt paring knife—and gouge at the fruit, taking away a thick layer of the flesh along with the peel. But eventually—after she stubbornly refused to use several vegetable peelers that I gave her as gifts—I realized that she would never change. Whether it was efficient or not, peeling a pear with her dear old butter knife made her happy.

Mistrust any guru who suggests that good cooking cannot start until you have spent thousands on shiny cookware. You don't need a lot of gadgets or a big kitchen to cook a delicious meal. Consider India, where millions of home cooks still produce miraculously varied and flavorful meals every day with no oven, no countertops, no fancy electrical gizmos, no fridge, and no kitchen sink, never mind an espresso machine or glossy stand mixer costing hundreds of dollars. According to food writer Julie Sahni, as of 1980, cooking in most Indian homes was done on a wood or coal-burning stove while sitting on a low stool or "from a squatting position on the floor." The traditional Indian kitchen contained nothing but a heat source, some pans and griddles and chopping boards, a few knives and sieves and graters, spoons for stirring, a wooden rolling pin for flatbreads, a grind-stone, and a woman with the skill and energy to bring all these tools to life.

Having said this, when given the choice between an easier way of doing something and a harder way, most traditional cooks would quite naturally choose the easier way. There is no point in making life more of a grind than it needs to be just because we have some romantic ideas about what hand-cooked food should be. Julie Sahni describes how transformative it was to discover "the virtues of the phenomenal food processor" for speeding up Indian dishes by making ginger-garlic purée, or slicing onions to "wafer-thin shreds," or mixing the dough for flatbreads.

Never hesitate to go high-tech with kitchen tools when it makes your life easier. I can't imagine cooking without my cheap hand-held immersion blender, my battery-operated digital scales, and my electric beaters. My food processor and my Instant Pot (of which more, later) are also beloved friends. And though I never thought I would say this, I'm endlessly grateful to my microwave oven for its ability to melt chocolate without a double boiler, soften butter for making cakes, and reheat leftovers. My microwave would pass the William Morris usefulness test (if not the beauty one).

Then again, it would be a mistake to assume that the high-tech way is always better, or quicker, or that it leads to a more enjoyable time in the kitchen. Once a gadget enters your house, you have to find space for it, and many expensive electrical gizmos cause more trouble than they solve. As food writer Sarah Beattie has remarked, "Do stop and think ... sometimes a knife is quicker."

Sharp knives and imperfect pans

"Remember that knives are dangerous tools and that
people are seldom hurt by those things that they fear;
more often than not, they are hurt by those things of
which they feel sure."
Burt Wolf, *The New Cook's Catalog*, 2000

A sharp knife and a good board; a trusty pan and a wooden spoon: you can cook
almost anything if you have these plus a decent stove (I still use gas, out of habit and
because I like the control of turning a flame up and down, but I now see that it is
only a matter of time before I switch to one of the new-generation induction stoves,
which are so much more energy-efficient). The problem is that most of us fall at the
first hurdle because we don't have a single sharp knife to call our own.

The most overlooked of all kitchen tools is the knife sharpener. Nothing you can
do as a cook will ever give you the feeling of power and freedom you have when you
are dicing or slicing something with a really sharp knife. It's as if the food is a slab
of marble and you are a master sculptor.

Yet very few people whom I know, even keen cooks, keep their knives sharp. You
know your knives are too blunt when you try to slice into a tomato and your knife is
so feeble it can't even make it through the top layer of skin. Another sign that your
knives are too blunt is that you keep them in a drawer without any fear that you will
cut yourself when you reach inside. Dull blades slow you down and make cooking
so much harder than it needs to be every single time. When your knives are blunt,
even chopping an onion becomes a frustrating obstacle course. My friends with
blunt knives will often say self-deprecatingly that they don't have very good knife
skills when actually it is a miracle that they are managing to chop food at all with
blades so ineffective they might as well be spoons. Every time we cook with blunt
knives, we are sabotaging ourselves as cooks. Buying a knife without the means to
sharpen it is a bit like buying a beautiful plant without the soil that will keep it alive.
Why do we do it?

The best answer I have come up with—other than inertia—is that there is a
kind of mystique about knife sharpening that puts some of us off so much that we
can't bear to do it at all. We have a sinking feeling that whatever we do, it will be

wrong, and so we don't sharpen our knives at all for fear of ruining them. The whole process perversely feels even more intimidating if we have bought expensive knives, because it feels as if there is more at stake. And then over time, your knives get so blunt that they require drastic action to restore them to sharpness, which makes it feel even more futile to attempt action with the sharpener you have, which you are convinced is the wrong sharpener. I used to be this way myself. I had read so many pieces of advice about how to sharpen knives—some of them contradictory—that I no longer trusted myself to do it.

When I asked people on Twitter to describe why they did or didn't sharpen their knives, many reported a deep sense of insecurity about sharpening. One person said that she constantly beat herself up for not sharpening her knives. "Every time I read about it, it seems complex, and the sharpener I do own, which was simple to use the one time I did it, doesn't seem like what Real Chefs think is best. So I just don't do it." Another person said that she had taken a knife skills course and been told that she could ruin knives by improper sharpening, so it was best to leave the job to professionals. But it isn't so easy to find a professional knife sharpener these days. My brother-in-law Gonzalo, who grew up in Argentina, remembers the neighborhood knife sharpener cycling around the barrio calling for people to bring out their knives to sharpen. In most cities of the world, those days have gone.

Here's what you need to know about knife sharpeners. The best knife sharpener is simply *the one that you will use the most*. That's it. It's much easier to keep knives sharp than to resharpen blunt ones. Rather than telling yourself that whatever sharpener you choose is wrong, find the one that you can bear to fit into your routines and on your kitchen counter *and actually use it*. You can buy little pull-through sharpeners that are cheap and foolproof to use and easy to store in a kitchen drawer. They may not give your knives the most perfect edge imaginable but what they will do is give you knives that are *not blunt* any more, and a not-blunt knife is worth its weight in gold compared to a blunt one.

Purists will tell you that a knife can only be properly sharpened using a water stone (AKA a whetstone) and elbow grease. The purists have a point. A whetstone—a set of brick-shaped tools with different levels of abrasion—will give you the best edge and it will also be gentle on the knife, removing the least amount of metal as you grind it. What's more, the process of using a whetstone can be deeply meditative and relaxing. There are now plenty of good quality videos on YouTube showing you the correct way to use a whetstone: what coarseness of grit to choose for the stone, how to soak it, what the proper angle is to hold the knife at in relation to the stone and how you know when you have a burr, how to strop the blade with leather, and finally, how to polish the blade using a stone with finer grit.

But I hesitate to recommend the whetstone as the best or only way to sharpen knives, because it is not a process that everyone can or will fit easily into their lives. I love using my whetstones, but it takes me around 15 minutes per knife to get the job done and sometimes I just can't find the time. Everyone deserves to cook with knives that are not blunt but not everyone has the inclination or time or ability to use a whetstone. I suspect that many of the whetstones that are purchased end up sitting unused in kitchen drawers.

My own preferred way to sharpen knives is with a little hand-held pull-through Japanese sharpener called a shinkansen, with sets of ceramic wheels set at exactly the right angle for Japanese knives, which are sharpened to 15° rather than the 20° that is standard for a German or French knife. Other than my knives themselves, it is the single most useful item in my kitchen. You fill it with water and draw the knife through the successive wheels to sharpen, then hone. It works brilliantly (until the ceramic wheels wear down, but you can buy replacements). If this is still too pricey, you can get plenty of nifty little pull-through ones for not much more than ten bucks, which will do the crucial job of giving you not-blunt knives.

The second crucial thing you need to get at the same time that you buy your sharpener is a honing steel, which you should ideally use every time you use your knife. This looks like a heavy metal or ceramic pole with a handle on the end. These honers are often misleadingly labeled as "sharpening steels" even though they don't actually sharpen the knife. Make sure that you do buy a honing steel and not a diamond sharpening rod, which is coated in a harsh abrasive that will chew up your knives. The honing steel keeps a sharp knife sharp by straightening it out, realigning the microserrations along the edge. Unlike a sharpener, the honer doesn't actually remove any metal from the blade.

For years, I couldn't see how adding an extra stage after sharpening could make much of a difference. Then I started doing a few strokes on the honing steel every time that I got my knife out and couldn't believe the extent to which it improved the knife's cutting edge. As with sharpening, you need to ignore the mystique around honing and forget any memories you may have of chefs doing it super-fast like Samurai. The technique that works for me—and does not leave me terrified that I am going to stab myself—is holding the steel vertically on the chopping board and then cutting down onto it lightly with the knife a few times on each side. Try to angle the knife at around 20° for European knives and 15° for Japanese knives, but do not fret if your sense of geometry is not this precise. Just cut down into the steel slowly at an angle, making sure that every part of the blade has touched the metal and you will be doing it fine. By giving my knife a few gentle swipes on the steel every time I use it, I am also reminding myself just how sharp it is and that I need to be careful.

A word to the wise. If you have been cutting with blunt knives all your life, go carefully when you switch to sharp ones. For one thing, make sure you have a safe place to store them. I like having my knifes on a strong magnetic strip over the sink, and knife blocks are also good, but if you don't have either of these, you can buy blade protectors or sheaths for storing sharp knives safely in a drawer.

As no end of experts will tell you, a sharp knife is the safest knife, but it can take time for you to adapt your technique if you are used to bluntness. It's almost shocking how little effort you need from your arm and hand with a truly sharp knife. But once you do adapt, you will never want to go back.

On the subject of knives, you really don't need many. To start with, you can get by with three knives: a good 8- or 10-inch chef's knife (or a Chinese cleaver if that's what you prefer, or a smaller 6-inch chef's knife if you are someone who just can't bear big knives), plus a little paring knife and a serrated bread knife (that you can also use for cutting tomatoes). Don't be swayed by those huge knife sets that look like a bargain until they clutter your kitchen with knives you never use. It's much better to choose the three knives you actually need individually, going for the best quality you can afford. The chef's knife is the one you will end up using the most, so read some reviews and pick one that feels comfortable in your hand. You want a knife that is full tang, where the metal of the blade extends all the way through the handle, giving you a balance between the blade and the handle. These three knives should see you through almost every eventuality.

The only strong reasons to buy additional knives would be a) because you'd like to share the cooking with other people from time to time, or b) because you see another knife that you love so much you just have to buy it. I used to think I needed a wide range of knives to allow for them getting dirty as I cooked, but then I realized that the best way to use a knife is to rinse and dry it constantly as you are going along. If I cut some meat and then want to cut some vegetables, I simply wash and dry the knife in between. I also wash and dry it and return it to where it is stored the very moment I have finished cooking, before we sit down to eat. Once you get in the habit of this, it becomes as natural as brushing your teeth before bed.

Now that you have your knives, you need a board. I would always go for wood, big enough to give you space to work on and heavy enough that it doesn't slide around too much. There used to be a worry that wood wasn't hygienic compared to plastic, but the evidence now suggests that it is every bit as safe because wood has antibacterial properties, as long as you scrub it well with dishwashing liquid and hot water between uses. Some people like to keep separate boards for fish, meat, and vegetables. I don't, but you might disagree. Wood is much the kindest chopping surface for knives, so you won't have to sharpen as often as you would with plastic.

A wooden chopping board also has the crucial quality that all the best kitchen utensils need, which is lovability. The right chopping board should feel like an old friend when you get it out. Ideally, you would have several boards so you can spread out your work and share the burden of vegetable prep when cooking for big meals.

TO RECAP, ALL YOU NEED FOR A LIFETIME OF HAPPY SLICING AND CHOPPING IS:

—One chef's knife (8–10 inches) or a Chinese cleaver (*tou*): for slicing, dicing, mincing, hacking, and everything in between.
—One paring knife: for peeling, paring, cutting grapes or cherry tomatoes in half, mincing garlic, checking whether fish is done, coring apples, and any time you just want the comfort of a little knife in your hand.
—One serrated bread knife (10–12 inches): for cutting bread and cakes as well as for cutting tomatoes and lemons.
—One knife sharpener.
—One honing steel.
—Several wooden cutting boards.

OTHER KNIVES THAT ARE NICE TO HAVE BUT NOT ESSENTIAL INCLUDE:

—A Japanese santoku knife with a dimpled blade is handy for chopping vegetables, and some prefer it to the Western chef's knife because it is smaller and more maneuverable.
—A petty knife or utility knife is good for anyone with small hands, or a child.
—A second chef's knife, perhaps smaller than the first, is handy if you want to cook with other people.
—A smaller serrated knife to use for tomatoes (so that you can keep your bread knife for bread).

Once you have your knives and board sorted out, I would celebrate by preparing something simple that requires fine slicing, such as Olia's tomato, cucumber, and radish salad (page 168).

Having figured out the knife situation, the next thing to consider is pans. While most cooks give sharp knives too little attention, we obsess far too much over precisely which cooking pot to buy. You can cook perfectly lovely food with very imperfect pots and pans. This is just as well, since imperfect pots and pans are the only kind for sale.

In 1988, an American engineer named Chuck Lemme set out to analyze how to design the ideal cooking pot using nine different criteria. His categories were:

1. Temperature uniformity (My translation: will the pan even out heat spots?).
2. Reactivity and toxicity (Will it poison my guests?).
3. Hardness (Will it get dents in it?).
4. Simple strength (Will it cope with being dropped?).
5. Low stick rating (Will my dinner get stuck?).
6. Ease of maintenance (Can I stick it in the dishwasher?).
7. Efficiency (Does it heat up quickly?).
8. Weight (Is it easy to lift?).
9. Cost per unit (Is it affordable?).

Lemme examined a range of metals including copper, aluminum, cast iron, and stainless steel and collected his findings into an idealness rating, with 1,000 as the perfect score. What he found was that even the top performing metal for cooking pans—which was cast iron—got a very low score (544.4). Most pans are brilliant at one thing but terrible at another. Copper pans, for example, got a perfect score for efficiency on Lemme's scale but a low score for ease of maintenance and cost.

Lots of the things we want from a cooking pot are contradictory. The ideal pan would be very thick to ensure hardness and heat retention but it would also be very thin so that it's easy for weak wrists to hold it and so that it heats up quickly. It's a physical impossibility to have a pan that is thick and thin at the same time. Lemme found that you could get closer to the perfect cooking pan by combining various metals together in a sandwich-type formation. This is how a lot of top-of-the-range cookware such as the All-Clad brand is now constructed, with high conductivity aluminum layered together with stainless steel for stability. The trade-off here is the price tag, which can be close to a couple of hundred dollars for a single pan.

You need to give up on the idea of perfect pans. To me, a good cooking pan is one that can be appreciated, flaws and all, like a member of the family. All that really matters is whether you feel affection for it or not, in which case you can forgive the pan its foibles and cherish its scars. On the other hand, if a pan is causing you nothing but grief, or you haven't cooked with it in years, then it might need a new home.

For good but basic pans, I would go to a restaurant supply store, where you will find pans aimed to withstand the heat of a professional kitchen, though I would also consider browsing thrift stores and garage sales, where beautiful old bakeware and Dutch ovens can be picked up for a song. As with knives, there will probably be a single pan that you reach for more than any other. For many, this universal pan will be a wok, ideally one with a lid and a steaming rack, which is perhaps the greatest multi-functional pan ever invented. As well as using it for stir-frying, you can use a wok for steaming, poaching, and deep-frying.

My favorite pan by far is nothing special but I am almost as attached to it as I am to my laptop. It is just a 12-inch/30cm shallow stainless-steel pan with a lid. Technically, it is a big sauté pan, but if you start talking about sauté pans these days, most people look at you blankly, because home cooks are not as wedded to classical French haute cuisine as they used to be. It is my most faithful companion in the kitchen. I use it for every kind of risotto, paella, and curry, for browning meat and for sweating vegetables, for poaching fish and making sauces. Because it has short metal handles, it goes easily from stovetop to oven and back again. I recommend getting something similar (Netherton Foundry have a lovely version in spun iron called a Prospector Casserole): a pan that is wider than most saucepans and deeper than most frying pans, with a lid and ovenproof handles. Once you get your own version of a pan like this—whether in stainless steel or another metal—you will never look back.

You'll also want a few more workaday pots for boiling things in (again, I would go for stainless steel). You want a vast one for boiling pasta or poaching chickens or making stock plus a couple of medium or small ones for cooking vegetables or whisking up béchamel sauce or making your morning oatmeal. All these pots should have lids, because you always want the option. In addition, you'll want some kind of device for steaming. I favor having a large stainless-steel steamer to fit over one of your saucepans, but another cheap option is the excellent bamboo steamers you can buy in Asian grocery stores.

When it comes to frying pans, the most useful sizes are either big or tiny, which is annoying because most of the ones you find for sale seem to be middling in size. You will need to make a decision about whether to buy nonstick or not. The sheer slickness of a brand-new nonstick pan is undeniably exciting: the way a tiny drop of oil dances across the surface, like water on hot rock. But there are serious questions over the safety of Teflon, a plastic polymer: when heated to very high temperatures (which isn't recommended), a Teflon-coated pan releases toxic gases. Newer nonstick technologies can be safer and slightly more durable, such as anodized aluminum. Yet every nonstick pan is a life lesson in disappointment and decay because no matter how promisingly it starts off, it ends up losing its nonstick properties over time.

Personally, I never cook with nonstick any more because I would rather have a pan that gets better rather than worse as it ages. You can make the surface of any pan more nonstick—even stainless steel—if you season it with oil. Seasoning a pan sounds like an intimidating process but the best way to keep a pan seasoned is simply to cook with it a lot. Ella Risbridger put it best in her book *Midnight Chicken* when she said that all you need to season a cast-iron pan is: "oil; hot oven; time; Google." If I think a pan is starting to stick, I just heat it for a few minutes on the stovetop with neutral oil until shimmering hot, then allow it to stand for a few minutes and wipe it out with a kitchen towel or paper towels. You will need to do a slightly more lengthy initial seasoning if you have pans made from cast iron (or spun iron, an up-and-coming material that has most of the virtues of cast iron but is lighter), but usually the pan will come with advice on which oil to use and what to do with it. The basic principle of seasoning is to rub your new cast-iron pan (that you have washed and dried) with a thin coat of oil and put it into a very hot oven, face down, for half an hour. Turn the oven off and let the pan cool completely. Repeat this process a couple of times until the surface looks slicker and glossier than before. To test whether it is nonstick enough, fry an egg.

Nothing will ever make you feel as capable, as pioneering, as utterly Little House on the Prairie-ish, as a cast-iron pan and they don't cost much, considering how solid and durable they are. My cast-iron pan—which I love—is a deep, 10¼-inch/26cm skillet with pouring lips on both sides. I use it for everything from frittatas to cornbread to searing a couple of steaks to making a shakshuka for two people to baking a small-pan pizza. You can even use it as a cake pan. There's a clever cookbook by Charlotte Druckman called *Stir, Sizzle, Bake* consisting of nothing but recipes for a cast-iron skillet. If you season it before the first use, wash it up gently, and rub it with a bit of oil every time you put it away, it will get better each time you use it. Another type of pan that improves rather than deteriorates over time is an aluminum omelet pan. I bought one decades ago after watching Delia Smith recommend it on TV and have been super strict ever since about using it for nothing but omelets and pancakes and oiling it after every use. This pan is battered and blackened but my weekend crêpes don't taste as good when cooked in any other vessel.

You also need some kind of hefty Dutch oven for braising or roasting things. I have three Le Creuset pans in three different sizes, acquired many years ago. They retain heat beautifully and look as reassuring on the table as they do on the stove. But when I looked up how much it would cost to replace them in today's prices, I gasped. When it comes to heavy cast-iron enameled Dutch ovens, there are now cheaper options than Le Creuset; or there is eBay.

Lid on or off?

On the subject of pans, some people seem to get very worried about whether the lid of a pan should be on or off. Try to start thinking about the purpose of the lid and you will usually figure out the answer for yourself. Lid on is good for any time you

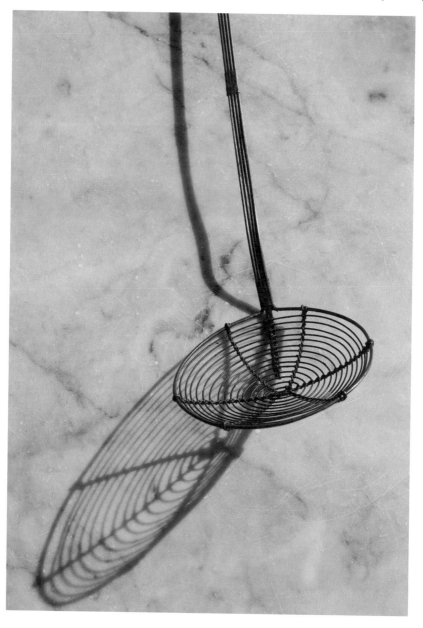

want things to cook in a moist and steamy way or if you want something to reach boiling point faster. Lid off is good when you want to see what is happening, when you want things to reduce down, or you want to brown the top of something when baking it in the oven. When boiling things such as pasta or vegetables, I would usually leave the lid off. But there are times when putting the lid on can make a huge difference. I now put the lid on when frying eggs, which removes any need for basting because by being enclosed, the top of the egg becomes surrounded by heat. As mentioned earlier, you can also speed up the stir-frying of tough vegetables by adding a couple of drops of water to the pan and putting a lid on for a minute or two so that the vegetables steam-sauté.

As for other vessels, it's useful to have a few cheap ceramic or enamel gratin dishes, metal tart pans, cake pans, and pie dishes (for making desserts and gratins and pies and crumbles), not forgetting that, as mentioned above, you can always use a cast-iron pan instead if you are short on space. Another thing I would splash out on is baking sheets and roasting dishes—at least two of each because by the time you've got the oven on, you may as well cook more than one thing, plus it is a rare cookie recipe that doesn't require two sheets. The better quality ones will last for years and can go straight over the stovetop when required, whereas a poor quality baking sheet will buckle and need to be replaced. The roasting dish will hold anything from lasagne to roasted chicken, from a big batch of lemon squares to branches of roasted cherry tomatoes. Good roasting dishes and baking sheets are another thing that you will never regret spending money on. A muffin pan is also useful if you are of a baking disposition.

What else do you need to make your kitchen life happier? I often think it is the modest hand-held utensils that really make the difference. Your list may well be different from mine, but here are twelve small items I use constantly (in addition to wooden spoons, which I am taking as read). These are by no means the only utensils in my kitchen but they are the ones I would save if my house was flooding.

Spider

I have already mentioned this, but I won't stop until you actually get one. A spider is like a small sieve on a long handle. Why these skimmers are not included in those useless utensil sets sold in kitchenware stores is beyond me. You can buy one cheaply from an Asian grocery store and once you have it, you will use it every day, whether for lifting short pasta out of boiling water, draining anything deep-fried or scooping vegetables from pan to plate. It can also double up as a serving spoon, if you are short on those.

Tongs

What would it feel like to have metal fingers? I imagine it would be a bit like using kitchen tongs. Mine are cheap and stainless steel, with scalloped edges. I have two sets, one longer than the other. I use my tongs to test strands of spaghetti, to toss things in a pan, to serve vegetables, to retrieve bay leaves from a pot of soup, to flip a flatbread, or to hold an eggplant direct in the flames of a gas stovetop to make it taste smoky. Other than a wooden spoon, they are the trustiest utensil in my possession.

Dough scraper

This cheap, simple tool is a calming thing to have around even if you never bake bread. Dough scrapers are designed to keep a work surface clean when you are working with wet dough. But I use mine almost like an extra pair of hands, to carry, cut and tidy. Use it to scoop up prepped items such as chopped nuts (it lifts every last crumb) or to scrape your chopping board clean.

Silicone spatula

There is a kind of Italian cookie called "ugly but good." I feel this fits my black silicone spatula too. It doesn't look pretty—like a plastic spoon-shaped spade—but it is amazingly effective at scraping out every last bit of batter from a bowl or stirring scrambled eggs.

Digital scales

You probably have these already, but if not, they are transformative: incredibly easy, quick, and precise compared to any other measuring method. I constantly marvel at the fact that 100ml of water weighs exactly 100g. Any time I can weigh something rather than measuring it by volume, I do, because it is so much more accurate.

Parchment paper

We don't usually think of paper as a technology, but I consider parchment paper one of the great inventions of modern times. Compared to the old greaseproof paper—which was useless—it is genuinely nonstick. With a roll of this in your kitchen drawer, your cakes will never stick to the pan again (unless you have a castle-shaped

bundt pan) and unlike plastic wrap or foil it is compostable after use. You can also use it when roasting vegetables and you feel that you just can't face washing up.

Immersion blender

This is another truly great modern invention and just about the most affordable electrical kitchen item you can buy. The immersion blender was first patented by Bamix in Switzerland in 1950, but it wasn't generally used in home kitchens until the 1980s. As with many things in life, you need to be middle-aged to appreciate how great it is. I can remember how annoying it was to attempt to purée a big pot of soup in a countertop blender. You had to do it in batches and if you didn't wait long enough, the hot soup might burst out of the lid, spraying you and the kitchen. Every day I give thanks for the convenience of being able to bring my blender to the pot rather than the other way around. I use it to blitz tins of tomatoes (canned tomatoes taste much better when you buy them whole, then blitz them), to make smooth soups and sauces and chutneys such as the green cilantro chutney on page 256, to whiz up smoothies from frozen berries, and so much more.

Electric beaters

Another hugely underrated device. You could spend $500 on a heavy stand mixer, which will admittedly look magnificent on your kitchen counter. Or you could spend $30–$60 on highly functional electric beaters plus a couple of dollars more for a stainless-steel mixing bowl. One of these mixers is all you need for making cakes and meringues and bowls of dreamy whipped cream and mayonnaise.

Whisk

Even though I have electric beaters, I wouldn't be without at least one of these too. It is an agent of alchemy: a tool for capturing air. This elegant and economical design has been around in some form at least since the sixteenth century. The bulbous shape increases the contact area of the metal wires, enabling more air to be whisked into the egg or the cream. As well as using it to mix eggs for an omelet, I use my whisk for taking the lumps out of a béchamel sauce or whisking air into hollandaise. I also reach for it any time I want to whip cream and actually experience the controlled magic of watching a milky-white liquid turn into snowy peaks.

Lemon squeezer

Yes, you can squeeze half a lemon with your bare hands. But when you have a Mexican elbow-style squeezer—designed for squeezing limes—you get more of the juice and none of the seeds. It's like a tea strainer attached to a cup with a hinge and it is a marvel. But actually, I am also fond of those wooden citrus reamers and of the old-fashioned glass or steel lemon squeezers with a ridged dome on top and a bowl to catch the juice below. In the end, you have to choose the one that feels right in your hands.

Mortar and pestle

When I get down my big granite mortar and pestle, it pleases me to think that the technology has been around unchanged for at least 20,000 years. No matter how many whizzy electrical devices you own, there are times when a big mortar and pestle is better. Or it *feels* better, which maybe amounts to the same thing. I use mine for grinding spices, which is pure kitchen aromatherapy, and also for making guacamole and other slightly chunky salsas and sauces such as pesto. Because it weighs so much, it also comes in handy as a weight for squashing things that need pressing, such as firm paneer.

Salad spinner

This is a toy as much as a tool. In days gone by, cooks would rinse and dry salad by spinning it in a clean kitchen towel. A salad spinner does the same thing at the push of a button. Watching the basket spin with centrifugal force reminds me of being a child feeling the headrush of spinning on a roundabout at the playground. Use it not just to rinse and dry salad greens but for rinsing and drying herbs, and soaking gritty sliced leeks or spinach leaves. If you buy unwashed greens from the farmer's market, rinse and dry the greens as soon as you get them home and store them in the salad spinner in the fridge until you are ready to eat them.

If this has sounded a bit like a shopping list, I apologize. Unless you are starting absolutely from scratch in the kitchen—maybe as a student—you don't actually need to go and buy lots of things to improve your cooking life. The secret of satisfaction in the kitchen is less about buying expensive new stuff than it is about using what you already have. A case in point is the box grater.

In praise of the box grater (or using what you have)

"A good many cookery books start out by requiring a vast battery of equipment without which the simplest dish is doomed to failure (I always burst into tears when I get to the bit about the little porcelain ramekins)."
    Katherine Whitehorn, *Cooking in a Bedsitter*

Imagine a kitchen tool powerful enough to do the work of a hundred small knives all at once. This miracle machine would be able to shred cheese in seconds and mince garlic with ease. It would have the ability to release the hidden fragrance from a nutmeg and to reduce a hard butternut squash to a pile of soft strands. And it would do all this without electricity.

Most of us already have one of these wondrous gadgets in our kitchens. It is the old-fashioned box grater. As food writer Burt Wolf observes, a grater should really be understood as a complex kind of knife because the whole surface is covered with cutting edges that slice efficiently in unison. One idle morning, I decided to count the perforated holes on my box grater. There were 50 holes on the coarse side and no fewer than 315 holes on the fine side. In addition, there was the underrated third side with its single slicing blade, which is surprisingly handy for making paper-thin slices of anything from radish to cucumber, though I tend to forget about it. Finally, there is the fourth side with its rasp-like raised surface which looks more like a vicious foot file than a kitchen utensil. I suspect that most people who say they don't like box graters have had unpleasant experiences with this side and its stabbing star-like holes. Food writer Rachel Roddy refers to it as "the bastard side of the grater that you never want to use." Certainly, it does a terrible job of grating things such as orange zest, which get mashed up and encrusted on the rasps, and it is a pain to wash up. But Roddy explains that its one great use is for grating the pecorino for cacio e pepe pasta into a powder fine enough to emulsify the cheese into a rich, creamy sauce.

In its way, the box grater is the ideal kitchen tool: it achieves great results with a whole range of ingredients from very minimal technology. (In this, it is a world away from all the high-tech single-function cupcake makers and overwrought coffee machines in the average cookware store, which promise so much but often end up as mere clutter on the kitchen counter). Homespun versions of a box grater used to be made at home from a tin can or a cookie tin, drilled with a few holes. This was how Irish cooks would traditionally grate the potatoes needed for boxty—a hearty potato pancake.

I did not always recognize the exciting potential of the box grater. For years, I was seduced by the pricier Microplane grater, which originated as a woodworking tool. I loved the way these slim steel rectangles could turn a hunk of parmesan into cloudlike fluff. But then the handle broke off my Microplane and although I bought a couple of replacements, I somehow didn't trust them in quite the same way. I found myself gravitating toward my trusty old box grater that was there waiting for me at the back of a drawer, where it had always been.

Here are some of the reasons I love my box grater, which is stainless steel and made in Italy. It cost little more than a bag of coffee beans yet is as excitingly versatile as one of those old four-in-one ballpoint pens that I remember loving as a child. It can grate coarse carrots or beets for a wintry slaw and fine lemon zest for the dressing. You might find yourself making a lasagne that requires you to grate both nutmeg and cheese. The box grater can do it all and yet it lacks the hefty price tag or the bling of so many modern kitchen gadgets. It really does deserve the name of "greater," which was the name of an American cheese grater marketed in Philadelphia in the 1920s. You can even use it to make breadcrumbs, using the coarse side, if you don't want to get the food processor out (a tip I picked up on Twitter from someone who got it from *People* magazine, although only later did I start reading around and see that actually, graters have been used to make breadcrumbs for hundreds of years). I started collecting recipes that called for grating rather than cutting and was surprised to discover that ingenious cooks from Italy to India had long been using the grater for far more than just cheese.

When multi-functional box graters were first sold on a mass scale in America in the 1890s, they were seen as modern, clever, and labor-saving, even though the technology of grating itself was nothing new. Since ancient times, cooks have used rough-surfaced objects for shredding hard vegetables that might otherwise be too tough to chew. The Taíno people of the Caribbean used rough stone boards to grate root vegetables such as cassava and sweet potatoes before cooking them. Cheese graters also go back a long way. As long ago as the 1540s, a Frenchman named François Boullier invented a metal cheese grater as a way to use up the hard cheese generated by a sudden dairy surplus in Europe.

But the combination four-sided box grater made from tin in the 1890s was something new: a grater for all your cutting needs, from shredding cabbage for sauerkraut to zesting citrus peel and chocolate.

Really, all we need from a grater is that it should shred stuff in an easy and effective way and, for my money, the box grater does this better than all the fancy and overpriced deluxe cheese scrapers and rotary cheese graters. I used to think that the fine side wasn't fine enough for ginger and garlic but now, for most uses, I have come to prefer the slightly larger strands that it produces, which offer a stronger hit of flavor than Microplane-minced ginger and garlic. I am satisfied by the sturdy simplicity of the design and the way that the shreds of cheese or carrot or whatever pile up inside the grater. And it is *fast*. I recently grated 9 ounces/250g of peeled carrot for a solo lunch and it took me under a minute.

For making carrot salad for a crowd, I do sometimes set aside my box grater and use the grater attachment on my food processor instead, which has the added bonus of turning the carrots into long elegant strands, like the carrot salads you find in France. And sometimes, because I am fickle, I revert to the Microplane for ginger and cheese. But for everyday cooking, I always find myself returning to the box grater because it works and because it makes me happy every time I use it: to zest a lemon on the fine side and use my fingers to extract the fragrantly oily yellow peel from the inside of the box is a jolt of brightness on the way to dinner.

Grated tomato and butter pasta sauce (with or without shrimp)

When I mention grating tomatoes, not everyone is convinced. "Surely a tomato is too soft to grate?" said one friend. But that is exactly why it works so well. Because of their squishy flesh and tough skins, tomatoes are perversely difficult to cut with a regular knife whereas the box grater can turn a large tomato into skinless (or nearly skinless) pulp almost instantly. You cut the bottom off a tomato and grate on the soft cut side over a bowl to catch the juices. Most of the skin sort of peels itself away as you grate, so that it is easily discarded without any need for the usual palaver of skinning tomatoes by blanching them in a bowl of hot water. In mere seconds, you are left with a fragrant bowl of tomato flesh and juice that can be turned into a sauce with butter and garlic in the time it takes to boil pasta. It is excellent with shrimp but you can just as easily make it without. When a version of this concoction appeared in *Bon Appétit* magazine in 2016 from chef Ashley Christensen, it was immediately hailed as a hot new hack. But grated tomatoes are hardly a novelty. They have made a regular appearance in Madhur Jaffrey's recipes for Indian home cooking for decades. As so often with cooking, what seems new on the page is not new in the kitchen.

Serves 2

9 oz/250g small wild frozen shrimp, cooked and peeled (optional)
7 oz/200g dried pasta, any shape (to make it even faster, I sometimes use quick cooking Chinese wheat noodles)
1 lb/450g large tomatoes
¼ cup/50g unsalted butter, plus an extra slice
4 cloves of garlic, peeled and sliced
1¼ cups/25g basil
Chile flakes

If you have not defrosted the shrimp overnight, put them into a bowl and cover them with hot water from a kettle.

Place your biggest pot on your biggest burner, fill it with hot water from the kettle, and bring to a rolling boil. Salt well and cook the pasta according to the timing on the package, stirring with long tongs from time to time.

Meanwhile, cut a very thin slice off the stalk end of each tomato. Hold by the uncut side and grate over a bowl until you can grate no further. What you should have left in your hand is mostly skin. Discard the skin or save it for vegetable stock.

Melt the butter in a wide pan over medium heat. Cook the garlic, stirring with a wooden spoon until fragrant. Add the tomato pulp and a big pinch of salt. Almost immediately, you will see the color change from reddish to terracotta orange. After a couple of minutes more, the sauce will have reduced. Drain the shrimp well and add them, if using, along with the basil: just tear the leaves with your fingers. Drain the pasta with tongs or a spider straight into the sauce. Toss and add the extra slice of butter off the heat until melted. Taste to see if it needs more salt and add a big pinch of chile flakes if you like (I do).

NOTES

If you have raw shrimp instead of the cooked frozen kind, add them to the pot of boiling water before you cook the pasta. Drain with a spider when just cooked (2 minutes) and reserve until the sauce is ready.

For those who like aniseed, this is good with ½ tablespoon of Pernod added at the end along with the slice of cold butter.

Melting-soft zucchini

I would happily eat these alongside almost any meal and they happen to be the easiest of all vegetable dishes to make. I first made them because I was yearning to re-create a dish of zucchini pasta with fried spinach balls from the menu of the Carluccio's chain of Italian restaurants. Cooking zucchini this way makes them taste meltingly soft and buttery, whether or not you add butter. For a side dish for 4, trim the ends of 2–3 medium zucchini, rinse them, and grate them on the coarse side of the grater straight into a wide pan. Grate in 2 peeled cloves of garlic on the fine side of the grater. Add 1–2 tablespoons of olive oil or butter and a fat pinch of salt. Put the pan over medium-high heat and cook, stirring often, until the zucchini are bright green, tender, and most of the liquid has evaporated away. Last time I made this, it took around 5 minutes but it can take longer. Finish with any or all of: a grating of nutmeg, a pinch of chile flakes, a shower of mint leaves, a squeeze of lemon, a spoonful of chopped rosemary. With parmesan grated over the top, this makes an excellent quick sauce for pasta.

Zucchini and herb fritters

This is another direction you can go in with box-grated zucchini, though you can also adapt it to other vegetables such as butternut squash, beet, or celery root. Grating potatoes and other vegetables is one of the most obvious and venerable uses for the box grater, from Persian zucchini fritters to Jewish latkes. The great American food writer Mimi Sheraton has said that a good potato latke should always contain a little blood "from bruised knuckles." I don't share this sentiment but what I do feel is that I want as many of these delicious grated fritters in my life as possible. With a bright salad and yogurt mixed with garlic, it makes a winter vegetarian supper that is comforting but not too soporific. I was amazed one day when I realized I could cook the fritters all at once in a tray in the oven, which is so much simpler than batch frying them in a pan.

Serves 4 generously, as a main course, with a salad
14 oz/400g potatoes, peeled
1 lb 2 oz/500g zucchini (or substitute root vegetables such as celery root
    or carrot or parsnip)
1 medium onion, red or yellow, peeled
2 cloves of garlic
Olive oil
3 large eggs
A few sprigs of mint or thyme or parsley or any herb that you have,
    finely chopped
Zest of 1 unwaxed lemon
A couple of pinches of chile flakes (optional)
½ cup plus 2 tablespoons/75g all-purpose flour (can be gluten-free)
¾ teaspoon baking powder

Preheat the oven to 400°F.
    Grate the potatoes, zucchini, and onion on a coarse grater into a sieve over a bowl. Peel the garlic and grate on the fine side of the grater, adding it to the sieve. Sprinkle with 1 teaspoon of salt and let rest for 10 minutes. While the mixture is set aside, drizzle a generous layer of oil on two baking sheets and put them into

the oven. You want the oil to get hot before you add the fritters. Now return to the grated vegetables. Squeeze out the excess liquid with your hands over the sieve. Then crack the eggs into another mixing bowl and beat together with the herbs and lemon zest (grated on the fine side of the grater) and the chile flakes if using. Add the flour, baking powder, and the vegetables to the eggs and mix well. Remove the baking sheets with the hot oil carefully from the oven. Dollop out spoonfuls of the mixture, spacing them out on the sheets. It should sizzle as it hits the oil. If not, the sheet is not hot enough—return it to the oven for a couple of minutes. Give the fritters 10 minutes. Then remove from the oven, flip with a spatula, and return to the oven for another 10–15 minutes, or until golden and crisp. Transfer to a plate lined with paper towels to blot some of the oil.

VARIATIONS

—If you prefer, you can shallow-fry the mixture in batches in oil in a frying pan, transferring the fritters to a plate covered with paper towels when they are done.
—I like these with a salad of radishes and lettuce dressed with oil, lemon, and full-fat yogurt to which I have added half a clove of garlic, grated, a big pinch of salt, and some nigella or cumin seeds.
—These also go well with fried or poached eggs, with or without feta cheese crumbled on top.
—If you have fritters left over, they also make excellent sandwiches the next day, like falafel, with hummus.

Kim's gyoza

When my friend Kim Smith told me that she had taught schoolchildren as young as eight to make gyoza—little Japanese dumplings with delicate fillings—I felt mildly intimidated. My own attempts at gyoza had been clumsy at best, so how were such young children managing it? "Easy," said Kim, who teaches cooking in schools (alongside doing a PhD in food policy). "We use box graters for the filling." She told me that the children found it deeply satisfying to grate together various vegetables and stuff them into the little dumpling wrappers. After our conversation, I went back to my own kitchen and tried to make gyoza again and discovered that, with the box grater method, it was indeed much more like child's play.

Serves 4
7 oz/200g carrots, peeled and trimmed
9 oz/250g mushrooms, any kind (ordinary button will do fine)
4 cloves of garlic, peeled
½ oz/15g fresh ginger, plus extra for the dipping sauce
2 tablespoons oil, plus extra for frying
2 teaspoons miso (any kind)
½ teaspoon sugar
1 teaspoon sesame oil
40 round wonton wrappers
3 tablespoons rice vinegar
2 tablespoons soy sauce

Grate the carrots and the mushrooms on the coarse side of a box grater. Grate the garlic and ginger on the fine side of the grater. Warm the oil in a wide pan over medium heat and add the carrots, mushrooms, garlic, and ginger. Cook, stirring with a wooden spoon, until the vegetables have cooked down and lost their moisture. This should take no more than 5 minutes, during which time the mushrooms will shrink and the carrots will turn from orange to yellowy orange. Off the heat, stir in the miso, sugar, and sesame oil. Taste to see if it needs salt (miso is salty).

Now, use the filling to stuff the dumpling wrappers. As a lazy and hurried person, I usually use a technique I learned from *Vegan Japaneasy* by Tim Anderson. Have a bowl of water ready, plus a wooden chopping board on which you can make the dumplings, and a large plate lined with parchment paper on which to put them when they are finished. Spoon a little filling into the middle of each wrapper— around 2 teaspoons. Wet your fingers with a little water from the bowl and dampen the edges of the wrapper. Fold it over the filling and pinch it shut in a little half-moon shape, then pinch the two ends together like tortelloni. If you want to know how to pleat gyoza the proper way, have a look on YouTube. As each dumpling is complete, put it on the parchment-lined plate. Keep them covered with a damp cloth until ready to cook.

Or you can freeze them on the plate before transferring them to an airtight container. Use within 3 months. You can cook them from frozen exactly as below (just give them a couple of minutes longer at the steaming stage).

To cook the gyoza: heat ½ tablespoon of neutral oil over medium heat in a cast-iron pan or any shallow pan with a lid. Put about 10 dumplings in the pan and let them brown and crisp on the bottom—1–2 minutes—moving them around in the pan so that they brown evenly. Add ¼ cup/60ml water, put the lid on, and let them steam for 4–5 minutes. Lift the lid. The water should have mostly evaporated. Carefully lift the gyoza out onto a warmed plate and cook the rest of them in batches.

While the batches are cooking, you will have time to make a quick dipping sauce by whisking together the vinegar, soy sauce, and a little fresh grated ginger. Ideally you should also have a second dipping sauce featuring chile, but this can be as simple as a squirt from a bottle of sriracha or a spoonful of crispy chile oil.

When all the dumplings are cooked, devour, with the sauce on the side.

OTHER VEGETARIAN GYOZA FILLINGS:

Tofu and Chive

This variation is based on a Hetty McKinnon recipe for wontons. Drain a 14-oz/400g package of firm tofu in a colander for 10 minutes to remove some of the moisture. Crumble it into a bowl and add ⅓ cup/30g of finely chopped chives, 1½ cups/30g of cilantro, finely-chopped, 1 tablespoon of soy sauce, 2 teaspoons of rice wine, 2 teaspoons of sesame oil, 2 garlic cloves, peeled and finely grated, a chunk of ginger, finely grated, 2 teaspoons of cornstarch, ½ teaspoon of salt, and ½ teaspoon of sugar.

Eggplant, lemon, and sesame

Slice and roast 2 eggplants with olive oil (see ideas for roasting vegetables on page 21) and combine in a bowl with the grated zest of a lemon, 2 teaspoons of sesame oil, 2 teaspoons of toasted white sesame seeds, 2 teaspoons of miso, 1 garlic clove, peeled and finely grated, and ½ teaspoon of sugar. Check for seasoning. This is also excellent with chopped roasted cabbage instead of the eggplant.

Three other tools you already have

Chopsticks

Wooden chopsticks—ideally long-handled ones—are one of the most underrated of all kitchen utensils. Used to toss salad, they are both more precise and more thorough than most salad servers. You can use them instead of tongs to move or retrieve food in a pan or instead of a skewer or cake tester to tell when a cake is done. They are also great for whisking eggs (or if you are feeling experimental, for making the extraordinary "tornado omelet," which was a viral sensation a couple of years ago—look it up and prepare to be amazed). Because chopsticks are made of wood, they are gentle on pans.

Jars

A clean empty jam jar or mustard jar is the best thing for emulsifying a salad dressing. It can also double up as a cookie cutter and a measuring cup. It's worth knowing that the standard Bonne Maman jar measures exactly one cup or 250ml up to the line where the lid screws on. I also use jars for storing my own home-made spice mixes and for keeping things like pumpkin seeds and pine nuts. In a pinch, you can even use a jar as a drinking glass.

Scissors

How useful are kitchen scissors? So useful that they regularly get stolen from the kitchen and carried off to other rooms of the house. Scissors are really just two knives joined together but compared with chopping food with a knife on a board, you are closer to the ingredients, whether you are snipping herbs, trimming green beans, or removing the fat from the edge of a chicken thigh. Or opening a package, which in all honesty is probably their main use in most kitchens. The real pleasure of scissors is the way they make your own hands feel like powerful shears. Using my strongest pair of kitchen scissors makes me feel like Wolverine, even if all I am doing is snipping chives.

AND ANOTHER THING: READ THE INSTRUCTION MANUAL

"I got a slow-cooker, it's meant to be really good," said another parent at the school gates one day. "And is it good?" I asked her. "I don't know; I haven't figured out how to use it yet so it's still in the box."

Sometimes, the most life-changing thing you can do in the kitchen is not to buy yourself a new gadget but to familiarize yourself with the instruction manual of a tool you already have. This even applies to something as basic as your oven. For many years, most electric ovens have come with timer delay functions as standard. In other words, you can put food into a preheated oven and set the oven to switch itself off automatically. Or you can put food into a cold oven and set the oven to come on and off automatically. This is incredibly useful and clever because it means you can put food into the oven, go out for an indeterminate amount of time and come back to find an oven full of beautifully cooked—but not burned—food.

Yet how many people do you know who ever use the timer delay on their oven? Almost no one. I understand this, because I didn't use the time delay on my own oven until very recently. Just the thought of trying to master this function made my head hurt. I couldn't be sure whether I had pressed the right buttons, and I didn't want to risk leaving the house and coming back to raw food. But then I realized I could experiment by cooking something on timer delay while I was still in the house, to make sure I had not completely misunderstood how to do it. It was perfectly easy and I have never looked back. I often use it on the weekend, when I take my dog for a walk and want to have the luxury of wandering without a fixed schedule. I might put some stuffed tomatoes and peppers into the oven or something like the roasting-tin chicken with fennel and citrus on page 320 or mushroom and pearl barley stew on page 323. When you arrive home to the scent of cooked food, it is as if the kitchen itself is greeting you.

Bells and whistles

"Good workmen blame their tools too;
there's such a thing as bad tools."
    Don Paterson, *The Fall at Home*, 2018

When buying bigger electrical gadgets, how can you choose the ones that won't gather dust or be discarded? The clutter in our kitchens is like a mausoleum of infatuations that didn't go the distance.

A good rule of thumb is to choose your devices based on things that you actually *want* to eat and drink rather than what you think you ought to consume. I recently met a brilliant cook who said she would give up almost every other electrical device in her kitchen (except for her toaster and her kettle) before she relinquished her heavy-duty ice-cream maker, the expensive kind that sits permanently on the countertop. She grew a lot of fruit in her garden and made different fruit gelatos several times a week, with unusual flavors such as mulberry and fig, which were far more refreshing and nourishing than any ice cream she could buy.

The best tools are the ones that enable you to live the life you want to live and to eat the foods you most desire. I am convinced that most of the unused kitchen gadgets in the world are linked to some kind of unrealistic weight-loss diet: the high-speed blender that you bought in the hope of making green juice every day, only to abandon it when you stopped the diet. A good kitchen gadget is one that is there to help you cook rather than one that gives you a twinge of guilt. A second rule of thumb is to think of the consequences. If you buy a coffee-maker that uses those little metal pods, it may feel opulent to start with—like being in a hotel—but you will be stuck buying those wasteful pods forever, whereas if you stick to a French press or Moka pot, you can compost the grounds and you are also free to experiment with whatever interesting beans you like. On the subject of waste, it's always worth considering buying your tools second-hand. Thrift stores and garage sales are usually full of perfectly good kitchen gadgets that people bought and then didn't want.

A few years ago, I wrote a book about kitchen technology (*Consider the Fork*). Every time I gave a talk to promote the book, people in the audience told me the kitchen machines they adored and the ones they hated. I loved these conversations.

What struck me was that there was no rhyme or reason to it. I met people who got daily joy and comfort from tools that I had written off as absurd or excessive, such as avocado cutters, mini cupcake makers, vegetable spiralizers, electric egg boilers, and automatic soup makers. I would look at these gizmos and think: why do you need that contraption when you already have a saucepan, an oven, and a knife? Yet many of their owners assured me these things were marvels.

When it comes to gadgets, the only fixed rule I can see is this: no tool is useless if it is actually used. Take the electric pancake maker. This is a kind of electric hotplate with six circular indents for making six small crêpes at a time. Until recently, I would have regarded this gadget as utterly pointless. But then my son went on his first sleepover after Britain's lockdown restrictions ended in the spring of 2021 with a friend who has a crêpe maker. The sight of five twelve-year-old boys all making breakfast pancakes simultaneously was one of the happiest visions of communal cooking I have ever seen. The beauty of the machine was that no one had to ask for another pancake when they felt hungry, they could just pour in more batter and make their own while chatting companionably.

What matters with a kitchen tool is what it can bring to your particular life. In this spirit, I will tell you about the three miracle machines I wouldn't want to be without in the kitchen, on the understanding that you may well violently disagree. In my life, all three of them enable me to cook things that I just wouldn't attempt otherwise. More than that, they make me want to cook.

My first and most obvious essential choice is a food processor, which I use five times a week *minimum* for blitzing of many kinds. It simply takes the grind out of grinding and makes daily cooking more of a pleasure than it would otherwise be. As great as an immersion blender is, there are tasks it can't easily handle. I will never forget how I felt when I got my first food processor, a gift from my sister-in-law Cathy. Suddenly, I actually *wanted* to chop and grate and pulverize things, the finer the better. When a gnarly celery root came into my kitchen, I no longer saw an annoying thing that I needed to peel: I saw beautiful strands of céleri rémoulade. My food processor can turn stale bread into herby green breadcrumbs and watercress into watercress soup. It can make cake batter or cookie dough in seconds. While I feel that stand mixers are not necessarily worth the space or expense, my food processor earns its keep many times over. When making a ragù of any kind, knowing that I can fine-chop the onions and carrots and celery in the food processor makes all the difference. I also love this machine because when you use the slicing attachments, it can slice potatoes and other vegetables micro-thin, thus sparing me the trauma of attempting to use a mandoline.

The second machine I would not be without is the Instant Pot, which is a Canadian brand of multicooker: an all-in-one electric pressure cooker with slow cooker, rice cooker, yogurt maker, and three other functions that no one remembers. I didn't expect to like the Instant Pot anything like as much as I do. For a while, a few years ago, it was horribly over-hyped. Every other new cookbook had an Instant Pot angle. I was getting bored with reading about these machines. And then I bought one and the very first time I used it, I cried from sheer gratitude. This may say more about me than it does about the Instant Pot (I cry easily), but still. For me, this machine has become the best answer to how to combine cooking with the rough and tumble of family life. My youngest child plays a huge amount of sport and almost every weeknight I was getting depressed by my inability to combine cooking a family dinner with taking him to a sports practice that didn't finish until 7:30 p.m. Sometimes I phoned home and begged my long-suffering teenage daughter to cook. Sometimes I was organized enough to have made something the day before, ready to heat up. Very often, we had a 5-minute omelet when we got in: no hardship, but it felt like a rush and a compromise. Then I got the Instant Pot and found that I could make nourishing one-pot dishes like pilaf on timer delay so that a piping-hot dinner would be ready the moment we stepped through the door. I also use my Instant Pot for soups and stews, for cooking legumes such as chickpeas to perfect tenderness without soaking, for no-stir risotto with a near-perfect texture, and as a rice cooker any time I want fluffy steamed rice. It is that rare thing: a genuinely labor-saving device. Unlike my old pressure cooker that went on the stovetop and needed a close eye, the Instant Pot tactfully switches itself to warming mode when the time is up, thus sparing me the prospect of burning dinner. My son is now so familiar with the Instant Pot that he can hum the jaunty little tune it makes when you open the lid.

My third miracle machine seems more frivolous. It is a waffle maker: a tool that gives you a huge reward simply for being a cook. For people without a waffle maker, the options are either: buy frozen or pre-made waffles, which don't taste good and contain too much sugar, spend a fortune on waffles at a café, or live a life without waffles. None of those sounds very appealing compared to owning a waffle maker and making your own whenever you feel in need of a boost. I was delighted to learn from the food historian Jeffrey Rubel that in nineteenth-century America there was a special kind of party called a "waffle frolic." With their crisp exterior and patterned shape, waffles are still one of life's small joys and sometimes, these are the only joys on offer. Here are two of my family's favorite waffle recipes.

Heavenly overnight waffles

A couple of years ago, I took my children to Brussels with a dream of waffles in our heads but on the whole trip we didn't taste a single real Belgian waffle that could match these. This formula is more than a hundred years old but tastes like something invented yesterday. It has a rich doughnut yeastiness. The secret ingredients are just yeast, butter, and time. The basic recipe for these raised waffles goes back to *The Boston Cooking-School Cook Book* by Fannie Farmer, published in 1896, but they were adapted and popularized by the great Marion Cunningham in *The Breakfast Book*, 1987.

Serves 6, with leftovers
1 x ¼-oz/7g envelope active dry yeast
2 cups/480ml whole milk
½ cup/115g unsalted butter, melted
1 teaspoon sugar
2 cups/250g all-purpose flour (again, this works fine with gluten-free flour)
2 large eggs
¼ teaspoon baking soda

You need to start these the night before for breakfast the next day. In a large mixing bowl with room to rise, mix together the yeast and ½ cup/120ml of warm water with a whisk and allow to dissolve and activate for 5 minutes. Add the milk, butter, sugar, flour, and ½ teaspoon of salt and whisk together well. Cover the bowl with a plate and let rise at room temperature. When it's breakfast time, preheat the waffle maker. Whisk the eggs and baking soda into the batter and cook in the waffle iron until golden and crisp. The batter will seem on the thin side, but it will puff up beautifully. They are hard to overcook because the mixture is so custardy and soft. I give them maybe 3–4 minutes in a shallow waffle maker or 5–6 minutes in a deep one (but machines vary, and so do people's taste in waffles, so it's always worth checking 1 minute before you think they are done). The batter will keep for a day or so in the fridge, so if there are only one or two of you, this quantity would be good for a whole weekend of waffles (just rewhisk the mixture slightly, then proceed). Or another way to go is to cook the whole batch of waffles, let them cool, and freeze them in freezer bags. They reheat easily in the toaster for weekday breakfasts.

Anne's hazelnut waffles

This works beautifully with any kind of nut you can imagine. My friend Anne, who first served me a version of these with fresh strawberries and cream, uses ground almonds. Just substitute weight for weight for the hazelnuts. Pistachio waffles are divine. I used to pre-grind the nuts for this but then I realized you can skip this step if you just blitz whole nuts in with the eggs, butter, sugar, and milk, which also creates a better texture.

Serves 4
6 tablespoons/80g unsalted butter, melted
2 tablespoons/20g granulated sugar (use less if you like)
2 large eggs
½ cup/80g whole blanched hazelnuts (preferably roasted)
¾ cup/180ml whole milk (or almond or coconut milk)
1 teaspoon vanilla extract (sometimes I leave this out and sometimes I use
    ½ teaspoon almond extract instead for a marzipan taste)
¾ cup/100g all-purpose flour (I've made these with gluten-free flour for celiac
    friends and it works fine)
1 teaspoon baking powder (make sure this is gluten-free if making for celiacs)

Preheat the waffle maker. Put all the ingredients except the flour and baking powder in a bowl, add a pinch of salt, and blitz with an immersion blender until the nuts are fully blended. Add the flour and baking powder and blitz again. Check for any unmixed floury patches and blitz one more time before giving the whole thing a quick stir with a spatula. Make the waffles as per the instructions for your machine. These might take 2–3 minutes in a shallow waffle maker or 3–5 minutes in a deep one. Opinion in my house differs on whether they are better crisp all the way through, which is how my son likes them, or soft in the middle (my preference). I have them for breakfast with maple syrup, frozen blackberries warmed in the microwave, and Greek yogurt or crème fraîche.

Treat cooking as a remedy (because it is)

"...it is the last pleasure that remains when the others have gone, to console us for their loss."
     Jean Anthelme Brillat-Savarin, *The Pleasures of the Table*, 1825

"Life goes on, mostly in the kitchen," became my stock answer for a while when friends emailed to ask how I was after my husband left. The more often I said it, the more I found it to be true. There were days so sad that I couldn't even bear to watch a film or open a book, because everything seemed to hit the wrong nerve. But there was no day so desolate that it couldn't be brightened at least momentarily by the familiar sound of eggs cracking in a bowl or the wheaty scent of noodles boiling. The late food writer A. A. Gill spoke of the therapeutic powers of cooking as "four and twenty black thoughts baked in a pie." By the time the pie is out of the oven, your thoughts are usually at least one notch brighter. If not, then at least you have pie.

I sometimes think how crazy it is that we spend so long talking about cooking as a problem (it supposedly takes too much time, costs too much, is too difficult) and so little time talking about all the things to which it provides cures (soothing a busy mind, bringing friends together, helping us to eat more vegetables). Consider cooking not as a problem but as a remedy, and it becomes easier to find the motivation to do it. At its most enjoyable, cooking is like meditation but with added butter and garlic. As many of us discovered during the pandemic, planning and cooking dinner can give pattern to the most patternless of days.

The original meaning of the word *recipe* was a formula for medicine. The root is Latin and it means "take" as in "take this and feel better." As I mentioned at the beginning, hundreds of years ago, cookbooks were not just collections of delicious things to eat but assortments of remedies for any problems that life might throw at a person, from baldness and stomach aches to the need to preserve a strawberry before it spoiled. Until modern times, most people understood that food was itself a kind of medicine.

After all this time, cooking is still one of the closest things we have to a panacea: a series of remedies, large and small, for making life better. It is sometimes said that if exercise were a pill, everyone would be taking it, because the benefits across the board—both physical and mental—are so great. The same is true of cooking, only more so. Home cooking is one of the very few things we can do that reconnect us both with nature and our own senses. It is an antidote to our screen-obsessed lives and a form of self-sufficiency that can be both soothing and confidence-boosting. Cooking is health and wellbeing but also fun and games. Cooking is culture and also community. Cooking can be a mindful break from our endless screens or it can be an expression of love. It is also a prerequisite to eating more sustainably, because only when you cook can you make choices about which ingredients to source and how many of them should be plants.

It's important to remember that cooking is not an all-or-nothing game. No one should feel obliged to cook (as generations of women did, trapped at the stove). In the modern world, assuming you have enough money, you can nourish yourself deliciously without ever picking up a saucepan.

But if you *never* cook, you can never know the sheer visceral joy of eating a pancake that you have made yourself, hot from the pan, or turning out a dish of green Persian rice onto a plate. You will never know how good a mayonnaise can taste, not just when it is finished but as you make it.

Cooking doesn't have to mean creating a five-course French dinner for eight from scratch, unless that's your dream (in which case, don't let me stop you!). Sometimes it means taking yesterday's curry and heating it up in the microwave, or the prosaic satisfaction of prepping a whole week's worth of packed lunches on a Sunday night. Other times, it means making your own cheese or tofu not because you need to but for the sheer heck of it. You could get started by learning to cook yourself a more delicious plate of eggs, or throwing together a series of salads that really delight you. In this world of tears, it's about finding your own remedies.

The only diet

Some so-called experts tell us to fear fat; others tell us to fear sugar or carbs or salt. But over the past decade, a new way of thinking about nutrition has emerged that suggests that all these food fears are misplaced or at least that they are leading us in the wrong direction. According to a mass of evidence from Brazilian scientists, the line between healthy and unhealthy diets is not marked primarily by some abstract idea of nutrients but by the percentage of whole foods a person eats. The obvious way to increase whole foods in your diet is to eat more home-cooked food, whether it's cooked by you or someone else—and to stop fearing food, full stop.

Depending on your own particular dietary needs, here is the only diet that most of us will ever need. Eat savory home-cooked food as often as you can, avoid what doesn't agree with you (including anything you have an intolerance to), and eat more vegetables. Manage portions by using smaller plates (a modest portion heaped on a small plate looks more generous). Eat more meals and fewer snacks. Treat any drink that isn't water or unsweetened tea as a snack, which isn't to say you shouldn't have it but do notice that you have swallowed it, just as you would with food. Oh, and allow yourself to feel moderately but not ragingly hungry at least once a day (I used to find this near-impossible but now find that I enjoy dinner so much more when I am actually hungry for it). Finally, eat with a view to maximizing your own pleasure. This means no guilt. Never allow yourself to see any of your eating—from chocolate cake to salad—as a failure. Whatever you ate today, tell yourself that you were allowed to eat it. Nothing tastes good when it's eaten in a spirit of self-recrimination, and tomorrow is always another breakfast. If you follow those basic guidelines, pretty much everything else will fall into place.

Almost all our current health problems with food seem to be associated with something called "ultra-processed food," which sounds obscure but is anything but. Ultra-processed food is basically the opposite of homemade food. The term was first coined in 2010 by a Brazilian doctor named Carlos Monteiro, who was alarmed to see how many people in his country were suffering from a new range of diet-related health problems—such as type 2 diabetes and tooth decay in children—seldom seen in the past. Monteiro knew that many nutritionists were laying the blame for these problems with sugar, but he wasn't convinced. During the period that obesity in Brazil had escalated—since the 1980s—surveys suggested that Brazilians were actually buying *less sugar* to use in the home, not more. To Monteiro, a bag of sugar on the kitchen counter can be a healthy sign because that bag of sugar belongs to someone who cooks. Monteiro's hunch—which has since been confirmed with evidence from dozens of studies—was that the greatest problem with modern food wasn't sugar or fat per se but the ultra-processed foods in which sugar and fat are now delivered to us.

More than half the calories the average person eats in the UK and US now consists of these ultra-processed foods (which are what Michael Pollan has memorably called "foodlike substances'). These products are ubiquitous, aggressively marketed, and consist mainly of refined starches, oils, and sugars made more palatable with the help of various additives. We are not talking about old-fashioned processed foods such as cheese, cured meats, canned tomatoes and beans, or smoked fish. The category includes everything from ready meals to snacks, from vegan hotdogs to meaty fast-food hamburgers, from sugary breakfast cereals to protein bars, from diet sodas to low-fat fruit-flavored yogurts. The saddest part of all is that many ultra-processed foods are labeled as health foods.

Over the past ten years, high consumption of these products has been consistently linked to elevated risk of depression, heart disease, asthma, breast cancer, type 2 diabetes, and eating disorders. There is also now evidence that diets high in these foods actively stimulate us to over-eat and hence to gain weight. A study from American scientist Kevin Hall in 2019 found that when twenty people ate a highly processed diet in laboratory conditions for two weeks, they ate on average 500 calories more per day than they did on a diet of mostly unprocessed and home-cooked food. What makes me so sad—as someone who used to be a compulsive eater—is that over-eaters tend to blame themselves for bingeing on salty snacks or ultra-processed ice cream when really it is in the nature of these foods to be overeaten. The more you can avoid having them in your house, the easier it becomes not to over-eat.

It is difficult to avoid ultra-processed foods altogether, precisely because they are so ubiquitous. With some categories of food such as bread, it is very hard to find any affordable versions in the supermarkets that are *not* ultra-processed. Most of us don't have the time or money to avoid ultra-processed foods altogether. Food is not an all-or-nothing game. A diet that is more than 50 per cent ultra-processed (which is the current average diet in the UK and US) is very different from one that is only 10 per cent or 20 per cent ultra-processed. Rather than trying to cut out ultra-processed foods altogether, I would notice which ultra-processed products are ones that you personally find really useful or really delicious (or both). Keep those and lose the rest.

The simplest way to cut down on these products is to eat more freshly cooked food. You don't have to deny yourself anything or force yourself to eat anything that you despise, and nor do you have to worry about the minutiae of whether what you are eating is healthy enough. Cook any main course that your heart desires without fear or guilt. Ignore all those angry diet wars between the low carbists and the low fattists and eat what you like. Brazilian food writer Rita Lobo told me that when she explains the concept of ultra-processed foods to people in Brazil they often say they are relieved, because they realize they can start eating homemade desserts they really love again and stop eating the ultra-processed low-fat flavored yogurts they have been eating out of self-denial.

We would be much healthier—mentally as well as physically—if we spent less time searching for perfect superfoods and more time dreaming up an easily made, affordable, and delicious lunch for ourselves. Am I promising that if you cook every day you will definitely lose weight? Of course not. Life doesn't work like that, and anyway, we are all far too obsessed with slimness as the only metric of wellbeing. There is far more to health than a person's weight. What I can promise for sure is that cooking on more days than not is the best step you can take toward a kind of healthy eating that—unlike those miserable diets—actually lasts.

The real secret of eating healthily is to reach the point where the foods you think are healthy and the foods you want to eat are one and the same. Along with all its other benefits, cooking is the most powerful way to change your own tastes: to unlearn old preferences and learn new ones.

In that spirit, here are a few of my favorite salads. These are not the kind of salads that I ate back when I was a dieter in the 1980s: dreary platefuls of dull iceberg lettuce with poached chicken breast and no dressing (or perhaps a gloopy low-fat dressing thick with emulsifiers and weirdly sweet from artificial sweeteners).

A good salad should be a joyous thing, full of contrasting colors and flavors and textures. It should be nourishing, but never punishingly so. North Carolina-based food writer Emily Nunn is the author of a glorious newsletter called "The Department of Salad." She has written that salads make her happy because they are "dazzling and delicious, like bouquets of flowers that you could eat."

Salads to savor

Mushroom noodles with peanut dressing

I got this idea from a recipe by the Chinese-British food writer Ching-He Huang in her book *Asian Green*. Vermicelli noodles are one of the best things to put in a main course salad when you are pushed for time because they cook in a bowl with water from a hot kettle. I often choose mushrooms when I am trying to eat less meat because they are so meaty, both in texture and flavor, and shiitake are meaty even by the standards of mushrooms. But you could adapt this recipe with its rich peanutty dressing to button mushrooms or actually to any vegetables you have in the fridge. It's quick enough to make last thing at night or in the morning before work to put in a lunchbox.

Serves 2, heartily

3½ oz/100g vermicelli dried rice noodles or (most delicious of all, if you can find them) vermicelli sweet potato noodles, which I buy from a Korean grocery store

1 large green onion, trimmed and cut very fine lengthwise (julienne)

1 tablespoon light oil

7 oz/200g shiitake mushrooms, stalks removed, thinly sliced (substitute any fresh mushrooms)

1 tablespoon soy sauce

A pinch of Chinese five-spice powder (leave out if you don't have any)

½ a cucumber, peeled and grated

2 large carrots, peeled and grated

2 tablespoons white or black sesame seeds

1 tablespoon sushi ginger, shredded (optional)

For the dressing

2 tablespoons smooth or crunchy peanut butter

1 tablespoon sesame oil

½ teaspoon chile flakes

1 tablespoon soy sauce

2 tablespoons rice vinegar

A thumb of ginger, finely grated

1 teaspoon agave syrup or honey

Take all the ingredients for the dressing, add 1 tablespoon of warm water, and shake together in a jar. Taste for seasoning. You might want more chile, a splash more vinegar, a touch more agave.

Put the noodles into a bowl or pot and cover with boiling water (check the package instructions to see how long they need to soak). Put the green onion slicles to soak in a bowl of cold water. This will remove some of their bite and make them curl up delightfully, like a vintage phone cord.

Heat a wok or a large frying pan over high heat and add the oil, mushrooms, and soy sauce. Season with the five-spice and cook, stirring often, for 2–5 minutes or until very savory and brown.

To serve, drain the noodles and divide between two plates or lunchboxes. Top with the cucumber, carrots, and mushrooms. Drizzle with the dressing, followed by the sesame seeds, drained green onions, and sushi ginger, if using.

Ten-minute cashew-noodle salad

Skip the mushrooms, make everything else as above, and add a big handful of cashews and any herbs you have (mint and cilantro are best) at the end instead.

Olia's tomato, cucumber, and radish salad

Sometimes people say that a good salad is all about the dressing, but summer vegetables, especially tomatoes, can make their own dressing if you salt them assertively enough. The word *salad* derives from the Latin word *sal*, for salt.

I first came across this combination in *Mamushka* by Olia Hercules. If I've eaten masses the day before and don't feel hungry, I might have this for lunch all by itself, just with some bread, but it's also a great side dish to fish or lamb chops. If you can find the tiny Persian cucumbers, they make a huge difference: they are so much crunchier and tastier than those vast watery ones. Think of this as a blueprint. In the summer, when I want a quick packed salad, I will take any crunchy vegetables in the fridge, chop them, and transfer them straight to a lunchbox with herbs, salt, and yogurt or oil.

Serves 4 as a side dish
1 lb 2 oz/500g ripe tomatoes, large or cherry or a mixture, any colors,
    the best you can buy or grow
4 Persian cucumbers (or 1 large English cucumber)
3½ oz/100g radishes
2 green onions
A handful of dill or fresh fennel
7 tablespoons/100ml full-fat yogurt (substitute 2 or 3 tablespoons
    of olive oil or tahini if you don't eat dairy)

Chop the tomatoes and put them into a big serving bowl. Slice the cucumbers (halve them lengthwise first if they are large and peel them if the skin is tough), radishes, and green onions and add them to the bowl with the chopped dill or fennel, the yogurt (or oil or tahini), and a big pinch of salt. Mix it all together until the tomatoes and radishes give off their pink juices.

Bread salad with zucchini and grapes

This—a great way to use up stale bread from a good loaf—is pretty much my perfect stand-alone lunch-salad, whether boxed up and taken somewhere or eaten from a plate at the table. What I love most about it is the way that the crispy pieces of bread become impregnated with vinaigrette. It is inspired by the chicken and bread salad in *The Zuni Café Cookbook* by Judy Rodgers but I've replaced the roasted chicken in her recipe with earthy roasted zucchini and green onions, plus grapes for juicy sweetness and feta or goat cheese for a salty tang. It comes together easily on a couple of baking sheets in the oven.

Serves 4
¼ cup/30g pine nuts
3½ oz/100g green onions
1 lb/450g zucchini, the freshest you can get and ideally yellow or pale green
    (I get pale green ones from my local Turkish grocery store)
6 tablespoons/90ml good olive oil
7 oz/200g substantial bread such as sourdough, sliced and torn
    into bite-size pieces
1 tablespoon rice vinegar
1 lemon
7 oz/200g salad greens, rinsed and dried (I usually use spinach leaves but
    arugula plus lettuce would also be good, and if you have any mint
    leaves, throw them in too)
5¼ oz/150g red grapes, rinsed and halved
3½–7 oz/100–200g crumbly white cheese such as feta or goat cheese

Preheat the oven to 400°F. Put the pine nuts on a baking sheet and into the oven for 3 minutes or until toasted (this can happen incredibly fast and a burned pine nut is not a happy thing). When they are done, tip them into a bowl to cool. Meanwhile, trim and thinly slice the green onions, cut the zucchini into rounds, and combine them with 2 tablespoons of oil and a few pinches of salt on the now-empty baking sheet. On another baking sheet combine the bread with 2 more tablespoons of oil. Put both sheets into the oven. After 10 minutes, check to see if the zucchini are roasted and if the bread is golden and crisp. You might need to give the zucchini another 5 minutes. When they are ready, tip the crispy bread onto the zucchini sheet. Mix together 7 tablespoons/100ml of water, a large spoonful of oil, a big pinch of salt, and the rice vinegar. Pour this all over the sheet and return it to the oven for another 5 minutes.

Meanwhile, juice the lemon and combine it with the final 1 tablespoon of olive oil and a pinch of salt. Put the rinsed salad greens into a big bowl and mix with the lemon-and-oil mixture, the zucchini, and bread. Scatter the grapes, the pine nuts, and cheese, crumbled or cubed.

Ruth's tuna salad with anchovy dressing

If you like mayonnaise-type dressings, this is salad as pure comfort food. My mother-in-law, Ruth, is the only person I know who always refers to tuna as tunny-fish. Someone else might call this a kind of salade Niçoise, but to Ruth it is always tunny-fish salad. I have lost count of the number of times I've eaten this at her table. Everyone who eats it falls in love with the dressing, which is based on one in *Keep It Simple* by Alastair Little, although Ruth changed it quite a bit. It sounds unlikely: a kind of mayonnaise-like concoction including ketchup and anchovies. But somehow, it works. The dressing mixes deliciously with the tuna, and it is as if the green beans, tomatoes, and eggs are dressed with anchovy-infused tuna mayonnaise. This is the one salad I make that my twelve-year-old son begs for second and third helpings of.

This makes enough dressing for 2 salads for 3 people. What I usually do is serve it the first night as written, and then to mix it up, the second night we have it without the potatoes in the salad but with baked potatoes on the side.

Serves 3 (with leftover dressing)

For the dressing
1 large egg
1 small tin of anchovies (the ones I buy weigh 2 oz/55g)
1 clove of garlic, peeled
Juice of 1 lemon
2 tablespoons ketchup (or tomato paste)
¾ cup plus 2 tablespoons/200ml neutral oil (or a mix of half and half light and
    extra-virgin olive oil)

For salad for 3 (double for 6 people)
10½ oz/300g small new potatoes, cut in half or quarters, depending on size
7 oz/200g green beans, topped and tailed
7 oz/200g cherry tomatoes, rinsed and halved
3½ oz/100g radishes, rinsed and sliced as thinly as you can (this is my innovation;
    please don't tell Ruth)
4 large eggs
1–2 cans of tuna
Wedges of lemon, to serve

First, make the dressing. Put everything except for the oil into a large bowl and thoroughly blitz with an immersion blender. Now slowly drizzle in the oil, continuing to blitz until you have a thick mayonnaise-like dressing. Taste a bit on a piece of bread or raw vegetable. It should be ambrosial. I don't usually add salt because anchovies are so salty. Adjust for lemon and ketchup.

Now for the salad. You need two medium saucepans. Boil the kettle. Put the potatoes into one of the saucepans, add boiling water and a small spoonful of salt, and boil for 10–15 minutes, or until tender. Drain in a sieve or a colander. Meanwhile, boil the kettle again. In the second pan, boil the green beans with a pinch of salt. They may take 4 minutes or they may take 8. It hugely depends on how fine they are. You want them properly tender, not squeaky (or at least, that's how I like them). When they are done, remove them from the pan with a spider and put them into a big salad bowl. Add the eggs to the pan and boil for 8–9 minutes until hard-boiled but still with a tiny bit of squidge in the yolk. Plunge into cold water and peel.

Drain away any water that has accumulated in the salad bowl with the green beans. Add all the other ingredients except the eggs and toss with a little under half the dressing. Halve the eggs, arrange them on top, and serve with extra dressing on the side plus wedges of lemon, lots of black pepper, and perhaps some bread to mop up the dressing.

A FEW MORE SALAD IDEAS

Most of the salads I make are not really recipes but combinations of a few delicious things, to which I add olive oil and salt. Think of having: one crunchy raw thing, one sweet soft thing (possibly a roasted vegetable), and something else with a strong flavor such as olives or nuts or dried fruit. Here are a few of my current favorites either by themselves or combined with green leaves:
—Shredded raw Brussels sprouts, fish sauce, lime juice, mint, sugar, toasted cashews.
—Slices of apple and cubes of hard cheese tossed with green leaves, walnuts, and a cream dressing.
—Pink grapefruit, avocado, shrimp (so much better than you remember).
—Borlotti beans, basil leaves, pitted black olives, roasted onions, torn mozzarella.
—Sliced orange, radishes, toasted cumin seeds, sautéd green onions, feta cheese, mint.
—Radicchio, pomegranate, pistachios, seared carrots, cilantro leaves (add pomegranate molasses to the dressing).
—Le Puy lentils, roasted beets, chopped dates, sliced of fried halloumi, cucumber.
—Peaches, goat cheese, raw fennel (fronds and bulb), toasted almonds.

Every day a feast (delicious eggs)

If you can cook eggs, you can cook anything. And the good news is that anyone can cook eggs.

There are all these emotional and convoluted reasons why I cook—to express love, to create a home that smells like home, to eat in a more sustainable way—and then there is another far more basic reason which is: eggs. Eggs are so immediate and satisfying both to cook and to eat, and once you have a few techniques under your belt you have the power to give yourself pleasure and sustenance at short notice from an almost empty fridge. The late Kenny Shopsin, owner of Shopsin's restaurant in Greenwich Village, noticed that when his customers ate any dish involving eggs they tended to "get a peaceful look on their face and go someplace else." Eggs give most of us a comfort that takes us straight back to childhood. Nothing will ever make me feel quite as safe as a soft-boiled egg with a plate of toast soldiers and a mound of salt and pepper mixed together to sprinkle on top at regular intervals as the egg goes down, just the way my father used to make it for me. Yet eggs are also the most shape-shifting and spectacular of ingredients, from the snowy whites of a meringue to the yellow yolky richness of a hollandaise sauce. More than any other food, eggs offer both the anchor of generations-old ritual and the thrill of the new. The ability to cook yourself more delicious eggs at the drop of a hat is reason in itself to cook.

"An egg that cooks," writes food scientist Hervé This, "is one of those everyday miracles we no longer recognize." But when you pause to notice the miracle, it really is astonishing to observe how a gloopy clear gel turns in a matter of seconds into an opaque white solid.

Once you start on the adventure of egg cookery, you see that as a cook, you can make yourself egg dishes that are much more luxurious and interesting than you can get in the average café. You can learn to make eggs exactly the way you like them—you need never suffer another rubbery omelet and you can boil your eggs as soft or as hard as your heart desires—but you can also tempt yourself with new egg dishes that you never tasted before or even imagined. Our usual repertoire of boiled, fried, scrambled, and poached hardly scratches the surface of egg possibilities. In nineteenth-century Paris, it was said that the standard number of egg dishes served by the average caterer was forty-two.

Even something simple such as a fried egg is not one thing but many. Before you fry an egg, ask yourself what you want from it. There are two distinct schools of thought on the texture. Some believe a fried egg should be silky and soft with no hint of crispness. If you agree, heat a small frying pan or blini pan over low heat, add a smidge of oil or butter, crack the egg into a cup and slide it into the pan. Season the yolk with salt, put a lid on the pan, and 3 minutes later (check after 2½) you should have a perfect fried egg. The lid is the crucial tip, because otherwise the bottom of the egg will be overcooked before the top is set. I know whereof I speak.

But there's another completely different way to go with fried eggs, which is to maximize those crispy bubbles at the edges because they are actually the tastiest part. For these, heat a generous amount of oil in a wok or saucepan until shimmering hot, slide the eggs into the pan, and use a large metal spoon to baste the top of the eggs with hot oil—i.e., pour some oil from the spoon over the eggs. They should instantly bubble up, like a cloud of lace. When they are done (about 1 minute), lift the frilly fried eggs carefully from the pan to paper towels, using a spider or a slotted spoon. I like these with the Burmese carrot salad on page 36.

Experimenting with eggs is one of the simplest ways to start seeing yourself as a cook and feeling excited about that prospect rather than daunted. If you are bored by cooking—or by life—one way to get your spark back is to set yourself a goal of trying a new way of cooking eggs every week. After years of cooking scrambled eggs low and slow, I recently found I could get results I liked just as much by adding a large spoonful of heavy cream for every 2 eggs and whisking the seasoned eggs over medium heat for just a couple of minutes until creamy-set. For poached, I use Nigella's formula: add a small spoonful of vinegar to the cracked egg in a cup, then pour the egg gently into a tea strainer to strain off some of the water and give it 4 or 5 minutes in a pan of hot water with the heat turned off. Here are some of the other egg dishes that currently excite me the most. I hope you will find them happy-making too.

Amulet eggs with Dijon mustard

This was a revelation to me and I am eager to share it with you because I have met hardly anyone who knows about it. When you are making a simple basic omelet and want an instant fix to improve the texture, add a dab of Dijon mustard. That's it. Unless you have perfected the French way of making beautifully tender rolled omelets—see the soft-centered lemon omelet on page 180—this is a fast route to better omelets (assuming you like mustard). I have called this omelet "amulet eggs," because the mustard works like a charm and because amulet was what omelets were sometimes called in the eighteenth century. Cookbook author Eliza Smith gave a recipe in 1732 for "An Amulet of Eggs the Savory Way."

For twenty years, I have had a lovely little cookbook called *Country Egg, City Egg* by a couple of chefs (who are also a couple) named Gayle Pirie and John Clark. Pirie and Clark used to be the lead brunch chefs at the Zuni Café in San Francisco, which tells us that their egg credentials are unimpeachable. I've made various dishes from the book over the years and loved them all but usually turned the page when I came to a recipe for ham and Dijon mustard omelet because it sounded unexciting. I am almost never without Dijon mustard and have it on the side of any omelet, so I couldn't see the rationale in adding it to the egg mix itself.

What I didn't realize—because Pirie and Clark don't mention it—is that the Dijon would enhance not just the flavor but the texture of the eggs. Dijon is both an acid and an emulsifier and these two things together do transformative things to the texture of the omelet. When I finally made Pirie and Clark's recipe, I found it so much more tender than most other omelets I have made, with a savory tang.

What you are doing when you cook eggs is taking a gel and causing it to coagulate using heat. What makes the process so delicate is that the egg starts to coagulate at such relatively low temperatures—around 142°F/61°C for the whites and 149°F/65°C for the yolks—and so it is very hard to make an omelet that is cooked without being tough. What the mustard does is accelerate the coagulation, so that you can pull the omelet off the heat sooner, before it has toughened. When I tasted a mustard omelet side by side with an omelet seasoned with nothing but salt, it was noticeably more tender. I wanted to know why and wrote to the food science expert Harold McGee to ask for his thoughts. He said that I should try making it with mustard powder instead of Dijon to see whether it was the mustard itself that was making the difference or the vinegar and other ingredients in the Dijon. The mustard-powder omelet was tough and charmless, which suggests that it is probably the acid in the Dijon that makes the difference. Whatever the reason, after years of searching, I have now found my perfect 2-egg omelet recipe (although for larger frittata-style omelets, I prefer to add cream or crème fraîche instead).

For each omelet (if you are cooking for more than one person, make them in succession because each omelet only takes a minute to cook)

2 large eggs, the best you can afford

½–1 teaspoon Dijon mustard

Optional: a large spoonful of finely chopped herbs such as parsley, chervil, chives, tarragon, in any combination, some grated Gruyère, a few spoonfuls of soft goat cheese, or a slice of good ham—or a combination

1 tablespoon unsalted butter

Beat the eggs with the mustard and a pinch of salt. Before you start, make sure you have your plate ready to turn the omelet out onto and that you have prepared anything you want to eat with it (a pungently dressed green salad flecked with slices of raw button mushrooms or fennel and maybe some parmesan shavings would be my preference).

When omelets outright fail, the main reason is a sticky pan. Make sure that your pan—which should be 7 inches/18cm or 8 inches/20cm in diameter—is seasoned well; I have a battered old aluminum pan that I only use for omelets and pancakes. Heat your omelet pan until it is very hot. When the pan is hot, add the butter. Swirl the pan as you watch it foam. Pour in the eggs, which will start to set instantly. Using a wooden spoon or a spatula, push from the edge of the pan to the center, letting the raw egg run underneath. Repeat this a few times until the bottom is set but the top is still wet. This whole process from the moment the eggs hit the pan should take no more than 1 minute. Scatter the herbs, spoon on the Gruyère or goat cheese, or lay on the slice of ham, if using. Gently fold the omelet in half and turn it out onto your plate. Devour, imagining that you are having a love affair in a bistro in Paris, the kind that sells rough red wine by the carafe.

Soft-centered lemon omelet

For a long time, I had a dream of making a lemon omelet. I had never seen one in my cookbooks and deluded myself that I had invented something completely new and exciting. And then I was reading a French cookbook from 1656 called *The Perfect Cook (Patissier françois)* and I found a recipe for "an Omelet with Lemmon-Peels" made with preserved lemons and I realized that I was more than 300 years behind the curve and there is nothing new under the sun.

Serves 1
3 large eggs
Zest of ½ an unwaxed lemon
1 teaspoon lemon juice
1 tablespoon finely chopped green herbs: chives or tarragon or parsley are all good, or any combination
2 tablespoons unsalted butter

At this point, I should really stop writing and tell you to look up a video of the French chef Jacques Pépin making a classic French omelet. Watching Pépin will teach you more than my words ever could. This is a completely different style of omelet from the more standard country-style omelet on the previous page.

Crack the eggs into a bowl and beat them very well with the lemon zest and juice and herbs and a big pinch of salt, using a fork. Before you start to cook the omelet, make sure you have a plate handy because the cooking itself will take you no more than 30–40 seconds.

Heat a nonstick pan or a seasoned omelet pan (6–8 inches/15–20cm) with the butter in it over medium-low heat. When the butter is foaming, pour in the eggs. Hold a fork or spatula in the center of the wet eggs and shake the pan like crazy. Every 5 seconds, pause and use the fork or spatula to scrape the side parts of the omelet into the center. After 30 seconds or so, while the eggs still look very moist, gently use the fork or spatula to roll the omelet from one end of the pan to the other— Pépin says it is like rolling a carpet. When you have rolled it as far as it will go, use the fork or spatula to ease the other side over to make a long oval. Transfer to a plate, as gently as you would lift a kitten from a sofa.

Buttery steamed eggs with vinegar and herbs

Soft-boiled eggs will always be my first love for weekend breakfast but these are my second love. There's a cozy elegance to a soft-yolked egg in a little dish. Again, I have Pirie and Clark's book to thank for turning me on to these. Considering how easy they are, they taste and look deeply luxurious and can be varied with any additions you like, such as a spoonful of cream at the beginning plus parmesan at the end, with or without a drop of truffle oil; a splash of soy sauce, a grating of ginger, and snipped chives at the end instead of the vinegar; a few flakes of smoked trout with crème fraîche and tarragon.

Serves 1
1 large slice of sourdough bread
1 tablespoon melted butter
Butter, for the ramekins
2 large eggs
A couple of sprigs of fresh thyme or marjoram
½ teaspoon red wine vinegar

I like to make special pre-buttered soldiers to go with this.

Preheat the oven to 350°F. Cut the bread lengthwise into long finger shapes and place on a baking sheet. Drizzle with the melted butter and bake until golden, 10–15 minutes.

Meanwhile, boil a kettle and pour the contents into a saucepan on which you can fit a steamer. Place the saucepan and steamer over high heat.

Rub butter over the bottom of two ramekins. Make sure you have a sturdy fish spatula or offset spatula on hand for lifting the ramekins out again at the end. Crack an egg carefully into each ramekin. Sprinkle with salt to taste and the leaves pulled from the sprigs of herbs. Place in the steamer, cover with the lid, and cook for 4 minutes. They will probably need 1 minute longer, maybe two. The second the whites look cooked, they are done. Carefully lift the ramekins out of the steamer and onto a plate using the fish spatula or offset spatula.

Eat with the toast soldiers, adding a tiny sprinkle of vinegar to each egg before you plunge your toast into the creamy yellow yolk.

Shakshuka

I nearly didn't include this recipe because the world is not short on recipes for shakshuka: a one-pot dish of eggs poached in a spicy tomato sauce that is popular all over the Middle East and that is thought to have evolved from an Ottoman meat stew. But then I couldn't bear not to give you this recipe because it is the glue that cemented my relationships with my two older children when they were teenagers. they would arrive home hungry at unexpected times of day. If I asked them "Do you want shakshuka?" they never once said no.

Serves 2, for lunch
1 tablespoon olive oil
2 large carrots, peeled and thinly sliced
2 cloves of garlic, peeled and sliced
1 teaspoon sweet smoked paprika
1 teaspoon ground cumin
½ teaspoon ground cinnamon
A pinch of cayenne
1 × 14–oz/400g can of whole, peeled tomatoes, blitzed with an immersion blender
A pinch of sugar
4 lalrge eggs
A small bunch of cilantro or parsley, chopped
Bread or toast, to serve (it's good with the focaccia on page 71)

Heat the oil in a medium frying pan with a lid (I use my cast-iron pan here). Soften the carrots for a couple of minutes, then add the garlic and cook for 1 minute more. Add the spices, stir until aromatic, then add the tomatoes plus a pinch of salt and a pinch of sugar. Turn the heat down and simmer the sauce for 5–10 minutes or until you like the way it tastes and looks. If it has become very thick, add a splash of water. Gently break the eggs into the pan, season each yolk with a pinch of salt, cover with a lid, and cook for 4–5 minutes. If the eggs are not quite set, give them 1 minute more (and maybe even 1 minute after that), until the whites are fully set but the yolks are still runny. When it is ready, gently transfer it with a large spoon to two shallow bowls. Top with a little chopped cilantro or parsley if you have some and eat with bread.

Something to take your mind off it (whatever it is)

In 2005, a little cookbook appeared with the title *The Soup Peddler's Slow and Difficult Soups* (the soup peddler was a guy who sold soup from a yellow bike in Austin, Texas). I didn't cook from it much but the title made me smile with recognition. We are endlessly bombarded with recipes that assume we only want dishes that are quick and easy. I can't deny I've done some of this bombarding myself in this very book. But sometimes—maybe because it's the weekend or because you are feeling blue or just because cooking is actually fun—the slower, more difficult, and therefore more meditative way is the one that you want. Sometimes you want to put some music on and lose yourself in a leisurely kitchen project. Here are a few ideas.

Homemade spice mixes

No spice mix that you buy is as thrilling as one that you toast and grind fresh in your own kitchen. Many people are intimidated by the idea of making their own, but assuming you have a small frying pan and a mortar and pestle, there is nothing to it. It's a far easier cooking project than making sourdough bread or kimchi, especially now that spices can be bought online. You simply toast the whole spices for a minute or so in a dry pan until fragrant, then grind to a powder and store in a clean jar.

If you're unsure how to start making your own spice mix, there is an excellent six-page primer with recipes in *India: The World Vegetarian* by Roopa Gulati. Gulati's version of a spice mix called chaat masala is one of the most delicious seasonings that I have ever tasted, let alone made: an extraordinary sour greenish powder that seems to wake up every taste bud. The key ingredients are dried mint and amchur (sour mango powder), plus various other aromatics such as ginger and chile.

Shaken over a salad, fried egg, or bowl of yogurt, this chaat masala is sensational. It is the only spice mix I know that is equally good sprinkled over fresh fruit for breakfast or used to enhance rice or to make plain grilled chicken less plain. If it were a perfume, it would be something green and angular like Chanel No. 19. The day I first made it, I had been feeling trapped and bored, wishing I could be somewhere—anywhere—else. And then I smelled the chaat masala, and suddenly I was.

Roopa's chaat masala

This should also contain black salt—an extraordinary South Asian rock salt with a sulphurous smell—but the first time I made it I couldn't find any and got used to it without (it still has sulphurous notes from asafoetida).

Makes about 3½ oz/100g
1 tablespoon cumin seeds
1 tablespoon black peppercorns
½ teaspoon carom seeds (ajwain)
1½ tablespoons dried mint leaves
A small pinch of asafoetida
2 tablespoons amchur (dried mango powder)
1 teaspoon ground ginger
½ teaspoon ground nutmeg
½ teaspoon Kashmiri chile powder (or substitute 1 teaspoon chile flakes)

In a small dry frying pan over medium heat, toast the cumin, peppercorns, and carom seeds for 1 minute or until fragrant. Off the heat, stir in the dried mint and asafoetida. Pour everything into a mortar and pestle and grind well, then add the mango powder, ground ginger, nutmeg, chile, and 1 teaspoon of salt. Store in an airtight jar for a few months.

SOME WAYS TO USE CHAAT MASALA

—Sprinkled over a crunchy salad.
—Used as a seasoning for bland white cheese such as roasted ricotta.
—Scattered liberally over a pilaf.
—To add excitement to a plain fried egg.

Aromatic all-purpose curry powder

Another spice mix that I love to make is this aromatic curry powder, which is what you need to make the red curry sauce on page 245.

Grinding this curry mix, which is adapted from one by the French chef Bruno Loubet (from a tiny 1996 book called *Chicken*), is a form of kitchen aromatherapy. Smelling the rich scent of toasty cumin seeds and perfumed cardamom lifts me on blue days, and the whole thing only takes a few minutes, assuming you have a mortar and pestle.

Makes enough for at least 3 curries

12 green cardamom pods—bash them to remove the black seeds, which is the part you need
3 tablespoons coriander seeds
1 tablespoon cumin seeds
5 whole cloves
2 tablespoons white or brown mustard seeds
1 tablespoon peppercorns
2 dried bay leaves
1 tablespoon ground turmeric

Put all the ingredients except for the turmeric into a small frying pan and heat gently, stirring, until the most wonderful aromatic scent fills your kitchen. After 5 minutes, or as soon as you feel it is toasty enough, tip it all into a mortar and pestle and add the turmeric. Grind until it is a powder. Think of someone who annoys you and pound even harder until the powder is fine. Store the mixture in a clean, dry jar. It will keep for ages, but the perfume starts to fade after 1 month or so.

SOME WAYS TO USE AROMATIC ALL-PURPOSE CURRY POWDER

—Mix with mayonnaise, mango chutney, and a squeeze of lemon to make a sauce for cold chicken.
—Add to sautéd onions and garlic before adding cubes of sweet potato and cooking (covered) until the potato is tender.
—Scatter over pieces of cauliflower with a drizzle of oil before it is roasted.
—Use to make katsu curry sauce.

Burmese chickpea tofu

Yes, you can make your own tofu! Not only that, but it will taste better than any tofu you can buy. As Mimi Aye explains in her wonderful book *Mandalay: Recipes and Tales from a Burmese Kitchen*, Burma has a version of tofu that is completely unlike the Japanese or Chinese beancurds made from soybeans that most of us know. It is made from chickpea flour and the process of making it is a bit like making polenta. The texture and taste are a world apart from soy tofu. As Aye says, it has a melting and custardy quality. When it's cut into pieces and fried, it's a bit like Sicilian *panelle*, if you've ever had that: crisp on the outside and soft on the inside. It's gluten-free, high in protein, cheap and sustainable. I love it, whether fried and added to noodle dishes or sliced in a salad. I've simplified the method a bit.

Makes enough for 4
Oil for the pan
1 cup/100g gram flour (chickpea flour)
½ a stock cube, crumbled, or 1 teaspoon vegetable bouillon powder
¼ teaspoon ground turmeric
¼ teaspoon baking powder (use gluten-free if cooking for celiacs)
2 tablespoons neutral oil

Oil a square (8 x 8-inch/20 x 20cm) or rectangular (6 x 8-inch/15 x 20cm) cake pan. Put all the ingredients into a medium saucepan and add 1¾ cups/450ml of water and ¼ teaspoon of salt. Whisk together over medium heat and bring it up to simmering point, stirring constantly with the whisk or a wooden spoon until it is bubbling up like lava and looks like a very thick and smooth lemon-yellow custard. This should take 6–8 minutes. Pour it into the oiled pan and let rest for 1 hour at room temperature or until set. Now cover it and transfer to the fridge until needed. It should be eaten within 2 days but can be used straight away.

Now that you have your very own tofu, what should you do with it? You could cut it into small triangles and fry it in a 2-inch/5cm depth of oil for a couple of minutes on each side. This will make fritters so delicious that, as Aye writes, people will "burn their tongues in their haste to eat as many as possible." She serves them with a dipping sauce made from tamarind, garlic, sugar, salt, fish sauce, and chiles.

Another way suggested by Aye is to cut it up and add it just as it is to a salad, preferably one with a pungent dressing.

Or you could make a very inauthentic but delicious sort-of pad thai, which to me is exactly what I want to eat on a Friday night with a cold beer: sweet and salty and hot, with a tangle of soft rice noodles and golden squares of crisp-soft tofu on top.

Sort-of pad thai with Burmese tofu

Serves 2

For the tofu
Neutral oil, for frying
½ batch × Burmese tofu (as on page 189), cut into small squares (about
 ½ inch/1.5cm)
4½ oz/125g flat wide dried rice noodles
9 oz/250g any firm green vegetable such as asparagus (trimmed and sliced into
 pieces) or broccoli (stalks sliced and the rest cut into small florets) or sliced
 runner beans or bok choy or a mixture of greens
4 green onions, thinly sliced
2 cloves of garlic, peeled and grated
¾-inch/2cm piece of ginger, grated
1 red chile, seeded and finely chopped

For the sauce
½ tablespoon fish sauce (or vegetarian fish sauce)
1 tablespoon tamarind paste
1 tablespoon rice vinegar
2 tablespoons maple syrup or agave syrup
1 tablespoon soy sauce

To serve
A handful of roasted salted peanuts
A handful of mint leaves and/or cilantro and basil leaves, shredded
1 lime, halved

After you have prepped everything, start by frying the tofu. Heat a fairly generous amount of oil in a large frying pan or a wok. Fry the cubes of tofu. Add them to the oil and immediately jiggle the pan a little, to stop them sticking. The cubes will need 2 or 3 minutes per side to form a crust and become beautifully golden and puffy.

While this is happening, put the sauce ingredients into a small bowl with 1 tablespoon of water and mix together. Put the rice noodles into a heatproof bowl, pour in enough boiling water to cover and set a timer for 3 minutes. When the timer is done, drain the noodles in a sieve and rinse them with cold water from the tap.

When the tofu is ready, transfer it to a plate with a spider and pour the oil into a bowl. Measure 1 tablespoon of the oil back into the pan. Add the green vegetables and cook over high heat for 2–3 minutes or until crisp-tender. Add the green onions, garlic, ginger, and chile and cook for half a minute more. Add the sauce, which will create a great whoosh of steam and fragrance. Add the noodles and gently toss them in the sauce until everything is well coated. Add water, a large spoonful at a time, if it seems dry. Transfer to two bowls and top each one with a handful of peanuts and a handful of herbs, and eat with the lime halves for squeezing.

Therapeutic baking

Another obvious way to take your mind off things in the kitchen is through baking. When I am so sad that even cooking doesn't lift my mood, sometimes the answer is making bread. It reminds me that at least something can still rise and turn golden. In their cookbook *Breadsong*, father and daughter Al and Kitty Tait write about how bread-making was the one thing that finally helped Kitty to get better after suffering from a depression so bad that she stopped going to school when she was fourteen. Kitty writes that the first time she watched Al make a loaf, it felt like alchemy. "Something so dull had transformed into something so brilliant."

Many people turned to sourdough making as something to hold onto during the strange, sad, uncertain spring of 2020. There is something about the process of nurturing a starter and seeing it gain in strength that can feel hopeful. I never quite managed it myself that year. My attention span was shot to pieces and there- fore my baking therapies of choice tended to be quicker, such as this soda bread, which offers the tactile satisfaction of bread-making but is also *fast*.

Molasses and oat soda bread

Even if you think you can't make bread, you can make this. I like to divide it into two small loaves, so that it bakes even faster. It is wonderful warm from the oven with butter and plum or damson jam. Adding molasses seems to bring out the maltiness in the grain, as does adding some pan-toasted oats.

1 tablespoon light oil
1 cup/100g rolled oats
4½ cups/500g whole wheat flour (or 2½ cups/250g white spelt flour and
    2¼ cups/250g whole wheat flour for a lighter loaf)
1 tablespoon cocoa powder
1½ teaspoons baking soda
3 tablespoons molasses (or honey or agave)
1⅔ cups/400ml buttermilk or 1 cup/240ml yogurt mixed with ⅔ cup/160ml whole
    milk or 1⅔ cups/400ml whole milk mixed with 2 teaspoons rice or wine vinegar
A little oil, for greasing
A handful of pumpkin seeds or oats for the top

Line a baking sheet with parchment paper. Preheat the oven to 425°F.

Heat the light oil in a large frying pan over medium heat and toast the oats in it for 2–3 minutes, stirring constantly, until they smell oaty and deepen in color around the edges. Tip them out into a large mixing bowl and add the flour, cocoa, baking soda, and 1 teaspoon of salt. Use your hands to dig a hole in the flour and pour in the molasses and most of the buttermilk (or yogurt and milk). Stir with a wooden spoon until it comes together as a sticky dough, adding more buttermilk as needed.

Transfer the dough to an oiled board or work surface and also oil your hands. Divide the dough into two pieces and work each one quickly into a round shape. Unlike with yeasted dough, you don't want to knead it too much. Place the two rounds on the baking sheet and mark a deep cross in the top of each of them using a knife. Sprinkle with the seeds or oats and bake for 30 minutes, or until they sound hollow when you tap the bottom. Check after 25 minutes. Remove from the oven and let cool on a wire rack. This bread only keeps for a couple of days, so if you don't think you can eat it all that quickly, freeze one of the loaves.

Reduce your options:
the sweetness of routine

'The problem with most home cooks is that
they have too many recipes rather than too few."
    Christopher Kimball

Before you can start cooking tonight's dinner, you need to say "No" to all the other equally lovely things that you might be eating at this moment instead. If you are naturally indecisive—as I am—all the hypothetical meals that crowd in your head can get in the way of your actual cooking. This might not sound like a big problem but if it gets repeated every day, this feeling of confusion about what to eat can tie you in knots and give you a sense of mild dissatisfaction with whatever you finally cook.

Cooking becomes a lot easier and more fun if you can trim down your options and build a repertoire of trusted favorites to rely on that give you pleasure every time, both to cook and to eat. This applies to ingredients and grocery stores as well as recipes. Simplicity will set you free. I'm not talking about eating the same old thing every night but about giving yourself the mental space and structure you need to make the most of your time in the kitchen.

When we speak of routines, it is usually in disparaging terms. We say that someone is a "slave to routine" or we use the word *routine* as an adjective to mean deathly boring. As Sherlock Holmes comments in *The Sign of Four*, "I abhor the dull routine of existence." But so far from being humdrum, a good routine is the surest path to living the cooking life you want to live. Like it or not, life is full of repetitive actions—cooking being one—and it would be exhausting to question the rules of our existence afresh every day. Routines don't have to be dull; they can be delicious. A happy cooking life is one in which your routines align with your desires. Try to adopt the routines and rituals that you actually want to live by until they become new habits, whether it's eating a leisurely breakfast of soft-boiled eggs every Saturday or buying your vegetables from the same market every week or deciding that Thursday is spaghetti night.

One of the most basic secrets of cooking is simply to establish that dinner is a given, a (more or less) daily commitment to yourself, like making your bed. The next thing is to decide what you want to make, and to go ahead and make it. In cooking, as in life, it is better to make a decision—any decision—than to spend too long worrying whether your decision is the right one. No meal that you want to eat can possibly be a mistake. (I can't pretend I've always lived by this motto. I have been known to go into hysterical spirals of regret when a meal goes wrong. Do as I say, not as I do.)

No one would have wished for the horrors of 2020. But one of the few upsides—assuming you were among the lucky ones who had enough to eat—was that it showed us a new and simpler approach to cooking, one in which we are not quite so overwhelmed by options.

Lockdown cooking gave us three things that have been in short supply in modern times: gratitude for food, time to eat it, and a clear head. The clear head part felt especially novel to many of us. Suddenly, much of the chatter about what to have for dinner was switched off. Shall we go out? Shall we stay in? Shall we eat Thai or Italian, shall we have jasmine rice or Basmati or brown rice or black rice, shall we try this or that recipe? Many of these questions were now irrelevant. Going out was sadly not an option. And we would eat whatever rice we happened to have in the house.

As time went on, we adjusted to a new way of cooking: one that was both more flexible and more forgiving than before. It is sad that it took a pandemic to make us recognize that it was OK—more than OK—to use light brown sugar instead of dark brown sugar or to leave out the ras el hanout if we didn't have it. A recipe writer might tell you to use fusilli, but if panic buying had stripped the pasta shelves of that particular pasta shape, you might discover that spaghetti worked just as well.

The real secret of making your cooking life easier is less about adding things and more about eliminating what you don't need. Subtract the things that you don't need or don't want to eat until the task in front of you is easy and clear. It's like the joy of pressing "unsubscribe" to a whole bunch of newsletters. This is one of the advantages of being vegetarian: you are cooking from a more limited palette.

You can give yourself a greater sense of calm and clarity with your own cooking simply by making a few decisions each week on what you really want to cook. I have met people who sit down with a notebook and some cookbooks every Friday night and plan out every meal in the week. Much as I admire these people, I will probably never be quite so organized. I like leaving a bit of spontaneity to my meal planning or else I feel trapped. But I have felt so much more serene about family cooking since I started deciding on at least a few of the week's meals in advance. It makes me feel like a frog who knows there are some safe lily pads ahead to hop onto.

Repertoires and rituals

"The chains of habit are too weak to be felt
until they are too strong to be broken."
    Samuel Johnson

For years, when we had guests coming to dinner, I would go into a blind panic and think: but I don't know anything to cook! This was, objectively speaking, crazy. I knew plenty of things to cook. But I didn't feel that any of the dishes I knew were good enough to offer to other people. I would skim through all my cookbooks, doubting every choice before picking something difficult and extravagant that I had never made before. I felt exposed and terrified, as if I were starting completely from scratch. This did not increase my sense of calm as I waited for the knock on the door.

If you want to be more relaxed as a cook, it helps to start to build a modest repertoire of *your* dishes that you actually look forward to cooking and eating, dishes that make you feel more yourself the minute you start to cook them and that you know so well you can rustle up on autopilot. It helps if you start to jot down favorite dishes that you make during each season of the year. This can become a comforting reference point when your dinner-planning mind goes blank.

A good repertoire will include dishes that are simple enough to be made at a moment's notice but special enough that you feel happy serving them to company. These don't have to be the most perfect or impressive dishes in the world (as if such a thing exists). They are ones that reflect your own tastes and that you find low-stress to cook. What these dishes are will obviously vary from person to person. Know your limitations and be kind to yourself.

When pondering what to cook, I sometimes find it comforting to think about house wine. When you order house wine in a good restaurant, you are making the decision to shut off all the countless other wine options in the world and trusting—for now—that this wine is the only one that need concern you. You are putting your faith in the restaurant's taste and saying: I know there are fancier, pricier options out there but for tonight, this one is good enough for me. Your only choice is red or white. OK, sometimes house wine is a bit ropey but there are nights when, with the right company, ropey wine drunk from a tumbler is perfectly fine.

It's a useful exercise to try to find your own house foods—reliable ones that you can reach for any day without too much thought, that suit your tastes and your way of life. If life is made up of days and days are made up of meals, it stands to reason that these kind of cooking routines can help you enjoy life more.

One of the main ways that traditional cooking varied from cooking today is that good home cooks in the past tended to make a much more limited set of dishes, often patterned in some way by the days of the week or the month. Everyone knew how these dishes were meant to taste and through repetition they became so familiar that cooks could make them almost on autopilot. My brother-in-law Gonzalo, who is from Argentina, says he will always think of the 29th of the month as gnocchi day. Traditionally, the 29th was the day before payday, so Argentine families would make potato gnocchi—a very inexpensive dish consisting of little but potatoes and flour—and put a coin under each plate in the hope of prosperity for the month ahead. Gonzalo learned this gnocchi tradition from his mother in Buenos Aires, just as he learned almost all the dishes that he makes on a regular basis, such as steak with chimichurri sauce and Milanesa with purée: breaded escalope (either veal or chicken) served with very smooth mashed potatoes strongly flavored with nutmeg. When I talk to my niece and nephew, Frankie and Luke, they can recite the dishes their father makes like the words in a much-loved song.

There is a particular kind of solace that comes from ritual meals: ones that take the same form on the same day of the week, like fish on a Friday. In our house, Wednesday breakfast is Waffle Wednesday, a tradition that originally sprang up when my youngest son always used to get hungry after school on a Wednesday because he didn't like the school lunches that were served that day. But over time, the tradition took on a life of its own, as traditions tend to do. The beauty of Waffle Wednesday—or Taco Tuesday, as the case may be—is that it's one fewer decision to make.

Building a list of recipes to cook on repeat isn't just about flavors; it's also a way to give rhythm to your week and to anchor yourself to certain people or places. It's easy to flit through our cooking lives from dish to dish without ever settling on the ones that really matter to us. But the idea of a culinary repertoire can focus the mind on the dishes you really need to hold onto, the ones that tell us who we are when everything else falls away. As I began to think through my own culinary repertoire, the dishes I can rely on with absolute faith even in an indecisive mood, I realized that they were all connected with people that I love. When it comes to it, what dishes mean enough that you would want your friends or family to remember you by them?

Anthea's apricot cake

My friend Anthea Morrison was the kindest person I ever knew, a retired academic who lived alone in a spotless bungalow with tulips in her garden. She never forgot a birthday, and, after her death, it was discovered that her birthday card list stretched to more than 500 people: she sent more than one thoughtfully chosen birthday card for every day of the year. When we used to visit Anthea for morning coffee or afternoon tea—which happened a few times a year—she always gave us exactly the same assortment of sweet treats, beautifully arranged on tea trolleys. There were chocolate cookies and Café Noir cookies and freshly made scones, half of them spread with lemon curd and half with honey. There was strong Costa Rican coffee, about which she was very particular, made in a brown jug; and for the children, there was milk or Ribena in a mug. The centerpiece of the meal was her Victoria sponge cake, spread with apricot jam rather than the usual strawberry. I can never eat this very English cake without thinking of Anthea sitting and beaming in her pale blue Liberty-print blouse and tweed skirt, like a sweeter Miss Marple.

Adding a tiny bit of vegetable oil and cornstarch to the classic sponge cake formula makes for a tender and more delicate crumb.

Serves 8–10
2 cups plus 1 tablespoon/260g all-purpose flour
2 tablespoons cornstarch
1 tablespoon baking powder
1 cup/225g unsalted butter, softened, plus extra for the pan
1¼ cups/250g granulated sugar
5 large eggs
½ cup/120ml milk (preferably whole)
2 tablespoons vegetable oil
1 teaspoon vanilla extract
½ cup/150g apricot jam
Confectioners' sugar

Preheat the oven to 400°F. Rub butter on the inside of two 8-inch/20cm cake pans and line them with parchment paper.

Whisk together the flour, cornstarch, and baking powder. Put the butter and sugar into a mixing bowl and beat together with electric beaters until creamy (or beat in a stand mixer if you have one). Crack one of the eggs into a cup, pour it into the butter and sugar mixture and beat well. Then add a large spoonful of the flour mixture and beat well. Continue to alternate 1 egg and a large spoonful of flour until all the eggs are used up. The reason for going slowly with the eggs and adding the flour in between is to prevent the mixture from curdling. Now add the remaining flour mixture and fold it in thoroughly but gently with a spoon, followed by the milk, vegetable oil and vanilla. Using a spatula, divide the mixture evenly between the two pans and bake for 18 minutes or until golden and risen and a skewer inserted into the middle comes out clean. Let the cakes cool in their pans for 5 minutes before turning out onto a wire rack to cool.

When they are completely cool, put one of the cakes flat side up on a plate. Using an offset knife or spatula, spread it all over with apricot jam—Anthea's preferred jam was Wilkin & Sons Tiptree—and top with the second cake. Sift confectioners' sugar over the top.

If you really want to gild the lily—for a birthday, say—you could forget the sifted confectioners' sugar and instead spread a layer of chocolate ganache over the top. Put ¾ cup plus 2 tablespoons/200ml of heavy cream into a pan with 2 tablespoons of sugar and bring to a boil. Remove from the heat and whisk in 5¼ oz/150g of chopped dark chocolate until it is smooth and glossy. Wait a few minutes before spreading the ganache on the cake. To make this more dessert-like, skip the jam and fill it with a layer of sweetened whipped cream topped with sliced fresh apricots or peaches cooked with apricot jam (see the recipe for jammy plums on page 272)— let them cool before you add them to the cake.

Vietnam–Philadelphia tofu sandwiches

Tofu sandwiches have a special place in my family because my sister, who is vegetarian, lives near a great Vietnamese deli (Fu-Wah Mini Market) and every time we visit her and my nieces in Philadelphia, we have to get tofu bánh mì from Fu-Wah for at least one of our meals. These sandwiches are more than a sandwich: they are a shared rite, a focal point that comforts and deepens with each repetition. My sister thinks I obsess too much about food (she is probably right) but the glory of these sandwiches is something we agree on. We ate tofu bánh mì sandwiches at the Philadelphia zoo on a dazzling spring day a few weeks after my younger nieces' dad left. And we ate my version of the sandwiches again together in England by candlelight at the kitchen table (all the power in the house was out) during the cold autumn of 2020, a few months into my own separation.

The tofu in the Fu-Wah sandwiches always tasted better than any tofu I ever cooked at home (except for the Burmese tofu on page 189). It is savory, dark, meaty, and juicy. One day, missing my sister and nieces, I tried to re-create it. It took a few attempts to get the tofu right but this has now become one of our favorite things to eat at home, even if the Fu-Wah original will always be the best. The ones in Philly come in soft hoagie rolls, but back in Britain I tend to use small ciabattas instead and pink radishes instead of daikon.

The tofu is also delicious served as part of a rice bowl or with noodles and vegetables. The reason it tastes so deeply flavorful is that I marinate it twice: once before cooking and once after. This is one of the advantages of tofu over meat: you can use the marinade twice without fear of food poisoning.

Serves 4, generously

4 half ciabattas or 4 submarine rolls or baguette rolls or any soft fresh white bread
    rolls
2 blocks of firm tofu (they usually seem to come in blocks of 10½–14 oz/
    300–400g)
2–3 tablespoons neutral oil

For the marinade
2 tablespoons rice vinegar
3 tablespoons soy sauce
1 tablespoon date syrup or agave or maple syrup
1 tablespoon sesame oil
4 cloves of garlic, grated
A thumb of ginger, grated

For the carrot and radish pickle
4 large carrots
1 bunch of radishes (about 7 oz/200g)
1 teaspoon sugar
1 tablespoon rice vinegar

To serve
Sriracha, fresh sliced green chiles, fresh cilantro leaves, mayonnaise from a jar,
    sliced cucumbers

Supermarket ciabattas usually come half-baked, so bake them if you need to.

Take the tofu, place it on a clean kitchen towel (or a stack of paper towels), cover with another clean kitchen towel (or more paper towels), and weight it down with a frying pan or a mortar. This makes the tofu firmer and is worth doing even if you only press it for a few minutes.

While the tofu is pressing, mix together the rice vinegar, soy, syrup, sesame oil, garlic, and ginger in a large bowl. This is your marinade. Slice the tofu into fingers about ½ inch/1cm wide. Put it in the bowl with the marinade and gently turn it until it is coated all over. You can cover the bowl and let the tofu marinate for up to 12 hours in the fridge, or cook it straight away.

Heat half the oil in a large nonstick pan. Lift half the tofu pieces from the marinade into the frying pan and let them brown and turn crispy without turning them for at least 3 minutes. Flip them very gently and cook for another couple of minutes until crispy on both sides. Remove it to a plate. Repeat with the second half of the tofu and the second half of the oil. Return the cooked tofu to what remains of the marinade in the bowl. This will infuse the tofu with extra flavor.

Meanwhile, make the pickle. Peel the carrots and cut them into long ribbons using a vegetable peeler. If you like, you can then cut these wide ribbons into thin julienne strips, though it's not essential. Trim the radishes and cut them as finely as

you can (a mandoline is best here if you are brave enough, or use a food processor). Combine the carrot and radish with the sugar, vinegar, and ¼ teaspoon of salt. Taste for seasoning and add an extra splash of vinegar if you think it needs it.

Now bring everything to the table and let people assemble their own sandwiches from the tofu and the pickled vegetables plus sriracha, chiles, cilantro, and mayonnaise (I don't add mayonnaise but my daughter considers it essential). If you are my nieces you may want to eat a disassembled version, with separate mounds of tofu and bread with some sliced cucumber on the side.

This makes a lot of tofu, but leftovers are lovely in a salad or tossed into egg-fried rice the next day.

Ratatouille for Richard

My friend Claire Edwards is French and has a thing for ratatouille. As a joke, she adds a syllable and calls it ra-ta-ta-touille. When our children were little, we went on vacation together a few times and the thing I remember most is being in the kitchen with Claire for hours, roasting a big chicken, and making her ra-ta-ta-touille, a slow process that left lots of time to talk as we chopped the zucchini and peppers. She would make great vats of it, enough to last for several meals. I can remember the wide smile of appreciation on her husband Richard's face when she finally put it on the table.

In early 2021, Richard died suddenly of a stroke at the age of fifty-four, a loss that can hardly be borne. All I can think of is his lovely smile, his love for Claire and the children, and how happy we all were those times when we ate ratatouille together.

Technically, the ratatouille I now make is not ratatouille at all. It is—as requested by my youngest son—based on the one eaten by the food critic Anton Ego in the Pixar movie *Ratatouille*. Properly, it should be called a tian, because unlike classic ratatouille, it is not stewed in a pan but constructed from very thinly sliced vegetables, baked in the oven. It looks much fancier this way but the flavors are the same: the gentle fragrance of sweet garlic mingling with oil and eggplant and tomato. You can get it ready ahead of time and reheat, if it helps. This is something that I would happily serve to anyone, any time, as the centerpiece of a family lunch or dinner. People are super impressed by the look of it, but it's easy if you have a food processor (or a mandoline). It makes a spectacular vegan feast, perhaps with a simple pilaf of rice cooked with bay leaves, onions, oil, stock, and herbs; or with baked potatoes and guacamole. But my default is still the way Claire served it, with a roasted chicken and some roasted, boiled, or dauphinoise potatoes and a green salad.

Serves 4–6, depending on what else you are having with it
    (it's a good idea to double it and make two)
7 tablespoons/100ml extra-virgin olive oil
6 cloves of garlic, peeled and grated
1 × 14-oz/400g can of whole, peeled tomatoes
A pinch of sugar
3 large zucchini (about 1 lb/450g)
2 large eggplants
6 large tomatoes
A few sprigs of thyme, leaves stripped and chopped

Preheat the oven to 400°F.

In a medium saucepan, heat 1 tablespoon of olive oil over medium heat and sauté 2 of the garlic cloves for a few seconds before adding the canned tomatoes and a big pinch of salt plus a smaller pinch of sugar. Cook, stirring often, until it reduces down a bit. Now, either mash it a bit with your wooden spoon or blitz it with an immersion blender. Spread this sauce over the bottom of a large roasting dish or wide-lidded ovenproof pan.

Cut the zucchini paper-thin using either a mandoline or a food processor. Now cut the eggplants in half lengthwise and cut them too, using a mandoline or a food processor. Finally, slice the tomatoes as thin as you can using a sharp knife and a chopping board (I find they get mashed by the processor). Make stacks of the eggplant, zucchini, and tomato and arrange these in circles in the pan. When I first made this, I was completely obsessive and felt I had to alternate the vegetables one by one. This was time-consuming and it also didn't work, because I always ended up with lots of eggplant and zucchini left over (there are fewer tomato slices than eggplant and zucchini). So what I now do is take a little stack of eggplant, a stack of zucchini, and then a single tomato slice and go around like that. It looks just as good. When the pan is full, sprinkle with the thyme and distribute the remaining garlic as evenly as you can, tucking it into the crevices. Sprinkle the whole thing well with flaky salt and drizzle the remaining olive oil. Put it into the oven for 30 minutes, then put the lid on and return it to the oven for another 30 minutes, or until the vegetables are completely tender and a little bit shrunken.

Chicken Milanesa with nutmeg mashed potatoes and chimichurri

This recipe comes from my nephew and niece, Luke and Frankie, who love it because it's what their Argentine father Gonzalo cooks at home in London. When the twins were tiny, he used to call it "meat fingers" (a riff on "fish fingers," aka "fish sticks"). But to Gonzalo, the true owner of this dish is his mother. The reason he puts nutmeg in his mashed potatoes is because that is what she did as a single parent in Buenos Aires in the 1970s, struggling to work and bring up two children and put good food on the table.

In Argentina, land of the gaucho, a Milanesa would traditionally be made with beef or veal. But it's also good with chicken. Make some extra if you like, because cold Milanesa makes one of the great sandwich fillings with sliced tomatoes and lettuce (I would also add capers and/or some of the not-romesco sauce on page 276 if I had some knocking around). We eat it with a cloud of nutmeggy mashed potatoes, but a quicker way is to skip the mash and put a fried egg on top. Or you could just have them with the chimichurri, a squeeze of lemon, and a salad. The sharp and herbal chimichurri sauce perfectly cuts through the richness of the fried breadcrumbs. The reason the Milanesa itself tastes more exciting than some other breaded cutlets is because the eggs for the coating are mixed with garlic and parsley. For a gluten-free version, replace the breadcrumbs with crushed corn flakes (a Nigella idea).

Serves 4–6, depending on how many of you are children or how big your appetite is

For the chimichurri
3½ oz/100g flat-leaf parsley
2 tablespoons red wine vinegar
2 tablespoons fresh oregano leaves
1 clove of garlic, peeled
1 teaspoon smoked paprika
½ teaspoon chile flakes
7 tablespoons/100ml olive oil

For the mashed potatoes
2½ lbs/1.2kg potatoes, peeled and cut into chunks
⅔ cup/160ml whole milk
¼ cup/60g unsalted butter
Nutmeg

For the chicken
4 boneless, skinless chicken breasts
2 large eggs
2 cloves of garlic, peeled and grated or crushed to a paste
2 tablespoons finely chopped parsley
2 cups/200g fine dried breadcrumbs (Gonzalo uses breadcrumbs that have a very
     fine crumb, but you could also use Japanese panko whizzed a bit in the food
     processor)
Neutral oil, for frying

To serve
Lemons
10½ oz/300g cherry tomatoes
3½ oz/100g arugula

First, make the chimichurri. If you have a food processor, pulse everything together with a pinch of salt until combined and chopped but not smooth. If not, finely chop the garlic and herbs on a chopping board, then mix in a bowl with the oil and vinegar and the chile flakes, paprika, and a pinch of salt. Check for seasoning. It should be pungent but well balanced between the acid of the vinegar and the brightness of the herbs. This makes too much chimichurri for this one meal but it will keep in the fridge for 1 week and is great with roasted vegetables; with eggs; with plainly cooked fish or steak; or to give piquancy to rice or grains. My sister-in-law Cathy calls chimichurri "the gift that keeps on giving."

Next, get started on the mashed potatoes. Cook the potatoes until very tender in a saucepan of boiling salted water (15–20 minutes). Drain them in a colander (for once, the best utensil!) and let them cool for a few minutes so they can dry off a bit. Meanwhile, warm the milk together with the butter in a pan large enough to hold the potatoes. Return the potatoes to the pan and mash them until smooth (I push them through a potato ricer but if you don't have one of these, just use a masher). Stir with a wooden spoon until silken and cloudlike. Taste for seasoning—and to see if it needs more butter or milk—and add a few gratings of nutmeg.

For the chicken, lay a piece of parchment paper over a chopping board. Put 2 of the breasts on top and cover them with another piece of parchment paper. Bash them with a rolling pin until they are wide and thin. It's amazing how much they spread out, and the process of flattening them is strangely relaxing. Crack the eggs into a wide shallow bowl and add the garlic, parsley, and a pinch of salt. Put the breadcrumbs into a second large shallow dish. Dip each chicken escalope first into the egg mixture and then into the breadcrumbs, patting them gently to coat all over. My nephew Luke showed me how to do this by patting each escalope with the side of his fist. Put each coated escalope on a plate, and repeat the beating and coating process with the other 2 breasts. Heat 2 tablespoons of oil in a wide nonstick pan. You will probably have to cook 2 of them at a time because of the size. Fry the chicken carefully over medium heat for about 3 minutes per side. Repeat with the remaining 2 escalopes, wiping out the pan and adding more oil.

Serve the crisp-gold Milanesa with the mashed potatoes and chimichurri on the side, plus lemon wedges and perhaps a salad made from the arugula and tomatoes, very lightly dressed with salt and lemon and a tiny bit of oil (bearing in mind that the chimichurri is both oily and sharp). Or skip the salad and have it with buttery frozen peas for nursery food comfort.

"Take an onion" or learning how to substitute

"If there's no bread, tortillas will do."
   Mexican proverb

Henry David Thoreau said, "Beware of all enterprises that require new clothes." I have begun to feel the same about chile sauces. At one point, I had no fewer than seventeen different chile sauces and pastes in my fridge because I kept buying another bottle or jar every time a recipe called for a new and specific variety. I had so many chile pastes I couldn't keep track of them. But then one day, I had a small epiphany. I was following a recipe for black beans that asked for ancho chile paste and I used a spoonful of Chinese chile garlic paste instead. I added it with trepidation, fearing that something terrible might happen. Reader, it was delicious and ever since then I have been much more confident about using the wrong chile paste.

Cooking gets so much simpler once you start to give yourself license to substitute ingredients. Learning to be adaptable will help you to keep a much leaner pantry, which in turn will save you a huge amount of time because you won't have to spend so much time rummaging around the back of the fridge or making panicky trips to the supermarket for some supposedly essential ingredient. You will also waste a lot less food.

Recipes are not commandments trying to dictate how you live. Most of them are really just casual suggestions for how to make something delicious. Recipe writers—of whom I've met a lot—do not tend to be sadists. If they happen to suggest that you use fennel in a given recipe, they don't mean: I insist that you eat fennel even if it makes you feel sick to your stomach. They also don't mean: go out and buy a lot of fennel when it blows your budget and you already have a fridge full of other delicious vegetables. The recipe writer was working on the assumption that you like fennel as much as they do. They were also assuming that you would take the initiative to adapt the recipe to suit your own pantry and tastes. The main reason they did not tell you all the things you could use instead of fennel is because the list would be never-ending.

As a rule of thumb, any tender fresh green herb can be substituted for any other tender herb, particularly if it's just being used as a final scattering garnish at the end.

Yes, this means that you never have to eat mint if you don't like it. But you knew that anyway, right? Meanwhile, any strong woody herb can be substituted for any other, within reason: rosemary for bay, thyme for sage. Obviously the effect won't be the same, but you may discover something even lovelier.

The basic rule of all substitutes is to ask yourself: what is this ingredient really doing in this dish? Is it offering softness or crunch, sourness or sweetness? If the cookbook says strawberries but it isn't berry season, it's much better to use some ripe juicy plums (on the rare occasions you can find them) rather than buying dull disappointing berries. You are trying to replicate the function rather than the form. When you run out of lemons, you probably have at least half a dozen other things in your kitchen that could play the same role (unless you were trying to make something very specifically lemony such as a lemon drizzle cake). You might use another citrus fruit such as lime, grapefruit, or orange. Or you could use a small spoonful of vinegar or another sour thing such as tamarind or even a few pieces of pickle, depending on the dish.

This kind of substituting should not be seen as a worst-case scenario but as a normal and beneficial part of cooking life. The economy of substitution should be part of your thinking even when you do your grocery shopping. Do I really need to buy a bottle of pomegranate molasses for this one recipe when I already have date syrup in my cupboard? Does it make sense to clutter my cupboard with rigatoni, which I don't like, when I already have conchiglie, which I do like?

Other than salt, and perhaps oil, no single ingredient in the kitchen is indispensable. Even an onion. A few weeks into the first lockdown in the spring of 2020, the unthinkable happened. I ran out of onions. Gazing around my onion-less kitchen, I felt distraught. Surely cooking was now, if not impossible, then pretty much pointless. "Take an onion" is the "once upon a time" of recipes. A meal may end up in countless different places, but where it usually starts is with an onion. Onions are the bite in a Greek salad and the sweetness in an Irish stew; they are the soft heart of a Spanish tortilla and the body of French onion soup. Most of the time, I think of onions less as a vegetable and more as the foundation stone for dinner.

But there is more than one way to get oniony flavor into a dish, as I discovered when I set out on a trip to buy more, feeling out of sorts. Having failed to find a single onion in two local grocery stores—this was the height of panic buying in the UK—I got talking to the nice man behind the counter in the nearest Chinese supermarket. He had sold out of regular onions but he still had a few bunches of green green onions in the fridge, next to the bok choy and ginger.

"Have you thought of combining green onions with these fried shallots?" he quietly inquired, gesturing toward a jar of pre-fried crispy shallots on a high-up shelf. I hadn't, but as soon as he mentioned it, I realized what an inspired suggestion it was. I bought a couple of bunches of green onions and a jar of the fried shallots and restrained myself from kissing him out of sheer gratitude. Back at home, I chopped half a bunch of the green onions and softened them in butter with a stalk of celery before stirring in risotto rice. When the risotto was done, after stirring in a handful of parmesan, I added a final flourish of crispy shallots. When we tasted the risotto, it had green sappy sweetness from the green onions and an addictive savory crunch from the fried shallots, whose texture contrasted with the tenderness of the rice. It may not have been risotto as an Italian would recognize it but it was good. I was surprised to realize that I had achieved a multi-layered onion experience in a fraction of the time it takes to chop and soften a regular yellow onion. For weeks afterward, I found myself using the one-two punch of fresh green onions plus fried shallots in countless dishes, from soups to noodles, from stews to salads. I carried on doing this long after yellow onions became easy to find again in the markets. The process taught me to be more open-minded about onions and their various relatives such as shallots and leeks. Most of the time, any allium can easily stand in for another. The taste and texture won't be quite the same, but this only keeps life interesting.

This is a long way of saying that not all cooking has to start with an onion. You can use your judgement on how many to add and in what form and sometimes—shock!—you can leave them out altogether. Sometimes you can get that onion hit, if you want it, in a different and much quicker way.

Perhaps because it is something we do so habitually, the cooking of onions provokes fierce and fixed opinions. Many people will have you believe that onions require huge amounts of time and effort to prepare. There's a popular belief—that seems to make some of those who hold it genuinely angry—that recipe writers have conspired to hide the truth about how long it takes to cook an onion. In 2012, Tom Scocca wrote an article in *Slate* titled "Layers of Deceit," arguing that it was a "lie" to say that soft browned onions could be achieved in five minutes. "Onions do not caramelize in five or 10 minutes. They never have, they never will—yet recipe writers have never stopped pretending that they will." Scocca points out that to produce true caramelized onions takes at least forty-five minutes rather than the ten minutes often mentioned to cook an onion in cookbooks.

But how often do you actually want to caramelize an onion? Yes, yes, there is French onion soup, whose deep dark loveliness I find myself craving at least once every winter. This, at least, is an onion dish that cannot—must not—be hurried. You will only achieve the requisite melding of savory onion and stock with melted cheese after the onion has been given the time to get completely soft and mahogany brown. Another dish whose comfort depends on very thoroughly caramelized onions is mujadarrah from the Middle East. This is basically just three elements, plus a few spices: rice, lentils, and caramelized onions. Those three elements fuse into something savory and bolstering: the kind of frugal dish that can revive you when you feel both fragile and broken—but only when the onions are cooked long and slow to a jammy sweetness.

Most dishes do not require the dark intensity of a caramelized onion, however. Let's say you are making a fresh green watercress soup as opposed to an onion one. You'll probably start by sweating the onion in a generous amount of butter or oil with a pinch of salt. After ten minutes and likely before, the onion will be soft and sweet but not colored and this is exactly what you want. To spend ages more on caramelizing the onion would not only be a waste of time; it would actually spoil the subtle flavor and bright color of the soup. Likewise, when you cook a finely diced onion with some carrot and celery in olive oil and butter as the basis for a rich ragù to go with pasta, you are only aiming to reach the stage when the vegetables are fragrant, soft, and glistening in the oil: eight minutes should do it.

The most common instruction for cooking onions is not to caramelize but to soften them or to sauté until translucent, a process that can easily be completed in five to ten minutes, assuming you are using around a large spoonful of oil or fat per medium diced onion and a pinch of salt to prevent them from sticking to the pan. If you dial up the fat or dice the onion extra small, the cooking time can be even shorter. Another way to save time when cooking onions is to use shallots instead (ideally the large torpedo-shaped ones, which are quicker to peel than the tiny ones). As food writer Alan Davidson remarks, "onion" is really a catch-all word that can refer to any vegetable in the genus Allium. Because shallots have much thinner layers than onions, it's easy to chop them into a beautifully fine dice which softens in butter in a trice. Take ½ cup/80g of diced shallots, a generous 1 tablespoon of butter, and a pinch of salt. Two to three minutes—really!—are all it takes to turn the mass of shallot from pungent and purple to sugary-soft and golden.

In truth, there is no single right way to cook a sliced or diced onion. You may want to cook an onion more or less—or not to cook it at all and go the raw or pickling route—depending on how you want it to taste and what you are serving it with. Or you may use green onions, which can be cooked to perfection in under five minutes (see recipe for skillet scallions on page 226) and which to my mind qualify as one of the most underrated of all ingredients. Edna Lewis, the great authority on American country cooking, said that green onions took "4 to 5 minutes" in a pan and Miss Lewis was certainly no liar. Decide what role the onion is playing in today's dinner and cook it accordingly, without being guilted into feeling that you are somehow failing.

Like the grieving process, the cooking of an onion has many stages, each of which has its own particular qualities. First comes the brutal tear-inducing stage, as the half-raw onion assaults you with its pungent chemicals: the vegetable's vengeance for being chopped. Those tears come from chemicals called lachrymators, which are released when the onion's cells are broken open. The original purpose of these sulphurous chemicals would have been to protect the onion from being eaten by animals. Stand too close to the pan during these initial seconds of cooking and no matter how happy your mood, you may find yourself watery around the eyes. Personally, I don't mind this, as long as I'm not wearing too much mascara. I'd rather cry because of an onion than out of true sadness. But if your eyes are more sensitive than mine, you could try wearing sunglasses any time you chop and cook onions. An added bonus is that you will look like the coolest onion chef around.

After a couple of minutes in the pan, the slices of onion lose most of their fiercest pungency but still have a firm texture. You could call this the crunchy-sweet stage. Perhaps you will choose to stop here and make a focaccia (Marcella Hazan says that the onions for focaccia should not be cooked too soft). Or maybe you will blast the heat high for three minutes until your still-crunchy onions brown a little at the edges. In *The Geometry of Pasta*, chef Jacob Kenedy recommends frying red onions for three minutes in butter until they smell "like a hot-dog stand," to go with an unlikely but delicious pasta sauce made with sliced frankfurters and diced fontina cheese, plus the aforementioned onions and some rosemary, that is the sort of thing you might feel like on arriving home late from a party at which you have drunk too much and eaten too little. Try it.

If you want the onions to play a less assertive role in your dish, you might turn the heat down and wait it out a little, stirring constantly with a wooden spoon until the pieces are soft and clear. This kind of simply softened but unbrowned onion will be the perfect base for everything from tomato sauce to pilaf. It takes no more than ten minutes. After a few minutes more, the onion releases more of its sugar and becomes golden and unctuous. Or if you want to have meltingly sweet onions for liver and onions—or to go with goat cheese in a salad—cook them for a full twenty minutes until they are golden brown and very soft.

Or if caramelized onions really are what your dinner plans require, here's a slightly easier way that I adapted from watching a YouTube video from *America's Test Kitchen*. The two brilliant things about this method are using water to help the cooking process along at the start and baking soda at the end, which helps speed up the browning process. Take 3⅓ lb/1.5 kilos of yellow onions, peel them, and slice into fairly thick pieces, pole to pole. This will look like a gigantic pile of onions, but sweep your tears aside and remember that, like spinach, they will collapse

and shrink as they cook. Put the onions in your largest wide shallow pan with 2 tablespoons of olive oil, 1 cup/240ml of water, and ¾ teaspoon of salt and set over medium heat for 10 minutes with the lid on. Then remove the lid and keep stirring and scraping the onions until they have fully browned (which should take around 15 minutes). Finally, mix together ¾ teaspoon of baking soda with a small spoonful of water. Drizzle into the onions and continue to cook until as dark and sweet as your onion-hungry heart desires. All in, this will have taken around 30 minutes. You might feel tempted to add sugar to boost the caramel notes, but do taste the mixture first and notice how sweet the onion is all by itself. If you find them too sweet, take a page from Samin Nosrat's book and add what she calls "a rumor of red wine vinegar" to take the edge off the sweetness. You might also want to add a few sprigs of thyme leaves stripped from their stalks. Thyme and onion were made for each other.

So yes, caramelizing onions is a bit of a performance and yes, you may find that your hair and clothes have a whiff about them by the time you are finished. But you can always make life easier for yourself by portioning up a batch of caramelized onions in freezer bags. This is an idea I got from Nigella Lawson's *How to Eat* (she calls it "onion mush") and it changed my life because any time I want onions for something like a pilaf or a stew, all I have to do is reach into the freezer and microwave one of the pre-portioned bags of onions for a minute. If I didn't have a microwave, I would defrost the bag in a cup of hot water. With pre-caramelized onions on hand in the freezer, you never need worry again that you don't have time to cook an onion. It's a good idea to make a big batch of caramelized onions every so often on a Sunday night alongside whatever other cooking you are doing for the week ahead.

It's also important to remember that if you don't like onions or don't have any, you can simply leave them out. Not every dish calls for an onion, any more than it needs a default sprinkling of black pepper. Claudia Roden, the greatest authority on traditional Middle Eastern cooking, writes that "onions and garlic may be used abundantly or omitted entirely without spoiling a dish." Sometimes the absence of an onion can actually make a dish feel fresher and lighter. In India, Jain vegetarians—who follow strict laws of non-violence—never eat onions or any vegetables that grow beneath the soil. On a trip to Mumbai, I devoured all manner of delicious Jain dishes including deep-fried chickpea dumplings soaked in yogurt and eggplants stuffed with peanuts. I never noticed the absence of onion, perhaps because Jain cooks make clever use of a spice called asafoetida (aka hing) that, used sparingly, can give a satisfying illusion of onion (don't be put off by the strong smell).

Another time-saving trick is simply to use garlic instead of onions. A tomato sauce for pasta involving onions will usually take a minimum of twenty minutes but you can make a fast-simmered one with a couple of cloves of garlic sautéd in oil in a scant ten minutes. The effect will not be the same but that does not mean it is worse.

When you stop taking onions for granted, you start to see that these lily-like plants are a far more interesting ingredient than we often appreciate. Both onions and green onions deserve to take center stage now and then and be honored as a vegetable in their own right: a vegetable that when cooked combines the sweetness of squash with the tastiness of meat and a silky texture that is all its own.

Three ways to put onions center stage

Yogurt-fried onions with lemons and sage

You could travel the world in search of rare and expensive things and not find a more satisfying morsel than a plain fried onion ring. My favorite way to cook them is to omit the batter and simply dip the rings in flour (possibly mixed with polenta for crunch, though it isn't crucial). As well as being a lot simpler, this allows the onion to shine. I like these with some slices of lemon and whole sage leaves fried alongside, an idea from *The Zuni Café Cookbook* by Judy Rodgers where they form part of a "piccolo fritto," Italian for "little fry." The fried lemon pieces offer bursts of sharpness alongside the sweet pungency of the onion, and the sage leaves are simply one of the most delicious things you will ever taste. But don't deprive yourself of trying the fried onions just because you don't have sage leaves or lemons.

Serves 4, as a starter

¾ cup plus 2 tablespoons/200ml whole milk

¾ cup plus 2 tablespoons/200ml full-fat yogurt (to make these vegan you could use coconut milk and coconut yogurt)

All-purpose flour, around 3 cups/375g or enough to cover the bottom of a dinner plate

Polenta, around 1 cup/165g, for the crunch
    (you can sub with semolina or leave it out)

1 tablespoon nigella seeds (optional)

2 large sweet onions, peeled and sliced (about ¼ inch/½cm thick) and separated into rings

1 large unwaxed lemon, rinsed and sliced as thin as you can muster

Whole sage leaves, a dozen or so

Sunflower or peanut oil, for deep frying (about 2 cups/480ml, or enough to reach a depth of at least 1½ inches/4cm in your pan)

Lemons, yogurt, and a clove of minced garlic, to serve

Mix the milk and yogurt with a fork in a shallow bowl such as a pasta plate. Mix together the flour, polenta, and nigella seeds (if using) on a large dinner plate (or a baking sheet if none of your plates are large). Have a couple more large plates or baking sheets nearby for putting the onions and lemon on once they are coated. Working in batches, dip the onion rings, lemon rings, and sage leaves first in the milk and yogurt mixture and then in the flour mixture. Coat them in the flour as if burying toys in a sandbox, then gently remove, shaking slightly to remove any excess, and set them on the plates or sheets. Continue until you have used up all the onions, lemon, and sage leaves. This is a gummy business and you should have a clean kitchen towel at the ready so that you can rinse and dry your hands a few times.

Now you are ready to fry. From this point onward, you will need to give the cooking process your full attention and stand well back at all times. Put some layers of paper towels on a plate and turn on the stove hood. Pour oil into a deep, medium saucepan so that it reaches a depth of at least 1½ inches/4cm and heat it to 350°F, ideally on a burner at the back of the stove. Use a kitchen thermometer if you have one, or if not, you can simply drop a very small piece of coated onion into the oil and watch and listen. The oil is hot enough when the onion sizzles softly but immediately. Using long-handled tongs or a spider, add a few pieces of the onion to the oil at a time. Cook them without touching them for a minute or two and then turn carefully with your tongs or spider. Watch the rings like a hawk but do not stand too close. Being splattered with hot oil is no joke. When they are golden and crisp, lift out onto the paper towels and repeat with the remaining onions, lemon, and sage. When they are all fried, sprinkle evenly with salt and serve with lemon wedges and a quick sauce: thick yogurt mixed with a clove of garlic and salt or the green cilantro chutney on page 256.

Deep-frying isn't hard but you just need to stay with it calmly until you are completely done. Your main job is to regulate the heat and turn it down if the oil hints at looking angry. After each batch, use your spider to clean the oil of any blackened crumbs. As soon as everything is cooked, take the oil-filled pan and put it somewhere safe out of the way until it cools, after which you can usually reuse at least some of the oil by straining it through a fine strainer, leaving behind any floury sludge at the bottom of the pan.

Skillet scallions

This is adapted from *The Taste of Country Cooking* by Edna Lewis. Before I read this magnificent book, I never would have guessed that a green onion could taste so good. N.B. The onions in the photograph are depicted halfway through the cooking process—you want them a little softer than this.

3 bunches of green onions (scallions)
2–3 tablespoons unsalted butter

Trim the roots off the green onions and trim the top ends to fit the pan. Rinse the green onions but do not dry them (the drops of water that remain will help them to steam-sauté). Heat a cast-iron frying pan over high heat and put in the butter. As soon as it foams, add the green onions and cover the pan. Turn the heat down to medium-low. After 3 minutes, turn them over (with tongs) and cook for another 2 or 3 minutes. Miss Lewis explains that the white part should be crisp and the green part "tender, shiny and green" and that they need no salt or pepper. Taste them and see. Amazingly, this is true.

Onion butter (or what to do with the trimmings)

You might not think that a recipe for onions could inspire strong emotions but this one makes me happy and sad at the same time. The happiness is from the discovery that onion trimmings, rather than being wasted, can be turned into a luxurious butter sauce. The sadness is because the source of the recipe is the remarkable *Prune* cookbook by Gabrielle Hamilton, named after her legendary restaurant in New York's East Village that closed its doors early in the spring of 2020. I never went to Prune, though I always imagined one day that I would. In April 2020, Hamilton wrote a moving article in *The New York Times* about how Prune had been her life for twenty years but now, as she laid off all thirty of her employees, she wondered whether there would ever be a place again for restaurants such as hers.

In Hamilton's cookbook, the onion butter is designed to go with a huge array of sweetly roasted onions cut in different ways, from long green green onions to glossy red onions in wedges to white onions cut as disks. At the end, you sprinkle the onions with a mix of flax seeds, millet, sesame, and poppy seeds so they taste like an everything bagel and anoint them with the onion butter.

But the sauce is so good you can make it to go with anything from white fish to a risotto to green vegetables whenever you have a lot of onion trimmings to use up. If you combine it with roasted onions and seeds as per Hamilton it makes a wonderful sauce for tagliatelle. The "onion tea" boils away happily in the background while you get on with anything else you are cooking.

Serves 4
Trimmings but not skins from at least 2 lb 2 oz/1kg of onions
2 tablespoons unsalted butter

Boil the onion scraps in 2 cups/480ml of water to make what Hamilton calls a "strong onion tea." Bring to a boil and cook for at least 30 minutes, or until the onion flavor is extracted and the water has reduced in volume. Strain ¼ cup/60ml of this onion tea into a fresh saucepan and bring to a boil. Whisk in the butter and stir until it becomes a beautiful oniony emulsion. Season with salt to taste. Serve over tagliatelle with roasted onions and seeds or in any of the other ways mentioned above.

Formulas to live by

Everyone needs a few edible blueprints to fall back on for days when you feel overstretched. An edible blueprint is something you can summon up on short notice from the pantry and whatever's in the fridge. By definition, it is something that everyone in the family likes. It should feel as reliable and forgiving as an old friend. These, more than any fancy dinner party creation, are the formulas that we live by. Some would call them no-recipe recipes, but I'm never sure how much sense this term makes because (am I missing something?) a no-recipe recipe is still after all . . . a recipe. An edible blueprint is a recipe so sturdy and capacious that it can withstand almost any number of variations and substitutions and still come out tasting like exactly the thing that you want to eat.

Each household and each person may have their own edible blueprints depending on the foods you most love and the ones you grew up with. Here are a few of my own stalwarts to help you on your way as you find your own.

Adaptable âsh

When the first UK lockdown started in March 2020 and my two younger children were suddenly thrown into a world of Zoom schooling, my most urgent thought was: what will we do about lunch? The prospect of having to cook a meal for four every day instead of my usual makeshift lunch for one frankly filled me with dread. How would I ever write anything again if I needed to spend half the morning thinking what to cook?

The thought of soup—which has always been my regular family standby for Saturday lunch—popped into my head. But I felt we needed something heartier and more filling than the mellow vegetable soups in the first chapter. I found a can of chickpeas and some dried pasta in the pantry and a few onions, greens, and herbs in the fridge. Perhaps I could turn these into a quick version of one of those thick bean and pasta soups? As my children enthusiastically slurped their noodle-filled broth, I felt instantly brighter at the prospect of a few weeks stuck at home. This, more than sandwiches, was a meal we could gather around. It felt healthy but also rib-sticking.

When I made that first lockdown soup in the Instant Pot, I had no idea that I would still be making it at least three times a week so many months later. During those endless weeks at home, this frugal and warming soup was both always the same and never the same. Sometimes, I used a can of white or red beans instead of the chickpeas. The vegetables were whatever was in the fridge. One day, I used beet instead of the greens and the whole pot of soup took on a magenta hue. Often, I used a cupful of bulgur wheat or rice instead of the pasta. My daughter and I always embellished our bowlfuls with chile flakes or chile crisp and usually a spoonful of thick yogurt, while my son left his soup plain. The strange thing is that after days and weeks and months of eating it, none of us got bored. Repetition only seemed to make it lovelier. When my son's birthday came around, nearly a year after the first lockdown had started, I asked what he wanted for his special birthday lunch (he had already established that dinner would be steak followed by chocolate cake). "Well, soup," he said, looking at me as if I were stupid. I can't say how much it consoled me to know that he still found this soup a pleasure.

Over time, I realized that the herb-rich noodle soups I was making on repeat had become less like an Italian minestrone and more like a Persian âsh, a family of dishes that are a way of life in Iran. As Margaret Shaida writes in *The Legendary*

Cuisine of Persia, the importance of âsh can be measured by the fact that a cook is called an âshpaz (soup cook). At the heart of any âsh will be legumes and herbs but there are myriad variants, some with tiny meatballs, some with grains such as barley, some with pomegranate molasses, some with dried fruit, some with lamb on the bone. Âsh is a flexible dish. In summer, âsh may contain vast quantities of fresh greens but in winter it might be made only with legumes and dried mint.

My lockdown soup lacks the finesse of true Persian âsh, which may involve many types of beans. But the beauty of my version is how little headspace it takes, as long as there are canned beans in the house. It can be ready in under 15 minutes in the Instant Pot from chopping to eating and most of that time is hands-free. Even in a regular pot, it still takes only 30–40 minutes to make and I always feel soothed by the act of making it. When I feel broken, the near-daily act of pouring oil into the pan and adding chopped vegetables to start that day's soup can patch me together again, like glue restoring an old pot. It reminds me that the original meaning of the word *restaurant* was a soup that restores and, by extension, an establishment that served restoring soups. Make this soup and be your own restaurant.

Serves 3–4

2 tablespoons extra-virgin olive oil

1 small onion, finely diced (or a leek, or a bunch of green onions)

3½ oz/100g spinach, rinsed and shredded (or a bulb of fennel, chopped, or some kale, leaves pulled from the stalks and shredded)

3½ oz/100g fresh green herbs such as parsley, cilantro, or dill, or a few stalks of celery with its leaves, coarsely chopped

1 medium zucchini, green or yellow, finely diced (or 2 medium carrots, peeled and finely diced or 2 beets, peeled and finely diced, or a few diced potatoes or a handful of sliced runner beans or green beans)

3 cloves of garlic, grated

¼ teaspoon ground turmeric (optional)

1 × 15-oz/425g can of chickpeas (or borlotti beans or kidney beans or cannellini beans or butter beans/lima beans)

3 tablespoons/40g moong dal (or red lentils or nothing)

2 bay leaves (known as "leaf of fragrance" in Persian, or a whole dried lime, pierced with a knife, or nothing)

3 oz/80g dried noodles or broken-up linguini or spaghetti (or 1 cup/160g of coarse bulgur wheat or rice)

A squeeze of lemon or a spoonful of vinegar

To serve

Choose any you like of chile flakes, fresh chopped herbs, a dollop of Greek yogurt, olive oil warmed with some dried mint, pomegranate molasses, sliced onions cooked until caramel brown in hot oil in a wok

INSTANT POT METHOD

Heat the oil on sauté mode and soften all the diced vegetables, stirring often, for about 3 minutes. Add the garlic, turmeric (if using), 1 teaspoon of salt and 1 tablespoon of water, press cancel and set it to high pressure mode for 1 minute. Fast release and add the chickpeas or beans and their water. Refill the tin twice with water and add this too, along with the bay leaves or dried lime and the pasta (or rice or bulgur). Set it to high-pressure mode for 2 minutes (or 4 minutes for rice). Ideally leave it to stand for 5–10 minutes before releasing the pressure (be careful). Give it a squeeze of lemon, thin it with water if it needs it, check for seasoning, and serve with any of the suggested accompaniments.

STOVETOP METHOD

Heat the oil in a large Dutch oven and soften all the diced vegetables, stirring often, for about 3 minutes. Add the garlic, turmeric (if using), 1 teaspoon of salt, and 1 tablespoon of water and cover the pan, turning the heat down, allowing the vegetables to sweat for 10 minutes. Add the chickpeas or beans and their water. Refill the tin twice with water and add this too, along with the bay leaves or dried lime and the pasta (or rice or bulgur). Cook until the pasta (or rice or bulgur) is done: 5–15 minutes depending on the shape. Give it a squeeze of lemon, check for seasoning, and serve with any of the suggested accompaniments.

SOME MORE VARIATIONS

—Sometimes I leave the rice/pasta/bulgur out and decrease the amount of water slightly. When it is done, I take out a ladleful of soup and blitz it with an immersion blender before returning this to the pan. I recently made a glorious purple version of this with beet, chickpeas, yellow zucchini, and green bell peppers with a touch of vinegar at the end.

—For a summery version, which is especially good with white beans, add 3½–7 oz/100–200g of halved cherry tomatoes at the end along with some torn basil. Leave out the turmeric and moong dal or lentils for this version for a more minestrone-like flavor and texture and eat with a splash of olive oil and lots of grated parmesan sprinkled over each bowl.

Sri's donburi rice bowls

In my family, this—a kind of not-quite-Japanese rice bowl—is the evening counterpart to the lockdown minestrone. We eat it on average once a week in countless variations and everyone is always happy to see it on the table. My son's eyes light up every time I serve him sticky short-grain rice. For some reason—the reason being sushi—he sees it as a far greater treat than Basmati.

Donburi literally means "bowl" in Japanese. A typical donburi meal in Japan consists of short-grain white rice topped with some kind of protein and/or sauce, such as crab omelet or raw salmon or chicken and egg simmered in soy sauce and stock. My house version of donburi is adapted from *The Rice Book* by the great Sri Owen, an Indonesian food writer whom I'm proud to call a friend. In *The Rice Book*, Sri gives a few different versions of donburi: one with beef, one with tofu, and one with chicken and mushrooms. They all consist of vegetables (with or without meat), sautéd in butter and simmered with ginger, garlic, mirin, soy sauce, and stock. Sri notes that the butter "may not be authentically Japanese, but it is quite irresistible even so." She is right. The resulting broth always tastes delicately comforting but healthy, the way I want home food to taste. We tend to have our donburi with vegetables and some kind of white fish or seafood such as frozen clams (that I buy from Asian grocery stores). But it's just as good with vegetables alone; or with a quickly cooked omelet on the side. Once you have made this a couple of times, you will see how easily it slots into your life (assuming you have the mirin, sake, and rice in the house). You can make the rice an hour or so ahead of time and let it rest. The vegetable-broth element will then take you only 10 minutes.

Serves 4

For the rice
2 cups/400g short-grain rice (I buy huge bags of rice from my local Korean
    grocery store but most supermarkets now sell sushi rice)

For the broth
14 oz/400g small fresh white fish fillets such as lemon sole or some fresh clams,
    cleaned, or frozen clams (1 lb 2 oz/500g)

¼ cup/50g unsalted butter

4 cloves of garlic, thinly sliced or coarsely grated

¾-inch/2cm ginger, thinly sliced or coarsely grated

About 1 lb 5 oz/600g vegetables, anything you like, trimmed and thinly sliced
(for example, a bulb of fennel, some carrots and fresh shiitake mushrooms; or
leeks, broccoli and asparagus; or zucchini, green beans, peas, and bok choy; or
whatever oddments you have in the crisper drawer, including lettuce)

2 tablespoons mirin

2 tablespoons cooking sake (or use ½ cup/120ml dry white wine plus 1 teaspoon
sugar instead of the mirin and sake)

2 tablespoons soy sauce

½ a stock cube, crumbled, or a little instant dashi powder (optional)

5 green onions, rinsed, trimmed, and sliced

A dash of rice vinegar

Sushi ginger and black sesame seeds, to serve

Start by cooking the rice. First, put it into a sieve and run under cold water from the tap while massaging the grains with your fingers. You have rinsed it enough when the water starts to run clear or when you get bored, whichever is soonest. Sometimes, I feel too tired to rinse the rice at all and it is still delicious. Try to remember the ratio of rice to water: for 1 cup/200g of rice, it's 1½ cups/360ml of water. Here it's 2 cups/400g of rice so you need 3 cups/700ml of water. I always cook the rice in my Instant Pot: place it in the Instant Pot, add the water, and set to high pressure for 5 minutes before allowing to slow release. Or simply place the rice and water in a saucepan with a tight-fitting lid, bring to a simmer, turn the heat down as low as possible, and cook with the lid on for 12 minutes. Take the pan off the heat and let it rest. I find that cooked rice will happily keep itself warmish in a covered pan for up to 1 hour.

If you are using the frozen clams, defrost them before you start. I do this by keeping them in their plastic pouch and dousing them in hot water from the tap until they loosen.

In a wok or large frying pan with a lid, melt the butter over medium heat and add the garlic and ginger. Add the sliced vegetables but keep back anything really tender such as bok choy or asparagus. Sauté until starting to soften, about 3 minutes. Add the mirin, sake and soy sauce and let it bubble up. Add ¾ cup plus 2 tablespoons/200ml of water, the stock cube or dashi if using, and any tender vegetables plus the green onions. Lay the fresh fish fillets on top or add the clams (for the frozen clams, make sure you add all their juices too). Put the lid on and simmer for 2–3 minutes, or until the vegetables are just tender and the seafood is piping hot. Check for seasoning. Add a dash of rice vinegar, just enough to bring it all to life.

Divide the rice among four bowls, top with the broth, and eat with sushi ginger and black sesame seeds.

VARIANTS UPON VARIANTS

—For chicken donburi, brown 10½ oz/300g of boneless, skinless chicken thighs cut into very thin strips in the butter along with the vegetables, then proceed as above.
—For tofu donburi, add tofu cubes (preferably deep-fried) instead of the seafood.
—For beef donburi, stir-fry 9 oz/250g of very thinly sliced sirloin steak in the butter at the start, then transfer it to a plate with a spider. Proceed as above and put the steak back at the end.
—For poached egg or omelet donburi, leave out the seafood and add a poached egg or small plain omelet to each bowl at the end.

Treat time as an ingredient

"Sharing food ... with family and friends is about
the clearest and simplest way to express that you
care. So how can there be no time for that?"
   Roy Finamore, *Tasty*, 2006

Judging from cookbook bestseller lists, many of us are searching for a form of cooking that takes less time or preferably no time at all. There are books that promise us meals in 30 minutes, 15 minutes, the blink of an eye. There are books for Quick and Easy Ketogenic recipes and for Fast and Thrifty Vegan meals. The other day, I was startled to find that when I typed "quick and easy cooking" into the book section of Amazon, there were more than 40,000 results. OK, so some of those are reprints. Even so, the market for quick recipes is crazily big.

But it seems we still haven't found what we are searching for where faster cooking is concerned. We may have time-saving recipes; but what we still don't seem to have enough of in our busy lives are the tools or headspace to use them. After another exhausting day, we look at the supposedly quick and easy recipes on the internet and laugh a bitter and hollow laugh at the notion that there is anything quick, let alone easy, about rustling up a dinner of grilled ribeye steak with asparagus and a red wine reduction sauce or a crispy-skinned fish with a multi-ingredient sauce when there is little in the fridge but a few vegetables and an old lump of cheese and we only have half an hour to spare to source, cook, eat, and wash up dinner.

The secret of time in the kitchen is not about forcing yourself to do everything in a tearing hurry (something that can increase a sense of panic rather than allaying it). It's about recognizing time as an ingredient in everything that you cook. Whenever you cook, time needs to be factored in, just as you would any other ingredient. Do I have butter? Check. Garlic? Check. Twenty minutes to brown the onions? Check. Just as you might decide against cooking something if the ingredients cost too much, you need to decide how much time you can afford to give to getting a meal ready on any given day. There are slow cooking days and fast cooking days. Neither is necessarily better or worse than the other but what matters is knowing where you stand and making plans accordingly.

The reason all those super-fast cookbooks don't necessarily work is that they perpetuate a mindset of scarcity around time. We have been told, over and over—often by the processed food industry—that we simply lack time to cook. And yes, most of us probably don't have time to make a three-course dinner every night. But this doesn't have to be a problem. The real question is to figure out how much time you can spare in the kitchen on any given week and tailor your food accordingly, just as you tailor the ingredients you buy to your budget. Time in the kitchen is a resource, like any other.

I think we often forget that time is not just an absolute concept but a subjective one. As well as trying to save time, we can also try to experience it differently. I've already mentioned this, but time spent in the kitchen can feel so much less onerous when you measure it by songs rather than by minutes. You might think you have no time to chop an onion but if you see it as three minutes to listen to your favorite song, it feels different.

In medieval China, cooking was timed using incense sticks. A recipe might mention that a dish would be done in the time it took to burn half a stick of incense or two sticks as the case might be. In this age of endless bleeping timers and phones that remind us what time it is down to the last second, this might sound an antiquated method to go about things but there is something calm about it that I like. In one thirteenth-century cookbook by a man named Lin Hong, a dish of fish in lotus leaves was said to take as long to cook as it took for him and his guests to walk around the lotus pond. "By the time we have circled the pond, the fish is cooked."

There is nothing wrong with a quickly made meal (except for our guilty sense that there is something wrong with us, for always running out of time). I find it consoling to remember that we are not the first cooks in history who sometimes needed to rustle something up in a hurry. Consider the Israelites who had no time to let their bread rise during their exodus out of Egypt and therefore they made flatbreads instead. Today, making your own flatbreads from scratch would not count as fast cooking to most people, but the point stands.

History is full of references to casual meals and cooking and eating on the go. In *The Taste of Country Cooking*, Edna Lewis explains that growing up on a Virginia farm in the 1920s, her family cooked differently on days when they knew they were going to be extra busy. They prepared a few things ahead of time and also relied on quick recipes such as something that Lewis calls Busy-day Cake, a simple sweet yellow cake. "Busy-day cake was never iced, it was always cut into squares and served warm, often with fresh fruit or berries left over from canning."

Obviously, quick cooking is a different proposition now that we can summon up food almost instantly on our phones. But I often think that convenience food is frequently not quite as fast as it seems, and that cooking, conversely, can be much faster than we imagine. As Michael Pollan describes in *Cooked*, microwave dinners can be slow to reheat if you are serving several people. Meanwhile, the stir-fried eggs with tomatoes and green onions made by every Chinese mother are done in the time it takes you to crack 2 eggs, heat a pan, and flick your wrist a few times. If you don't feel like cooking (or you feel like eating something that's slow to cook but quick to buy), that's another matter. Cooking is never an obligation, moral or otherwise. But if you want to cook, please don't let the thought that you have no time stop you. Most days have pockets of cooking time buried here and there if you know how to look.

Time to cook is not just one thing but a series of distinct problems. Prep time is often a much bigger hurdle than cooking time. Recipe writers don't always acknowledge, as Nigel Slater puts it, that "everybody works at a different pace, ovens do not have identical thermostats, and one person's idea of a minute can differ from the next's (even with one eye on the clock)." The single thing that makes any recipe faster, in my experience, is repetition, so that the prep gets faster and your hands start to work on auto-pilot. Something that might be a 30-minute recipe the first time you make it will often take half that amount of time on the second or third outing, because of muscle memory.

Another huge thing that doesn't get mentioned enough is shopping time, which if you ask me is a much greater cause of stress than cooking time. There are certain dishes that are super quick to cook, assuming you have had the time (and money) to purchase the ingredients. Take mussels. Mussels cooked in the French manner are heaven: so unbelievably delicious, cheap, and sustainable too, as well as rich in minerals, and all you need to serve with them is a baguette and a green salad. And they are so speedy and simple to cook. For 2–3 people, sauté some very finely chopped onions or shallots in butter. Add about 2 lb/1kg of cleaned live mussels and a glass of white wine. Clamp the lid on the pan and steam until the mussels open, shaking the pan a few times. This will take maybe 4 or 5 minutes. Swirl 2 tablespoons of heavy cream into the broth (or not—it's also good without) and check for seasoning (mussels are naturally salty, so for once I never add salt). Serve sprinkled with chopped flat-leaf parsley. After you have eaten your first mussel, use the empty shell as tongs to extract the remaining mussels and as you eat them, dip the baguette into the briny broth. Bliss.

But this kind of quick meal only counts as quick if you were able to visit a fish market earlier in the day or to order the mussels in advance. If you don't have access to a bag of fresh mussels, it is ludicrous to talk about them as a quick food, because you can't exactly summon them up from the small supermarket at the train station on the way home.

And grocery shopping isn't just about the shopping. It's also about making decisions, something I can spend all day feeling weighed down by. Before you can shop for food, you need an uncluttered moment or two to plan what you want to make and whether the other people in your house will actually eat it. This planning time is what really makes cooking a chore for so many of us: all those tiny decisions and calculations about what you've got in the pantry and how many extra things you need to buy to turn it into dinner and how many stores you will need to go to. This is why books of quick-and-easy recipes are not enough to solve the problem because you still have to spend time perusing all those recipes, choosing the ones that will actually work for you, and figuring out what ingredients they require.

All this talk about fast cooking can make us forget that sometimes slow cooking is strangely easier to fit into the day. Not all time in the kitchen is equally burdensome. There is hands-off time and hands-on time. Which kind you prefer will depend on your temperament and situation in life. Some people are driven to fury and despair by recipes that require you to start the day before ("soak the chickpeas for twelve hours," "marinate the chicken overnight"). But for others, this sense of getting ahead can be soothing.

Some kinds of slow cooking—such as a slow-roasted shoulder of lamb—require almost no active prep time on the part of the cook, but they do require planning ahead so that you put it in the oven at the right time. By the same token, some kinds of fast cooking such as a stir-fry can be on the table in minutes but may require ten minutes of concentrated peeling and chopping followed by another ten minutes of concentrated cooking, which is not always so easy to find when you have a toddler scampering at your feet or emails to answer, as the case may be.

What you need is a series of strategies to solve bad timing in different situations. Fast food takes many forms and flavors. Sometimes it means a microwaved bowl of a slow-cooked stew that you made the day before. Other times, it means a ten-minute couscous rustled up at the last-minute with a kettle and some frozen peas. You need dishes that you can conjure up from the pantry when you arrive home twenty minutes before you want to eat, with no inspiration. But you also need forgiving recipes you can start ahead of time that will give you a range of handy options to help you luxuriate more when you eat. As the great Edouard de Pomiane wrote in his classic 1930 book *Cooking in Ten Minutes*, the real goal of fast cooking is not speed per se but to give you more leisure time in which to relax, digest and enjoy your meals. Pomiane said he was writing "for everyone who has only an hour for lunch or dinner and yet wants half an hour of peace to watch the smoke of a cigarette while they sip a cup of coffee that has not even had time to get cold."

We could all still do with half an hour of peace over dinner (cigarette or not). In that spirit, here are a few ideas that have helped me feel richer in time, both when I cook and when I eat.

Getting ahead: universal sauces

Bottled cooking sauces sell by the million and it's not hard to see why. With a jar of savory sauce at your disposal, half the palaver of cooking is gone. That handy liquid saves you all the chopping and most of the simmering and the seasoning. It's just a shame that many of these bottled sauces taste so drab and dispiriting.

But what if a cook-in sauce could actually be delicious? It can and I will show you how. Imagine how reassuring it would be if you knew you had at your disposal in your fridge or freezer a series of elixirs that could become a meal for almost any occasion using almost any ingredients in the house. This is a very kind-on-yourself way of cooking. It's a way of bottling your own cooking energy for a day when you are flat-out or just plain flat.

Some cooks have freezers stocked with cartons of neatly-labeled batch-cooked stews and nutritious soups, ready to defrost for any occasion. If this is you, the following section may be irrelevant to your needs. Skip ahead a few pages. I wish I could be so organized. The only time I've managed to plan the food in my freezer to this extent has been out of sheer survival instinct, when my children were about to be born and I created a whole library of lentil soups to see us through the first few weeks. The rest of the time, my freezer is not quite so perfectly stocked. The problem is partly that there's something about fully finished pre-frozen dishes that makes me feel closed-in, as if all the options have been taken away from me. A frozen sauce, however, is another matter. It's something you can adapt to whatever needs using up in the fridge. It opens up possibilities instead of closing them down.

Wouldn't it be a boon to have a clutch of aromatic all-purpose curry sauces, one red, one green, and one yellow, each as fragrant as can be but not so hot that they frighten any chile-haters? Or what about having a stash of comforting tomatoey stew seasoned with paprika, orange zest, and garlic: the makings of a fish stew except that should you find yourself without any fresh fish, it would be just as good with potatoes or chicken instead. The joy of this kind of cooking is that it is flexible. Unlike frozen batch cooking, which can leave you feeling tied down—the stew that seemed so appetizing on the afternoon you made it can start to seem like a dead weight of obligation when it lingers in the freezer—these sauces leave you with options. If you suddenly realize you are cooking for vegans instead of meat-eaters, having these sauces will remove all panic.

I only started making these universal sauces a couple of years ago and they have genuinely transformed my cooking life for the better. For me, they are the secret of feeling as if I have more time in the kitchen as well as wasting less food. I've given some more polished ideas in this section on how to use the sauces—with meat, with fish, with paneer, or tofu—but the truth is that I most often use them when stocks are low to use up random assortments of vegetables. I now can't make a stew or a curry without wondering how it would work as a stand-alone sauce.

These sauces are also a great thing to have in your possession should you be a cook with control-freak tendencies like me. I am slightly ashamed to admit that part of the appeal of these sauces for me is that if I ask someone else in the family to make a meal out of one of them, I know they can't screw up the seasoning, because it is already done exactly the way I like it. The main thing to remember is that when reheating any of the sauces, add splashes of water as needed, if it's become too thick.

N.B. All these sauces will keep for 3–4 days in the fridge or up to 3 months in the freezer. I label and date them in portions (e.g., 1st March, 2 portions red curry).

The loveliest red curry sauce

What that makes this sauce especially lovely is using your own freshly ground curry powder (see recipe on page 188). But feel free to use store-bought curry powder brightened with a little cardamom and coriander if that makes things more doable from your end. Liberty hall. Either way, this sauce is pure comfort, though it makes no claim to be authentically Indian. The lemongrass means that it is still fragrant even after weeks in the freezer.

Enough for 2 curries for 4–5 people, or 4 curries for 2 people, to serve 8–10
4–5 tablespoons/60–75ml neutral oil
2 large onions or 4 small ones, peeled and very finely chopped
2 tablespoons aromatic curry powder (page 000) or 2 tablespoons of any curry
    powder plus ½ teaspoon ground cardamom and 1 teaspoon ground coriander
4–6 fat cloves of garlic, finely grated
A large chunk of fresh ginger, chopped or grated
4 stalks of lemongrass (remove the tough outer layers and when you get to the
    tender part inside, chop it finely, inhaling deeply as you do so to get the full
    uplifting effect)
1–2 red chiles, seeded and finely chopped
2 tablespoons soy sauce
2 × 14-oz/400g cans of whole, peeled tomatoes, blended until smooth with an
    immersion blender
1 × 13.5-oz/400ml can of coconut milk
2 teaspoons sugar
Juice of ½ a lemon or lime

REGULAR METHOD

Heat the oil in a wide heavy pan and soften the onions for 8–10 minutes, keeping the heat fairly low so they don't burn, and stirring often. Mix in the curry powder and notice the fragrance that suddenly fills the room. Add the garlic, ginger, lemongrass, chile, and soy sauce and stir for 1 minute more. Add 1 teaspoon of salt and everything else except for the lemon or lime, and simmer for 20 minutes. Taste. Does it need more salt? Add the squeeze of lemon or lime. The sauce will be a tiny bit textured from the onions. If you would prefer it totally smooth, blitz it with an immersion blender.

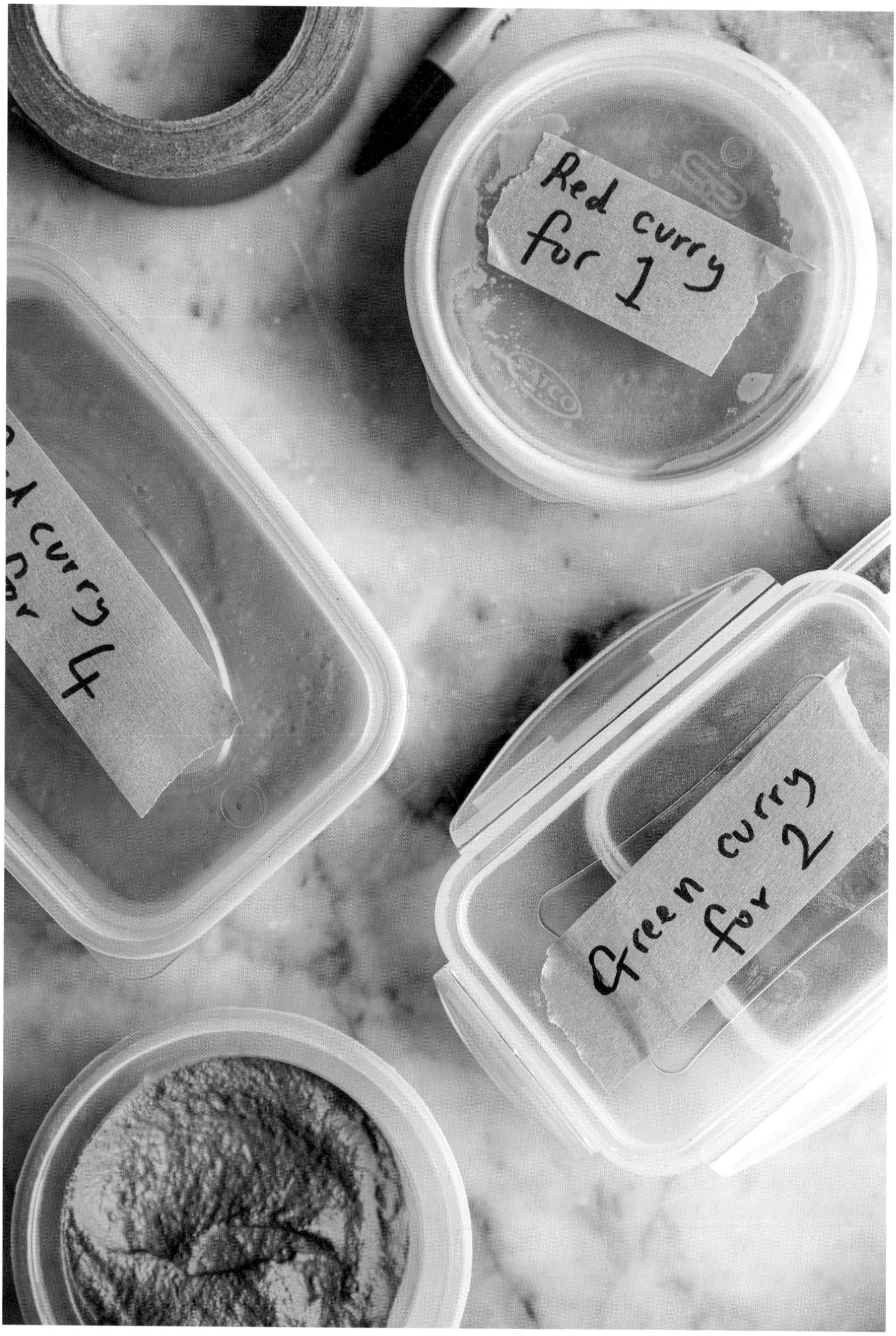
Red curry
for 1
Green curry
for 2

INSTANT POT OR PRESSURE COOKER METHOD

Set the pressure cooker to the sauté function. Add the oil and the onions and soften them for a few minutes. Mix in the curry powder and notice the fragrance that suddenly fills the room. Add the garlic, ginger, lemongrass, chile, and soy and stir for 1 minute more. Add 1 teaspoon of salt and everything else except for the lemon or lime, and cook at high pressure for 6 minutes. Let the pressure release naturally. If it is too thin, turn back to the sauté function for a few more minutes until it thickens a little. Taste. Does it need more salt? Add the squeeze of lemon or lime.

You now have in your possession a stash of the loveliest red curry sauce. I'm assuming you will want to use some straight away—see below for how. Keep the rest in the fridge (it will keep for 3–4 days, refrigerated) or freeze in batches (label carefully) for future meals.

Use this curry sauce with any ingredients you like. Remember: I can't see inside your fridge so you know much better than I do what needs using up. But here are some ideas to get started.

Chicken curry

Serves 4

1 lb 2 oz/500g boneless, skinless chicken thighs, with the largest pieces of fat trimmed off, or chicken breasts

1 tablespoon oil

½ × batch of Curry Sauce (page 000)

1 × 15-oz/425g can of chickpeas, drained (optional), or 7 oz/200g green vegetables such as bok choy or green beans

1–2 tablespoons heavy cream

To serve

Cooked rice, plus any combination of: plain yogurt, chopped fresh cilantro, wedges of lime, sliced chiles, Indian pickles

REGULAR METHOD

Cut the chicken into cubes of ¾ inch/2cm or so. Heat the oil in a large frying pan over medium-high heat. Add the chicken, stir it once to coat in the oil, and then cook it undisturbed for a few minutes until it takes on some color. Flip it over and cook until it is lightly browned all over. This should take around 10 minutes in total. Add the sauce and 7 tablespoons/100ml of water plus the chickpeas, if using, and simmer for 10 minutes. Add more water if the liquid has dried out too much. If using green vegetables, add them now and simmer until tender—1 minute for bok choy, longer for green beans. Taste for seasoning and adjust the salt. And does it need lemon? Stir in the cream.

INSTANT POT METHOD

Set to sauté mode. Heat the oil and add the chicken. Stir it once to coat in the oil, then cook it undisturbed for a few minutes until it takes on some color. Flip it over, add the chickpeas, if using, and the sauce. I don't add extra water here. Press cancel and then set to high pressure for 5 minutes. Slow release. Taste for seasoning and add more salt if needed. Add the green vegetables, if using, and set to sauté until tender. If the sauce is thin, set it back to sauté for a few minutes to thicken slightly. Stir in the cream.

Serve with rice, yogurt, cilantro, lime, fresh sliced chiles, and pickles.

OTHER IDEAS

Red cauliflower and shrimp curry

Cut a whole cauliflower into small pieces and cook it in a little oil in a large frying pan over medium-high heat until deeply bronzed all over (8–10 minutes). Add the sauce plus 7 tablespoons/100ml of water and simmer it for 10 minutes or until the cauliflower is tender. Add some cooked small wild shrimp and simmer them in the sauce until thoroughly hot (2–3 minutes). If the shrimp are frozen, first defrost them by putting them into a bowl, covering with hot water from a kettle, then draining in a sieve and rinsing with cold water. This version is especially good with a final sprinkle of fried crispy shallots for crunch as well as the cilantro leaves.

Sweet potato and kale curry (vegan)

Sauté some peeled, sliced sweet potato in oil until it has browned slightly (5–8 minutes). Add shredded cavolo nero leaves and sauté this too until slightly brown before pouring in the curry sauce plus an extra grating of ginger and a finely chopped seeded red chile. Simmer for 15 minutes or until tender. Stir in 2 cans of drained black beans and simmer a couple of minutes more until the beans are warm. Adjust with water as needed. This version is good with flatbreads and a simple salad made from avocado, green onion, olive oil, lime zest, green tomatoes or cucumber, and green chile. Personally, I'd like sour cream or thick yogurt with this, too. You can also make this with cabbage instead of kale, in which case sauté the shredded cabbage at the start with the sweet potato until it is sweet and slightly brown before adding the sauce.

Bouillabaisse sauce with orange and anise

I love the flavors of a French fish soup or bouillabaisse: the heady mixture of orange peel, fennel seeds, tomatoes, wine, and garlic. But you don't need to be a fish eater to enjoy this sauce. It is also incredibly good with sautéd chunks of celery root, a vegetable whose sweet-savory fleshiness is one of the best stand-ins for meat or fish. Making bouillabaisse from celery root is a trick I learned from *The Cranks Bible* by Nadine Abensur. This sauce also makes a fine stew with potatoes combined with other vegetables; or with chicken. Or, needless to say, with fish (simmer 1 lb 2 oz–1 lb 9 oz/500–700g white fish fillets, cubed, in half a batch of sauce, with or without fresh mussels or clams, for 3–4 minutes or until cooked, with flat-leaf parsley or fennel fronds sprinkled at the end).

Serves 8
¼ cup/60ml olive oil
6 cloves of garlic, peeled and chopped
2 bulbs of fennel or 4–5 stalks of celery, finely chopped
2 teaspoons fennel seeds
2 teaspoons smoked paprika
½ teaspoon chile flakes
2 star anise
A long strip of peel from an orange (preferably unwaxed)
4 × 14-oz/400g cans of whole, peeled tomatoes (in the summer, I sometimes make
  it with 2 cans of tomatoes plus 1¾ lb/800g chopped fresh tomatoes)
2 teaspoons brown sugar
¾ cup plus 2 tablespoons/200ml white wine

Heat the olive oil in a large, wide frying pan over medium-low heat and soften the garlic and chopped fennel or celery for 3–4 minutes, or until soft and fragrant. Add the fennel seeds, paprika, chile flakes, star anise, and orange peel and stir for half a minute more, or until all the scents rise up and mingle. Add the canned tomatoes, sugar, wine, and 1 teaspoon of salt. Simmer for 30–40 minutes, or until well reduced. Remove the star anise and orange. Transfer to a saucepan and blitz until very smooth. Check for seasoning. Divide up into whatever portion sizes you want and refrigerate or freeze until needed.

Celery root and white bean bouillabaisse

Serves 4
2 tablespoons olive oil
1 medium-large celery root, peeled and cut into cubes
1 × 15-oz/425g can of white beans, drained
½ × batch of bouillabaisse sauce with orange and anise (page 251)

To serve
A handful of flat-leaf parsley, chopped
Lemon, cut into wedges
Slices of baguette, toasted
3½ oz/100g Gruyère cheese, grated (1 cup), or vegetarian equivalent (optional)

Rouille
Mayonnaise (either a batch of homemade mayonnaise made with ¾ cup plus 2
    tablespoons/200ml oil and 2 yolks plus a little lemon juice and salt, or ¾ cup
    plus 2 tablespoons/200g store-bought mayonnaise)
1 roasted red bell pepper from a jar
2 cloves of garlic, crushed to a paste
½ teaspoon paprika (sweet or smoked)
A pinch of cayenne pepper

Heat the oil in a large, wide frying pan over medium-high heat and sauté the pieces
of celery root until nicely brown (8–10 minutes). Don't skimp on this stage; it adds
flavor. Add the white beans and the sauce and simmer until the celery root is tender.
As always, add a splash more water as needed. Serve in bowls with chopped flat-leaf
parsley, wedges of lemon, and sliced toasted baguette on the side.

   If you want to make the grated cheese and rouille to go with it (it's good either
way), blend the mayonnaise with the red bell pepper, garlic, paprika, and cayenne.
Check to see if it needs more lemon. Serve with the celery root bouillabaisse in wide
bowls. Put the rouille in a bowl on the table and the grated cheese in another bowl,
with the toasted baguette in a third bowl. Each person can take slices of toasted
baguette and top them with rouille and grated cheese, before floating them like little
rafts in the aromatic red soup.

Universal straight tomato sauce

If you prefer a plainer tomato sauce to this bouillabaisse sauce, try the all-in-one tomato sauce on page 20. This is very handy if you make it in big batches and store it in the freezer, not just to use as a pasta sauce but for simple stews—for example, you could turn it into homemade baked beans by simmering it with a couple of tins of drained white beans plus a little chopped rosemary, 2 teaspoons of dark brown sugar, 1 teaspoon of vinegar, 1 teaspoon of Worcestershire sauce, and ½ teaspoon of smoked paprika.

Green curry with crispy fish and peas

Serves 4
½ × batch of green cilantro chutney (page 256)
1⅔ cups/250g frozen pease
A handful of raw sugarsnap peas, shredded lengthwise
Oil or butter, for frying
1 lb 2 oz/500g lemon sole fillets or other white fish fillets, dusted with all-purpose
    flour and a pinch or two of salt

To serve
Rice
A few mint leaves, rinsed
Lime wedges
Fried shallots (optional)

I used to cook pieces of fish straight in the sauce but now I prefer the contrast of textures between crisply fried fish and soft curry sauce. Before you start, put some rice on to cook. Put the chutney into a wide pan with the frozen peas and 7 tablespoons/100ml of water over medium heat. When the liquid starts to bubble, put the lid on and cook for 3–4 minutes, or until cooked through. Add the sugarsnaps (they don't need to cook, only warm) and taste for seasoning. Meanwhile, heat up a wide shallow pan, add the oil or butter, and fry the fish fillets until crisp and just cooked: maybe 2 minutes on the first side and 1 minute on the second side. Transfer them to plates. Serve the fish and pea curry with rice and a scattering of mint leaves, and perhaps some crisp fried shallots for even more crunch.

Green cilantro chutney

I never realized that green chutney could be used as a curry sauce rather than simply as a condiment on the side before I read *Made in India*, Meera Sodha's first cookbook, in which she includes a recipe for cilantro chutney chicken. When I first tasted this, it instantly became my new favorite thing to eat: sour and sweet and deeply grassy-green. And then one day, I had vegetarians coming for dinner and wondered if it would work just as well with paneer.

It did. It's also wonderful with any kind of white fish, which can be turned into a curry in a scant 6 minutes (or 10, allowing for the kitchen prep) when you have a batch of this in the fridge. I've adapted Meera's recipe slightly, using cashews instead of peanuts and adding water to make it more sauce-like, but if you intend to use some of it as a condiment, cut the amount of water in half.

Makes around 14 oz/400g, enough for 2 curries for 3–4 people
7 oz/200g fresh cilantro
1 cup/150g unsalted cashews
Juice of 2 lemons
4 teaspoons brown sugar
2 teaspoons ground turmeric
2 small green chiles, seeded and roughly chopped (leave these out if serving this to
   children and instead serve the dish with fresh chiles on the side)

Rinse the cilantro by swishing it in a bowl of cold water. Put it into your largest measuring cup or a small saucepan. Add all the other ingredients plus ¾ cup plus 2 tablespoons/200ml of water and 1½ teaspoons of salt and blitz with an immersion blender until smooth. Taste to see if it needs more lemon, salt, or sugar to suit your taste.

Green spiced paneer with spinach

This can make a couple of blocks of quickly purchased supermarket paneer taste like a feast. Or substitute firm tofu to make it vegan.

Serves 4

14 oz/400g paneer, cut into ¾-inch/2cm cubes (or the same quantity of tofu)

2 teaspoons garam masala

3 tablespoons sunflower or olive oil

2 medium onions, peeled and finely chopped

4 cloves of garlic, peeled and grated

A thumb of ginger, grated

½ × batch of green cilantro chutney (page 256)

14 oz/400g fresh spinach leaves, rinsed

Dry the cubes of paneer with paper towels, season them with salt, and dust them with the garam masala. Heat the oil in a wide lidded pan over medium-high heat. When it is shimmering hot, add the paneer. Let it cook until it is browning at the edges before turning, otherwise it may stick to the pan. This is no disaster if it happens, just scrape up the sticky bits and continue. When the paneer is golden on both sides, transfer it to a bowl, leaving the oil in the pan. Add another 1 tablespoon of oil if it needs it and fry the onions until soft and golden, around 8 minutes. Add the garlic and ginger, stir until fragrant, then add the chutney. Return the paneer to the pan and stir in the spinach leaves in batches (it will look like masses but it wilts down to almost nothing). When the spinach is all wilted, check the seasoning and add a little water if you think it needs it. Serve with flatbreads or naan.

THE SECRET OF COOKING

Green pumpkin curry with potatoes and green beans

Take half a batch of the green cilantro chutney (page 256) and set aside a large spoonful of it in a small bowl. Put the rest into a medium saucepan with ¾ cup plus 2 tablespoons/200ml of water and add 1 lb 5 oz/600g of butternut squash or pumpkin, peeled and cut into large chunks, and 1¾ lb/800g of baby new potatoes, halved. Simmer for 15 minutes with the lid on, topping up with water if it evaporates too fast. Add 7 oz/200g of fine green beans, halved, and simmer for 5 more minutes. Stir in the reserved green chutney. Serve with lime wedges. Sometimes I add cream to this at the end.

Lemon-yellow laksa sauce

I became hooked on laksa while visiting Australia a decade ago. Almost every restaurant or café we visited seemed to have some version of this heady, coconutty noodle broth, which is eaten all over southeast Asia. The word laksa comes from the ancient Persian word for noodles. This bright yellow laksa sauce is not a true laksa as eaten in Singapore or Malaysia (it lacks the crucial ingredient that is laksa leaf) but was conjured from pantry supplies based on my memories of the ones we ate in Australia. I've made it with lemon peel instead of lemongrass because that was all I had the day I first made it and then I found I liked the lemony taste (lemongrass and lemon is even better). And I add a bit of miso as a vegetarian equivalent of the traditional shrimp paste. The sauce is good with any combination of vegetables plus rice noodles, or with seafood. Use half a batch any of the ways described for the green or red curry sauces above and add a final sprinkling of chopped cilantro and/or mint and a squeeze of lemon or lime.

Makes enough sauce for 2 laksas for 4
2½ oz/70g ginger, coarsely chopped (or 1½ oz/40g ginger and 1 oz/30g galangal if you can find galangal)
8 cloves of garlic, peeled
2 red chiles, seeded and chopped (if serving to children, leave out and add chile later)
The peel of 1 small-medium unwaxed lemon, cut off with a sharp knife (and/or 4 stalks of lemongrass, inner parts only, chopped)
A big handful of cilantro
1 teaspoon ground turmeric
1 tablespoon ground coriander
2 tablespoons neutral oil
2 × 13.5-oz/400ml cans of coconut milk
¼ cup/60ml fish sauce (or vegetarian equivalent, either soy sauce or vegetarian fish sauce)
2 tablespoons miso paste (any kind)
2 tablespoons brown sugar
Juice of 1–2 lemons

Put all the ingredients up until and including the oil in a large bowl and blitz with an immersion blender. Be patient, it may take a while for it all to break down.

Heat the oil in a large frying pan over medium heat and fry this paste for around 2 minutes or until fragrant. Add the coconut milk, fish sauce, miso, and sugar plus 1⅔ cups/400ml water and simmer for 8–10 minutes or until it smells and tastes really good. Adjust the seasoning with the lemon juice plus more fish sauce and/or sugar.

Divide into portions and keep in the fridge for up to 4 days or the freezer for up to 3 months.

Asparagus and pea laksa with fried tofu puffs

You can usually find deep-fried tofu cubes in Asian food shops. They are one of my favorite fast foods. With asparagus and peas, this makes a lovely spring-like laksa.

Serves 4
7 oz/200g thin or fat dried rice noodles
½ × batch of lemon-yellow laksa sauce (page 259)
9 oz/250g fried tofu
7 oz/200g asparagus, trimmed
5¼ oz/150g sugarsnap peas
⅔ cup/100g frozen peas
Fish sauce, to taste

To serve
1¾ oz/50g radishes, trimmed and very thinly sliced
Mint leaves, lime wedges, fresh red chiles

Soak the rice noodles according to the package instructions. Bring the laksa sauce up to a simmer in a wide sauté pan, thin with water as desired, then add the tofu followed by all the vegetables except for the radishes. As soon as the asparagus is tender (3–5 minutes), switch off the heat. Taste for seasoning. Does it need a splash of fish sauce? Rinse the noodles in hot water to declump them and divide them among four bowls. Pour the sauce over the top with the vegetables and tofu. Garnish with radish slices and mint leaves and serve with lime wedges, sliced red chiles, and extra fish sauce.

Cooking from a standing start

"I admire those who know what they will be eating
the following day. They are the sort who remember
to soak the beans overnight."
　Nigel Slater

I was walking the dog with my friend Sarah one afternoon when she said, "The thing
is, you can't cook from a standing start." She was talking about the fact that people
who didn't cook much (her husband, for example) didn't understand that cooking
isn't just about the action with wooden spoons and knives that happens just before
dinner. It's about all the stages that come before. The example Sarah gave was that if
she wanted to make a supposedly quick risotto in the evening, she would first consult
a couple of recipes and then check that she had risotto rice in the house and maybe
even sauté the onion ahead of time.

Afterward, I couldn't stop thinking about what Sarah had said because it suddenly
struck me that at least half of my cooking does happen very nearly from a standing
start. It isn't ideal, but sometimes it's the only way. As Edouard de Pomiane wrote
in his classic 1930 book *Cooking in Ten Minutes*, sometimes you need to put a pot of
water on the fire before you have even taken your hat off. I don't usually wear hats
but frequently start cooking before I take off my coat.

You should be able to find ideas dotted all over the book that would qualify as
cooking from a standing start. Take a look at the egg dishes in Every day a feast
(page 000) and the magic pasta in Have a backup plan (page 000).

When you are cooking from a standing start, it helps to have a few ideas up your
sleeve of ingredients that take almost no time to cook. Take grains. Grocery stores
now contain an array of tasty and interesting grains. The drawback is that some of
them take an age to cook. When I'm in a hurry, I try to steer clear of such things
as farro and barley and spelt grains, which can take as long as 40 minutes to fully
soften, and gravitate toward whole-wheat couscous or fine bulgur, which cooks
perfectly with water from a kettle in 5–10 minutes.

There are a few simple tricks you can use to make almost any meal much quicker
to cook. Here are some things that have worked for me:

—Tidy your fridge and your pantry so you can see what you have. I dread to think how much time I have lost over the years opening every kitchen cabinet searching for cumin only to find that I have three jars, all in the wrong place. I recently moved most of my spices from a cabinet to a drawer and it feels like a daily miracle to open the drawer and be able to see exactly which spices I have.

—The same goes for utensils. Cooking is so much quicker when you know where the spatula is.

—When trying to sauté anything, remember it will cook much faster in a bigger pan such as a wok (or a large sauté pan).

—It will also cook much faster if you cut the pieces smaller. This is another reason to keep your knives sharp. None of this is radical news to cooks in China, but it took me ages to figure out that tiny pieces of vegetable or meat cook so much faster than large chunks. Yes, they take longer to prep but you still end up saving time.

—Substitute green onion for regular yellow onion. It softens in one minute or so rather than 10 minutes and tastes lovely.

—Or leave the onion out altogether (see page 216).

—When in a hurry, use blitzed fresh tomatoes instead of canned. Fresh tomatoes don't need simmering time to taste good.

—Use couscous instead of rice. Use Chinese egg noodles (cook in 3 minutes) instead of spaghetti (cooks in 10 minutes).

—Reduce the ingredients list. If a recipe for a stir-fry calls for small quantities of seven different vegetables, use larger quantities of two different vegetables instead.

—Keep some basics on hand so that when the chips are down, you can rustle something up.

—Make use of frozen vegetables and fruits that not only cook fast but come pre-prepped.

—Whenever you are cooking a rice dish or a soup or stew, put it in the Instant Pot (if you have one). Hands-free risotto in 10 minutes. Not too shabby.

—Choose a recipe that doesn't require you to go to three different stores for the ingredients.

If it is really to be doable, this kind of cooking needs to be easy-shop as well as easy-cook. It also tends to rely heavily on having a well-stocked pantry, complete with cans of cooked beans, as well as oils and vinegars and things like jars of roasted peppers and cans of anchovies for flavor. I've lost track of the number of times that a can of beans has saved dinner for me.

Quick feasts from a can of beans

Lima beans with spinach, cream, and crispy prosciutto

Despite the speed, there is no compromise on flavor here. It's based on a recipe by Claire Thomson in her superb book *Home Cookery Year*, but I've exchanged the bacon for crispy prosciutto—a Mark Bittman idea for stretching a little meat a long way. I also like it as a vegetarian dish with some sliced mushrooms cooked with soy instead of the prosciutto. Going big on garlic and cream is always a good option when time is tight, because fat plus garlic will make anything taste good. This basic template will work with any canned beans, and you could switch around the spinach for other greens.

Serves 2
1 tablespoon unsalted butter
2 fat cloves of garlic, peeled and grated or crushed to a paste
7 tablespoons/100ml heavy cream
1 × 15-oz/425g can of lima beans (butter beans), drained
A grating of nutmeg
1 tablespoon olive oil
2½ oz/70g sliced prosciutto
2 thick slices of sourdough bread
3½ oz/100g rinsed spinach leaves
Juice of ½ a lemon
A handful of basil leaves or any herb you like

Melt the butter in a medium saucepan and add the garlic. Fry for 30 seconds, or until just turning golden. Add the cream, lima beans, and a grating of nutmeg, plus a big pinch of salt. Turn the heat down and cook, stirring now and then, for 5 minutes. Add a splash of water if it threatens to burn or dry up.

Meanwhile, heat the oil in a frying pan and cook the prosciutto until crisp, stirring often—3–4 minutes. Switch off the heat. Toast the bread. Returning to the bean pan, add the spinach and cook until it is wilted—maybe 2 minutes more. Taste it for seasoning and add a squeeze of lemon. Serve the beans on toast with the prosciutto and basil scattered on top.

Ten-minute chana masala

By using green onions instead of regular yellow onions and fresh tomatoes instead of canned, you can get a full-flavored chana masala (Indian chickpeas) on the table in under 10 minutes. I would happily eat this for lunch every day, and leftovers are good for breakfast with a fried egg.

Serves 2

    2 tablespoons oil
    4 green onions, trimmed and chopped
    2 cloves of garlic, peeled and grated
    ¾-inch/2cm piece of ginger, grated
    9oz/250g fresh tomatoes, rinsed and blitzed with an immersion blender
    1 tablespoon tomato paste
    1 teaspoon garam masala
    ¼ teaspoon ground turmeric
    ¼ teaspoon chile flakes
    1 × 15-oz/425g can of chickpeas, drained

In a wide sauté pan or frying pan, heat the oil and cook the green onions until just softened—1 minute. Add the garlic and ginger and cook for 1 minute more, then add the tomatoes and tomato paste plus ½ teaspoon of salt. Simmer for about 2 minutes, then add the spices and chickpeas and simmer for a couple of minutes more or until the sauce is thick and delicious. Check for seasoning.

Serve with flatbreads and cool yogurt or on hot buttered toast.

Quicker food for friends

It's one thing cooking from a standing start when you are doing it only for yourself or close family. The times when I find last-minute cooking most stressful, though, is when other people are coming over. Here are a couple of menu ideas that can be happily cooked—and shopped for—at short order after work without giving you a nervous breakdown.

Express vegan feast for two

Whether they were vegan or not, this is the sort of dinner I would make if I had a friend coming over and I didn't want my time in the kitchen to take away from the more important time we could be spending talking and catching up. The order in which I would do the cooking is: dessert first (and reheat the plums last-minute) then starter then main. It could all be done before your friend arrives, if that's what makes you feel most relaxed, or you could stand in the kitchen together having drinks while you finish the pilaf. If you are making this for a non-vegan friend, the orange and cardamom shortbread squares (see page 28) is a good alternative for dessert. You'll have leftovers, but to me that is a bonus.

It's up to you whether you want to serve the beet dip as a separate course or have everything on the table from the beginning. I prefer having it in separate courses, to spin things out more. One of the great advantages of quick cooking is that it gives you time to luxuriate over the eating part. But when you move on to the pilaf, don't clear the dip away—they go well together.

I first cooked this for my friend Miranda. I'd hardly seen her for a year because of the pandemic. Now, any time I make these dishes, I can hear the sound of her laughter that night.

Turkish beet dip (Kiz Güzeli)

This comes out deeply pink. Vacuum-packed cooked beets are one of the great convenience foods, in my view, but obviously if you have some fresh beets these will be even more delicious: rinse them and roast them with the skin on for around 45 minutes or until tender, then peel and proceed as below.

Serves 2
9 oz/250g cooked vacuum-packed beets (not cooked in vinegar)
1 clove of garlic, peeled and grated
2 tablespoons olive oil
1 teaspoon ground cumin
A squeeze of lemon
2 tablespoons coconut yogurt (or use regular Greek yogurt if you are not vegan), plus more to serve
Sumac or chile flakes

To serve
Flatbreads or pita or crackers plus lemon wedges and radishes and olives

Drain the beets and blitz with all the other ingredients in a large bowl with an immersion blender (or in a food processor). Pulse-chop until it is combined but not totally smooth. Taste for seasoning. Transfer to a bowl with a silicone spatula and swirl some more coconut yogurt over the top, followed by a pinch of sumac or chile flakes and another drop of oil.

Serve with warm flatbreads or pita or crackers, and a bunch of rinsed radishes and some olives.

Bulgur and eggplant pilaf with pistachio and lemon

Sometimes, even when your window for cooking is small, you want something that warms you deep inside and tastes as if it took hours to cook. This is when I turn to bulgur wheat pilafs, which I find nutty and healthy yet consoling. This is adapted from a Nigel Slater recipe. To make it even faster, cut the eggplants into extra-small pieces and use an extra-large pan.

Serves 2
2–3 tablespoons olive oil
1–2 fresh bay leaves
4 green onions, chopped
1–2 eggplants (total weight 10½–14 oz/300–400g), cut into tiny dice
⅔ cup/120g bulgur wheat (coarse bulgur wheat, not fine—I buy mine from
    Turkish grocery stores and love the one that has pieces of vermicelli mixed in,
    but any coarse bulgur is fine)
1¼ cups/300ml vegetable stock (made from half a stock cube), or water
Zest of 1 unwaxed lemon plus a squeeze of lemon juice
1 tablespoon chopped or nibbed pistachios (or any nut you like)

To serve
Coconut yogurt and garlic plus nigella seeds (or any seeds you have)

In a wide sauté pan, warm the olive oil over medium heat with the bay leaves and soften the green onion for a couple of minutes. Add the eggplant and cook until just tender. It will positively drink up the oil and you may feel it needs more, but instead you can add water, a large spoonful at a time, until the eggplant is completely tender and sweet. Tip in the bulgur and the stock plus a pinch of salt. Turn down the heat, put the lid on, and simmer for 10 minutes. While this is happening, whisk a grated clove of garlic into some plain coconut yogurt (or dairy Greek yogurt if you are not vegan). Season with salt and sprinkle nigella seeds over the top.

Now return to the pilaf. Lift the lid. It should be fluffy, with most of the liquid absorbed. Fork in the lemon zest and juice.

Check for salt and serve with the pistachios strewn over and the bowl of garlicky yogurt on the side. You could also strew the pilaf with pomegranate seeds.

Jammy plums with coconut cream

I sometimes think that jam—including marmalade—is the most underrated fast ingredient for dessert. The point is that it already tastes delicious without you having to do anything extra. You can use jam to glaze fruit tarts, to fill cakes, or to make these glistening sugarplums, roasted in minutes on the stovetop. If the plums seem like work enough, don't feel you need to make the coconut cream. Some plain coconut yogurt plus a drizzle of agave syrup or similar would be a fine accompaniment (you should have plenty of yogurt left over from the starter).

Serves 2
½ tablespoon neutral oil
4–6 plums (depending on size), halved and pitted
1 tablespoon granulated sugar
1 tablespoon plum or damson jam (or any jam you have)
½ teaspoon ground cinnamon
A pinch of ground cardamom
Rose petals, dry or fresh, to serve

For the coconut cream
1 × 5.4-oz/160ml can of coconut cream or, if you can't find this, use a can of regular
   coconut milk but make sure it is the good stuff, ideally Thai and not "lite"
2 tablespoons confectioners' sugar
½ teaspoon vanilla extract

First, make the coconut cream. Spoon off the thick top layer of the coconut cream into a mixing bowl. Save the watery part for another recipe such as soup, or use it to make oatmeal the next day. Add the confectioners' sugar and vanilla to the coconut cream and whisk—preferably with electric beaters but a whisk will do—until thick and cloudlike. No matter how long you whisk it, coconut never develops quite the same texture as dairy cream but it has another texture—half watery, half creamy—that is excellent in its own way when you develop a taste for it.

   Heat the oil in a medium frying pan—preferably cast iron—and cook the plums for 1 minute, cut side down. Add the sugar and continue to cook until the plums stick to the pan at the edges and become caramel-brown. Add the jam and gently

continue to turn the plums in the pan until they are thoroughly glazed. Sprinkle with the cinnamon and cardamom.

Put a dollop of the coconut cream on each of two plates with the plums on top, then scatter the rose petals over the top.

Elegant dinner for four (that happens to be gluten-free)

Lamb chops are not cheap but they only take a couple of minutes on each side to cook, there is very little waste, and as tender cuts go, they are more interesting-tasting IMO than filet mignon. I would happily serve this dinner to anyone who eats meat. The not-romesco sauce that goes with the lamb was a breakthrough recipe for me, because it was the first sauce my son Leo ever admitted liking. True romesco, as eaten in Barcelona, is made from dried Ñora peppers with roasted hazelnuts, almonds, vinegar, tomatoes, and oil. It is deep-tasting and utterly lovely but not quick to make (not least because Ñora peppers are not easy to come by). My not-romesco is nothing but roasted peppers blitzed with garlic, oil, and almonds. Make sure you buy a good-tasting jar of roasted peppers (they vary hugely). It is sweet and earthy, and if you don't want to make the lamb chops, it also makes a fine quick dinner tossed with cooked conchiglie pasta with a can of tuna and some wilted spinach or arugula and sautéd zucchini.

Smoky lamb chops with not-romesco sauce

Serves 4

10–14 French-trimmed lamb rib chops (you can make these by buying a rack of
    lamb and slicing it into chops)

2 teaspoons sweet smoked paprika

1 teaspoon ground cinnamon

1 teaspoon cumin seeds

½ teaspoon chile flakes

⅓ cup/80ml olive oil

3 cloves of garlic, peeled and grated

Juice of 1 lemon

For the not-romesco

2 large roasted red peppers from a jar (5¼ oz/150g)

1 large clove of garlic

3 tablespoons of your best olive oil

½ cup/50g toasted sliced almonds or almond flour

To serve

A bag of rinsed salad leaves (watercress is old-fashioned and nice), quickly dressed
    with oil and lemon

New potatoes

Put the lamb chops into a mixing bowl and add the paprika, cinnamon, cumin
seeds, chile, oil, garlic, lemon, and ½ teaspoon of salt, mixing well. Let sit at room
temperature for up to 30 minutes while you get on with the rest of dinner.

For the not-romesco, simply put everything into a large bowl with a pinch of salt
and blitz with an immersion blender. Check the seasoning.

Bake the pears (see page 277) and boil the potatoes. When you are almost ready
to eat, heat a large frying pan over high heat. Lift the chops from their marinade with
tongs and cook them for about 4 minutes on the first side and 2 minutes on the second.
You want them brown on the outside and pink within (or at least, I do). You don't need
to add any oil to the pan because the marinade has plenty already.

Eat the chops with the potatoes, not-romesco, and salad.

Marsala pears with clove cream

Pears are one fruit that can be quicker to eat cooked than raw because you can wait weeks for them to ripen. I love poached pears but find them time-consuming because of the peeling. These are so much less labor-intensive yet they look beautiful, standing proudly in the dish, like an autumnal still life from the Renaissance. I know that it's traditional to cook pears in red wine, but I find their delicate flesh is better suited to white wine or something fortified like Marsala or sherry. This is based on an Alice Waters recipe.

For the pears
10 under-ripe pears
1 cup/240ml dry Marsala or white wine (once I made this with leftover Cava and
    it was delicious)
½ cup/100g granulated sugar

For the clove cream
¾ cup plus 2 tablespoons/200ml heavy cream or Greek yogurt
1 tablespoon confectioners' sugar
A pinch of ground cloves

Rinse the pears and cut the bottoms off them so that you can stand them upright in a ceramic or enamel baking dish. Mix together the wine and sugar and pour this over the pears. Bake in the oven at 400°F for an hour, basting the pears every 15 minutes or until caramel-golden and slightly shrunken. Let them cool on the side while you eat your main course.

While the pears are in the oven, make the clove cream. Put the cream and confectioners' sugar into a mixing bowl and whisk with electric beaters until it forms soft peaks (be careful not to overmix or you get butter). Or beat together the sugar and Greek yogurt with a whisk. Add a pinch of cloves and mix well. Serve immediately, or keep covered in the fridge for a couple of hours.

Fast, medium, and slow: four ragùs

Cookbooks sometimes talk as if the only thing that matters, when we are choosing what to cook, is flavor. But in real life, our decisions about dinner tend to be much more pragmatic, determined by time and resources. The reason you added tarragon to a bowl of soup may not have been that you were craving its aniseed perfume but that you happened to have some in the fridge. And if you make a fried egg rather than a soufflé it was probably because the fried egg was all you had time for.

In that spirit, here are four different versions of ragù—a rich sauce that would be equally at home tossed with spaghetti or layered in a lasagne or eaten as if it were chile, with a baked potato or in a bowl with a spoon. I have categorized them not according to flavor or cuisine but according to how long they take to cook. One is super fast to make, two are medium, and one is slow. I promise that all of them are delicious. They are also all easy to shop for, with the possible exception of the short ribs one, for which you may have to go to a butcher. All of them serve 4–6 and can be frozen in individual portions if that helps.

Silky black bean ragù

I was making last-minute lunch for my extremely hungry older children one day and was elated to discover I could get something on the table in under 20 minutes that they both devoured that was also vegan and cheap as chips (the greatest expense is the miso but that has dozens of other uses). I timed myself last time I made it and it took me 19 minutes including prep time. There are a few tricks to achieving this. The silky texture comes from eggplants and, as in the pilaf recipe on page 271, it's crucial to cut the eggplant very small so that it cooks faster. The sauce contains no onion but it does include lots of garlic plus miso paste for near-instant flavor. My older son, a student, said he would make this for himself and his friends in his university kitchen.

TIME: VERY FAST

Serves 4–6
2 medium-large eggplants
¼ cup/60ml olive oil
7 oz/200g fresh tomatoes
2 × 15-oz/425g cans of black beans
4 fat cloves of garlic
1 tablespoon miso (I use white but any kind would do)
2 tablespoons tomato paste
½ tablespoon chipotle paste (or gochujang paste or chile crisp oil or any chile
    paste or sauce you have)

To serve
Chinese wheat noodles or spaghetti and a little oil or butter
Flat-leaf parsley, chopped

Boil the kettle for the noodles and find a big pot to cook them in. Before you do anything else, rinse the eggplants and cut them into ½-inch/1cm dice, i.e., very small. Take your time doing this as it's the one real piece of work in the whole thing. My method is to cut each eggplant in half lengthwise, then to cut each half in half again lengthwise before dicing. Heat the olive oil in your biggest frying pan over medium heat and cook the eggplant with a pinch of salt until completely tender, stirring

occasionally. I reckon on 10 minutes for this. While it's cooking, blitz the tomatoes and one can of the beans, juice and all, with an immersion blender. Drain the other can of beans in a sieve. Peel and grate the garlic. When the eggplant is soft, add the garlic and stir for 1 minute, then add the tomato-bean mixture, the other beans, miso, tomato paste, chile paste, and ¾ cup plus 2 tablespoons/200ml of water. Simmer until thick and delicious, which should take no more than 3–5 minutes.

While this is happening, cook the noodles (I prefer this with spaghetti rather than noodles but it will take longer), then drain and toss with a little oil or (if you are not vegan) butter. Divide the noodles among four plates or bowls and top with the ragù.

Serve with chopped flat-leaf parsley.

This is also great made into a not-quite-moussaka, layered with béchamel sauce and sliced boiled potatoes and baked in the oven until the béchamel is bubbling and brown.

Pickled ginger lamb keema

I've been making versions of Madhur Jaffrey's lamb and pea keema (keema matar) for years. It is the kind of family food almost everyone seems to be delighted and consoled by. Then one day, I had no fresh ginger in the house and wondered if it would work with pink pickled ginger instead (the kind you have with sushi), which I buy in big jars from my local Korean grocery store. It did: the pickled ginger brings a sprightly tanginess to the lamb. I've also increased the percentage of vegetables to meat so that I can serve this, lazily, as a one-pot dish with nothing alongside except for some plain-cooked Basmati rice or flatbreads (and maybe some chutney or a soothing bowl of yogurt).

This isn't as fast as the black bean ragù on page 280, but by chopping the vegetables in a food processor I find I can get it on the table in 45 minutes start to finish, which is still respectable for a midweek meal and most of that is hands-off simmering time.

TIME: MEDIUM-FAST

Serves 4–6
7 oz/200g onions, peeled
1 heaped tablespoon of pickled sushi ginger, plus more to serve
5 cloves of garlic, peeled
3 tablespoons oil
½ teaspoon chile powder (always optional)
1 teaspoon cumin seeds
1 teaspoon ground coriander
½ teaspoon ground turmeric
1 lb 2 oz/500g ground lamb or beef
12¼ oz/350g fresh large tomatoes, rinsed (or, in winter, a can of whole, peeled tomatoes)
2 tablespoons tomato paste
2 teaspoons garam masala
A couple of handfuls of spinach leaves (optional)
1⅔ cups/250g frozen peas

Blitz the onions, ginger, and garlic in a food processor or chop them all finely by hand. Heat the oil in a wide sauté pan. Add the onion mixture and cook until softened, about 5 minutes. Add the chile, cumin, coriander, and turmeric and stir until it becomes wonderfully fragrant. Add the meat and 1½ teaspoons of salt and break it up with a spoon while it browns. Blitz the tomatoes in a food processor and add them to the pan, simmer for 1 minute and then add the tomato paste and ¾ cup plus 2 tablespoons/200ml of water. Simmer the whole thing for 20 minutes. Taste to see if it is mellow and cooked—give it another 5–10 minutes if not—then add the garam masala, spinach, and peas and simmer for a final few minutes or until the peas are just cooked and the spinach is wilted. Serve with a little more pickled ginger on each portion.

Leo's lentil ragù

"It's not weird and I like it," was my youngest son Leo's final judgement when we ate this tossed with spaghetti. You would have to know the boy to understand what high praise this is.

I set myself the challenge of creating a meat-free bolognese that Leo would eat without complaining that it wasn't as good as what he still calls the "real" kind. It took many attempts and tweaks before I succeeded in getting something to satisfy him. I tried to keep the flavor profile similar to an Italian beef or veal ragù by using a base soffritto of celery, onion, and carrot plus a grating of nutmeg and some bay leaves for that all-is-well-with-the-world homely lasagne taste. The other crucial ingredient was some hidden blitzed mushrooms, a vegetable Leo generally hates but that add meatiness here without actually tasting mushroomy. There is sweetness from Marsala (or use the dregs of a bottle of port or dessert wine if that's what you have), and I decided to use red lentils instead of Le Puy or green because they cook down quicker and have a mushy nursery-food charm.

TIME: MEDIUM

Serves 4–6
2 medium onions, peeled (about 12¼ oz/350g but don't fret if it's more or less)
5¼ oz/150g carrots, trimmed and peeled
3½ oz/100g celery, trimmed
2 cloves of garlic, peeled
3 tablespoons olive oil
9 oz/250g white button mushrooms
1 × 14-oz/400g can of whole, peeled tomatoes
1 cup/200g red lentils
7 tablespoons/100ml Marsala or dessert wine or port (or red wine plus 1 teaspoon sugar)
¼ cup/55g tomato paste
A grating of nutmeg

Cut the onions, carrots, celery, and garlic into big pieces and blitz them in a food

processor until very finely chopped. (Or finely chop them by hand.) Heat the oil in a wide shallow pan, add the blitzed vegetables, and cook until softened—5–10 minutes. Meanwhile, blitz the mushrooms. When the other vegetables are softened, add the mushrooms and cook for 2–3 minutes. While this is happening, blitz the canned tomatoes in the food processor. Add the lentils to the pan, followed by the Marsala, blitzed tomatoes, tomato paste, nutmeg, 2½ cups/600ml of water and ½–1 teaspoon of salt. Give it a good stir and bring to simmering point. Cook over the lowest possible heat for 20–30 minutes, or until the lentils are completely soft. Check and stir often. You may need to add an extra splash of water toward the end. If you don't want to have this with spaghetti, it's especially good made into a vegetarian shepherd's pie crowned with mashed potato or a vegetarian lasagne, layered with béchamel.

48-hour short ribs with red wine and celery

Never make beef short ribs in a hurry. An undercooked beef stew will be gelatinous in all the wrong ways. But give it enough time and the texture of the meat on the ribs softens to something gloriously sticky that hits the spot, especially on a cold winter evening with a glass of red wine.

This ragù is best eaten the day after you make it, so this is a project you might want to start on Friday night to eat on Sunday evening. But if you can bear to give it some time, it is one of the easiest and most high-satisfaction things to have for dinner and it practically cooks itself while you get on with other things. One way that I've simplified the procedure is that I don't think you need to spend much time pre-softening the vegetables when they are going to cook for 4 hours or more.

This version of ragù, which is sticky and glossy, is especially good with pappardelle but I also love it with mashed potato or buttery soft polenta. I have gone heavy on the celery and don't use any carrots here because I find their sweetness dulls the flavor of the red wine sauce.

TIME: VERY SLOW

Serves 4–6
2 lb 2 oz–2½ lb/1–1.2kg short ribs
2 cups/480ml red wine
Olive oil
2 medium-large onions
7 oz/200g celery
½ cup/100g tomato paste
2 sprigs of fresh marjoram or thyme

Put the ribs into a mixing bowl, pour in the wine, then cover and put into the fridge overnight or for at least 5 hours. Remove the ribs from the wine, reserving the wine, and pat them dry. In a Dutch oven, heat some olive oil over medium-high heat and brown the ribs well on all sides until they smell deeply meaty. You will have to do this in batches. Sprinkle them with salt as you go. While this is happening, finely dice the onions and celery and heat the oven to 375°F. Transfer the ribs to a plate using tongs. Pour the red wine into the pan to deglaze the sticky bits of the meat. Add the onion and celery followed by the tomato paste, the marjoram or thyme leaves picked from their stalks, and ¾ cup plus 2 tablespoons/200ml of water.

Nestle the ribs back into the Dutch oven. Cover with a piece of parchment paper and the lid, then put into the oven for 2 hours. Turn the meat over and cook for another 1 hour, adding a splash more water if it seems to be drying out too much. When the hour is up, check to see if the ribs are cooked. The meat should be falling off the bone. If not, give it another half an hour or even 1 hour. Allow the stew to cool before transferring to the fridge. When it is cold, remove the solidified fat and strip the meat from the bones. Put the meat back into the sauce and reheat it gently before tasting for seasoning and serving over buttery pappardelle, with or without a final sprinkling of parsley and/or grated parmesan.

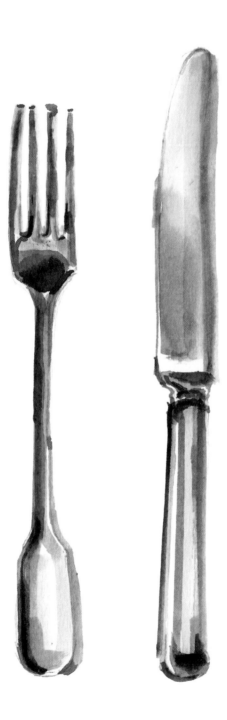

Be your own guest (cooking alone)

"Sometimes eating supper alone feels private,
quiet and blessedly liberating. You may eat
anything you want ..."
     Marion Cunningham, *The Supper Book*, 1992

Of all the tactless assumptions in cookbooks, one of the most pervasive is the default phrase "serves four." It sends a message that cooking is only worth doing if you have a neat nuclear family to feed, or an overflowing tableful of friends. It makes the person who cooks and eats alone most days feel that they—and their appetites— don't count. Yes, a single person can scale a recipe down or eat the same thing four days in a row. But it would be nice if cooking alone could sometimes be recognized as something rewarding in its own right, not to mention normal.

The person who eats alone, at least some of the time, is far from exceptional. In the UK, it is far more common to live in a two-person or one-person household than one with four or more people. In 2018, the number of people living alone in the UK exceeded 8 million for the first time. One of the biggest population trends in the world today is the rise of single-person households. In Stockholm, by 2012, 60 per cent of all households consisted of one person and a similar trend can be seen in most other European countries plus the US and Canada. Living alone is on the rise almost everywhere, from Japan to Ghana, although in low-income Asian countries it is still relatively rare.

Given that so many of us are living alone, it is strange how little the world caters to solo dining. Supermarkets make it hard for the person cooking alone not to overbuy fresh ingredients and the pages of food magazines are still full of the kind of large aspirational dinner parties that hardly anyone—single or not—seems to have much any more.

Cooking alone is completely different both in mood and content from cooking for others. But this isn't to say that it has to be less enjoyable. In some ways, it's the purest form of all cooking, because you can focus so completely on the process and your own pleasure without factoring in the judgement of others. I adore cooking solo meals, but I say this as someone who spent a quarter of a century almost always cooking for or with other people. For me, cooking alone now feels like a calm space all for myself. After my husband left, the sight of his empty chair at the table kept catching me in the throat. But when the children went off to have dinner with him, I found that I actually relished time alone in the kitchen, keeping myself company, listening to podcasts or music and adding as much garlic or chile to the meal as I liked without anyone complaining. I would light candles and pour a glass of wine (or fizzy water with a dash of Angostura and a slice of lime, which is what I drink when I am not-drinking). It felt selfish, in a good way.

But cooking and eating alone is not always easy. For anyone whose eating is disordered it can feel panicky to find yourself alone with a full fridge, without the structure of social meals to determine when eating will stop and start. Some of the loneliest times in my life were after my parents' divorce, as a teenager, sitting by myself at the kitchen table, bingeing on ice cream and sliced bread. My mother, who cried most days, was out at work. My sister was in her bedroom, reading and not eating. With no one else around, I made food my companion and my torturer. Alone in the kitchen, I felt two things at once: that no amount of food could satisfy my hunger and that any amount of food I ate was more than I deserved.

Even without an eating disorder, cooking alone can feel demotivating. Some of us choose our solitude in the kitchen while others have it forced upon us. A divorced friend whose children are grown up told me that he sometimes got a sense of deep futility when cooking his dinner: "Why cook this thing that will take an hour when it's just for me?" He did not mind so much if he could read a book while idly stirring something with his other hand, but settling on what to stir was also a problem. He missed having his children's preferences to think about. "When all you're consulting is your own taste, it can be hard to decide."

During the pandemic, I spoke to a surprising number of people who said that, stuck alone at home, they no longer saw any point in cooking. It seemed to be the most generous cooks who suffered the most, the ones who generally use cooking as a way of connecting with other people. A friend—one of the best and most sociable cooks I know—spoke of his boredom at the thought of eating lentil soup day after day with no one to share it with.

Whether you enjoy cooking alone or not depends partly on your relationship with food and partly on your relationship with yourself. But the good news is that neither of these things is fixed. One of the most promising things about being an omnivore is that we can change our relationship with food and our tastes at any time in the human lifespan. We can also learn to be kinder to ourselves. I know this often sounds like an empty phrase, but it becomes less empty when you actually put the kindness into daily practice with your hands. It might be a gesture as small as bothering to make yourself a cup of tea with fresh mint instead of a teabag.

It might be garnishing a plate of food to make it look extra beautiful (garnishes are one of the first things to go when we cook alone). Or it might mean making yourself a special surprise breakfast of pancakes (obviously you will have to pretend to be surprised when you see the pancakes, but aren't all surprise celebrations a bit like this?).

In the summer of 2020, I came across a remarkable little book from 1954 called *Cooking Alone* by a writer named Kathleen Le Riche whose writing seems to have been more or less forgotten. I found it comforting to realize that there have always been solitary cooks. Le Riche argues that the key to cooking alone is finding positive incentives to help you enjoy it more. She rightly sees that these incentives will be different for different people. For some, the incentive might be health; for others it will be pleasure. Le Riche describes a convalescent who nurses herself back to health with small nourishing meals of poached eggs or frozen raspberries and sugar. For others, cooking alone is a form of independence. One of Le Riche's chapters is about a happy putterer, a woman who loves puttering in the kitchen trying new recipes because it signals to herself that for once in her life "my time is my own." Another of her chapters is about a lonely mother who feels she doesn't really deserve food but who starts making herself nicer lunches by pretending she is expecting guests.

One of the secrets of cooking that has taken me a lifetime to learn is to try to cook for yourself as if you are company. Too many of us still see cooking alone as a kind of cooking that doesn't matter, compared to elaborate entertaining. But this reflects a false view of what home cooking really is, as if it were all for show. What could be more basic and essential than following your own instincts and cooking to please yourself? It's a way of making yourself feel more at ease in the world. The added bonus is that the better you get at cooking alone, the easier you will find it to cook for others, because you will feel so much more confident in your tastes and your cooking will come from a place that is authentic rather than rehearsed.

Screen out the voices telling you it isn't worth cooking for one. Kick off your shoes and pour yourself a nice drink. Let the world outside (or Twitter) continue to do all the maddening and unjust things that the world outside is always doing. All that matters now is the sound of your knife on the chopping board, the scent of the green herbs, the tickly feeling of rice falling through your fingers, the anticipation of good things, and the knowledge that you deserve to eat them.

Shop once, eat for three days

"Eternity is a ham and two people."
  A quotation attributed to Dorothy Parker

Cook once, eat twice is a great motto to live by. Cook once, eat four times is not quite so great, as any single person cooking from recipes for four soon discovers. The first night, it is cheering to ladle out a bowlful of chile from a giant pan. The second night, it is a pleasant surprise to realize that there is a generous batch of chile in the fridge and you don't have to cook again. The third night, your stomach starts to turn at the very sight of it. The fourth night, having lost all appetite for the chile, you stash the dregs of it in the freezer where it is never seen again until you defrost the freezer and chuck it out six months later.

Yes, I know it doesn't have to be like this. Batch cooking can be a brilliant way to live for the single cook: thrifty both on time and money. The key, I feel, is deciding what you are going to do with all this food from the offset. On the first night, decant the chile (or soup or stew or ragù, as the case may be) into a few neatly labeled containers with portion size, date you made it, and any other notes (i.e., chilli for one, April 10th—spicy and delicious!). It then seems a much more appetizing prospect in the freezer. Also consider ways to do something differently. To stick with the chilli example, a bowl of chilli could be eaten with a baked potato and sour cream one night, with rice, lime juice, and cilantro another night, and stuffed into tortillas and baked as enchiladas on a third night.

But batch cooking is not the only way. Another approach to shopping and cooking for one is to find alternative ways to cook the same thing to give it completely different flavors and textures on two or three successive nights. This approach suits those like me who actively relish a bit of cooking therapy at the end of a long day and who get bored easily (though it may seem less appealing if you are someone who enjoys cooking more when it's a once-in-a-while deal).

If this style of solo cooking appeals to you, I highly recommend a book called *The Pleasures of Cooking for One* by Judith Jones, written after the author was widowed and wasn't sure if she would ever enjoy cooking again. Jones suggests that the secret of making cooking for one more fun is to see the ways that one meal can connect with another through the same ingredient. The example she gives is a whole pork tenderloin, which could be used in at least three different ways on three nights: "one night, a few slices sautéd in a lemony pan sauce; another, a quick roast macerated first in garlic and ginger (any leftovers from that might go into a hash or rice dish); finally, the thinner end piece cut up for an Asian-type stir-fry with lots of vegetables."

Instead of cook once, eat twice, how about shop once and eat three times? To me, this keeps life more interesting, which is half the point of cooking. Here are two mini meal plans for getting three meals from one ingredient: the first for a whole cauliflower and the second for sausages. Obviously, if one of the dishes in the trio speaks to you more than the other two, you could double that one up and skip one of the others.

Three nights of cauliflower

A fresh whole cauliflower is a splendid thing—the cloudlike white florets, the sturdy green leaves—but the size can feel daunting when cooking for one. Here is how to get every ounce of goodness from it without getting bored. The flavors are Italian on one night, Chinese on the next, and French on the third. In the first two recipes you can use the green leaves as well as the white florets, but do taste a leaf first to check that it is fresh.

Crispy cauliflower with pasta and mustard croutons

This might be my favorite vegetable-based pasta sauce of all time, even though it's more dry than saucy. It's based on the spicy broccoli and cauliflower in *The Zuni Café Cookbook* by Judy Rodgers, but I've taken out the olives, anchovies and broccoli and added lemon zest for brightness and mustard croutons for crunch and joy. The secret is cutting the cauliflower small enough that it crisps up quickly in olive oil in a pan. If you double it up, it makes a good lunchbox meal the next day.

Serves 1

For the pasta
⅓ of a cauliflower (about 7 oz/200g, white and green)
3 oz/80g dried pasta, any shape (it's particularly lovely with orecchiette or shells)
1½ tablespoons olive oil
1 teaspoon capers
½ teaspoon fennel seeds
2 cloves of garlic, chopped
Zest of ½ an unwaxed lemon
A pinch of chile flakes
A handful of flat-leaf parsley, chopped

For the croutons
A thin slice of sourdough bread
A little olive oil
1 teaspoon Dijon mustard

Start by slicing the white cauliflower lengthwise and then crosswise into fine pieces. Some of the pieces will be no bigger than crumbs. This is good. Cut the leaves small.

Then make the croutons. Cut the sourdough into small cubes. Warm some oil in a frying pan, add the Dijon, and mix in the bread cubes, stirring with a wooden spoon until crisp and brown. Set aside in a bowl, wipe out the pan, and use it to cook the cauliflower.

Put the pasta on to cook in plenty of salted boiling water and set the timer. The cauliflower will be ready in roughly the same amount of time.

Warm the oil in the frying pan over high heat and add the cauliflower pieces. Cook without stirring too much until it is brown and crispy. Season with salt and add the capers, fennel seeds, garlic, lemon, and chile. Stir for 1 minute or so more. Add a couple of large spoonfuls of water and continue to cook until it is tender and the flavors have merged. Check for seasoning. It might need a squeeze of lemon. When the pasta is done, lift it into the pan of cauliflower with a spider or strainer, stir well, add the parsley, and serve, topped with the mustard croutons.

Sticky cauliflower with cashews

This reminds me of the chicken with cashews I ate the very first time I went to a Chinese restaurant as a child, which seemed unbelievably glamorous to me then. Here, the cauliflower is sautéd until richly brown and then simmered in a sauce of soy, water, and cooking wine seasoned with mouth-numbing Sichuan peppers or a little chile before getting a final scattering of crunchy cashews. It is dark brown and sticky.

Some might call this "Kung Pao Cauliflower" in homage to a Sichuanese Chinese dish called Gong Bao Chicken (named after an imperial governor of Sichuan), including peanuts and handfuls of seared dried chiles.

Serves 1
A handful of cashews, roasted and salted or unsalted and raw
1½ tablespoons neutral oil
⅓ of a cauliflower (about 7 oz/200g, white parts cut into bite-size florets
  and green parts shredded)
1 teaspoon cornstarch, plus extra to dust the cauliflower
1 teaspoon cooking wine (Shaoxing rice wine or cooking sake or
  dry sherry or Marsala)
2 teaspoons sugar
2–3 teaspoons soy sauce (it depends how salty you like things)
2 teaspoons rice vinegar
½ teaspoon sesame oil
½ teaspoon Sichuan peppercorns, ground with a mortar and pestle,
  or a pinch of chile flakes (optional)
3 green onions, trimmed and sliced
2 cloves of garlic, peeled and grated, plus the equivalent amount
  of ginger, grated

To serve
Cooked jasmine rice (½ cup/100g of rice simmered in a covered pot in
  ¾ cup/180ml of water for 12 minutes, then left to stand for 10–30 minutes)
Black sesame seeds

If the cashews are raw, start by cooking them. Heat 1 tablespoon of oil over medium-high heat in a wok or your largest frying or sauté pan. Add the nuts and cook, stirring often, for about a minute or two or until golden. Transfer to a plate with a spider or slotted spoon. If the cashews are roasted and salted, skip this step.

Dust the cauliflower with a little cornstarch and add it to the oil in the pan and cook for a good 8–10 minutes, or until nicely brown and softened. You may need to put the lid on from time to time to speed things up. Meanwhile, whisk together the cooking wine, cornstarch, sugar, soy sauce, vinegar, sesame oil, and ½ cup/120ml water in a bowl; this is the sauce. When the cauliflower is browned and tender-crisp, add the remaining ½ tablespoon of oil, the Sichuan pepper or chile and the green onions and cook for 1 minute. Add the garlic and ginger and after a few seconds add the sauce, scraping it up from the bottom to get all the cornstarch. Simmer for 1 minute or so or until shiny and sticky (but if it is too sticky, keep adding splashes of water as needed).

Add the cashews and serve with the rice, sprinkled with black sesame seeds. I like to take the cooked rice, pack it into a teacup or ramekin, and turn it out in the center of the plate before arranging the sticky cauliflower all around.

Cauliflower cheese soufflé

The food writer Elizabeth David described "an omelet and a glass of wine" as an ideal solitary meal. She was right (she usually was). But on days when you feel like some gentle kitchen therapy, a soufflé and a glass of wine is even better. It's far less work than you imagine (assuming you have cheap electric beaters) but the ethereal airiness of soufflé makes dinner for one feel like a grand occasion. To serve yourself a soufflé when there is no one else to be impressed by its rise is a deep form of self-care. Adding cauliflower to a cheese soufflé makes it a meal in one, but it's even better with a green salad and some baguette. I like to make this in a little 8-inch/20cm Falcon enamelware pie dish, but if you have a small soufflé dish that would also work. Soufflé sounds posh but it is actually no pricier or trickier to make than macaroni and cheese.

Serves 1
Butter, for greasing the dish, plus 1 tablespoon more
3½ oz/100g cauliflower (white parts only), cut into very small florets
1 tablespoon all-purpose flour
⅓ cup/80ml whole milk
A bay leaf (optional)
1½ oz/40g any strong hard cheese such as parmesan, Gouda,
    cheddar, or Gruyère, grated
A grating of nutmeg
A pinch of cayenne
1 large egg yolk
2 large egg whites
A few black sesame seeds (optional)

Rub butter around the inside of your pie or soufflé dish. Preheat the oven to 425°F.
    Cook the cauliflower in boiling lightly salted water for 8 minutes, or until soft and slightly overdone. As soon as the cauliflower has gone into the water, melt the 1 tablespoon of butter in another small saucepan over lowish heat and stir in the flour, using a whisk. Cook for around 1 minute, stirring constantly. Off the heat,

whisk in the milk, a bit at a time, still whisking thoroughly. It will look lumpy, but have faith. If you give it time and enough whisking, the lumps should smooth away. Return to low heat, add the bay leaf (if using), and simmer for 1 minute, stirring constantly, until it is thick. Stir in the cheese until melted and season quite strongly with salt and nutmeg and cayenne. Soufflé mix always needs to be seasoned a tiny bit more than you think because the flavor will dilute when you add the whites. Fish out the bay leaf.

Drain the cooked cauliflower and mash it into the sauce with a fork—a few pieces of cauliflower are nice. Mix the yolk into the sauce. In a clean mixing bowl, beat the whites with electric beaters until they are white and snowy. Add a dollop of the whisked whites to the sauce to lighten it. Now fold in the rest of the whites, using a large metal spoon or silicone spatula. Pile the mixture into your prepared pan or dish, sprinkle with a few sesame seeds, and bake for 15 minutes, or until nicely risen and browned. You can cut it in the middle to check if it is done, but know that a perfect cheese soufflé will always look a little wet (but not sloshing) in the middle. Eat with a green salad and good bread or toast.

Three days of sausages

These recipes are all designed to use a package of good-quality pork sausages, which usually seems to consist of 6 sausages, weighing 14 oz/400g. Buy the plainest fresh sausage you can find for these recipes, because you will be seasoning each of them in different ways. If you don't want three days of meat in a row, you could freeze a third of the sausages, then defrost and cook them next week. The recipes will also work with vegetarian sausages.

Sausage, greens, and polenta

This is based on a dish in *Home Cookery Year* by Claire Thomson, who comments that it is the kind of dish that makes you feel "replenished, and that all is well with the world." The sausages are removed from their casings, browned, and cooked with sturdy greens and chile before being piled on top of soft cheesy polenta. I've changed the method slightly, cooking the greens all-in-one with the sausage to simplify things and using quick-cook polenta to speed things up. However you make it, this is savory succor.

Serves 1

1 tablespoon butter or olive oil

2 sausages (about 4½ oz/130g), squeezed out of their casings (or if they are vegetarian sausages, just chop them)

5¼ oz/150g cavolo nero (or any greens such as bok choy or spring greens), finely chopped, any tough stalks removed

1 clove of garlic, peeled and chopped

A few rosemary or thyme or sage leaves, chopped

A pinch of chile flakes

Tiny dash of vinegar

¼ cup/40g quick-cook polenta

Some grated parmesan

Melt half the butter or oil in a frying pan over medium heat, add the sausage meat, and cook until well browned. Add the shredded greens, garlic, herbs, and chile and cook until wilted. Taste a piece of greens. If it's not tender, add a spoonful of water and put a lid on the pan for 1 minute. Keep doing this until the greens are cooked to your liking. Add a tiny dash of vinegar. Meanwhile, combine the polenta with 1 cup/240ml of water and a pinch of salt in a small or medium pan and cook over medium heat, whisking, until thick. Stir the remaining butter or oil into the polenta and add the parmesan. Serve in a shallow bowl with the sausage and greens mixture on top.

Buttery lima bean stew with kimchi and sausages

When I was a child, I believed that lima beans (aka butter beans) must be made of butter and was sorely disappointed when I first tried them. So here is a recipe for butter beans with lots of added butter, plus kimchi. The sourness and fire of the kimchi is softened by the butter and the pleasing blandness of the beans. It was a Korean-American consumer researcher named Eddie Yoon who first told me about adding butter to kimchi and I will be forever grateful to him. Kimchi varies hugely in quality (as do canned beans, come to that). If you can, I highly recommend buying your kimchi from an Asian grocery store (or making your own). This is about the easiest stew you will ever make—it's one of the simplest recipes in the whole book—because good kimchi will do all the work of seasoning for you. For once, no salt or lemon are needed. The cabbage-sausage combination reminds me of the classic French dish choucroute, made from sausages and sauerkraut (and indeed, you could substitute sauerkraut for the kimchi and add a bay leaf and ½ teaspoon of caraway seeds if you'd rather take it down that flavor route). You could absolutely make this vegetarian by leaving out the sausages and serving the bean stew with steamed rice and a poached egg. If you have some greens left over from the polenta dish, wilt them and serve alongside or shred them and add them along with the beans.

Serves 1
2 pork sausages (about 4½ oz/130g)
A dash of oil
1 × 15-oz/425g can of lima beans (butter beans)—you'll need half for this recipe and half for the koftas (page 311)
1 tablespoo butter
½ cup/80g kimchi
Flat-leaf parsley, chopped

First, put the sausages into a small frying pan with a drizzle of oil. Fry them gently, turning often, for about 15 minutes or until cooked through. After they have browned on both sides, I usually put a lid on but still check them every couple of minutes. While this is happening, open the can of beans and drain but reserve the liquid. Weigh the drained beans. Set aside half in a covered dish in the fridge for the koftas (page 311). Melt the butter in a medium saucepan or frying pan. Add the kimchi and stir for 1 minute. Add the beans plus half their liquid and the greens, if using. Continue to simmer while the sausages cook, until the liquid has reduced a bit and the sauce is mellow and smooth, with a consistency like a thinner version of canned tomato soup. When the sausages are done, transfer them to a board and chop them before stirring them into the stew and serving with a handful of chopped flat-leaf parsley.

Bean and sausage koftas with parsley salad

These have the comfort of a kebab: spicy patties rolled up in a flatbread with yogurt and a tomato and parsley salad. I buy flatbreads from my local Turkish grocery store and keep them in the freezer, which means I can defrost just a few at a time as needed. Pita bread, which you could use here if you prefer, also freezes very well. One of the things I find annoying when cooking for one is using up fresh herbs. If I've bought parsley in a big bunch, which is the way I like to buy it, I will try to feast on it for a few days before starting anew with another herb such as mint or cilantro. Here, there is parsley both in the green-flecked koftas and in the tomato salad. Use lettuce and/or cucumber instead of tomato, if that's what you have.

Serves 1

For the koftas
½ × 15-oz/425g can of lima beans (butter beans)
2 pork sausages (about 4½ oz/130g)
A large handful of flat-leaf parsley leaves (or any herb you like), chopped
½ teaspoon ground cumin
1 clove of garlic, peeled and grated
A pinch of chile flakes
A pinch of ground cinnamon
1 teaspoon all-purpose flour
Oil

For the salad
3½ oz/100g tomatoes, chopped
A large handful of parsley leaves, chopped
1 green onion, chopped, or a few chives if you grow them
A little oil

To serve
Warm flatbreads or pitas, a few spoonfuls of plain full-fat yogurt and any pickles you have in the fridge (sliced cucumber pickles, preserved lemons, or pickled chiles would all be good)

For the koftas, start by putting the beans into a bowl and mashing them with a large fork. Remove the sausage meat from its casing and add it to the bowl (or chop it if it's vegetarian sausage). Add the chopped parsley, the cumin, garlic, chile flakes, cinnamon, flour, and a minimal pinch of salt (the sausage will already be salty). Mix gently but thoroughly with your hands. Still using your hands, form the mixture into a few little oval-shaped koftas. Flatten them out (this will help them cook faster). I reckon this amount should give you 4. If you have time, put them into the fridge to firm up.

Heat some oil in a frying pan over medium heat and cook the koftas until browned all over and thoroughly cooked through. I usually give them 3 minutes on each side, then flip again for another 3 minutes on the first side, and finally, off the heat, cover the pan and let them rest in the hot pan for 5 minutes to continue to cook in the residual heat. The mixture is quite fragile. Don't worry if it breaks up a bit—if it collapses, just tell yourself it's sloppy Joes instead of koftas.

While the koftas are frying, make the salad by tossing together all the ingredients with a pinch of salt. Warm the flatbreads or toast the pita. Serve the koftas with warm flatbreads, salad, yogurt, and pickles.

A toolkit for solo cooking

When cooking for one, everything can be slightly different, and that includes kitchen equipment. You can't put ingredients for a solo casserole into a pot designed to feed six. Having said this, many of the tools you need will be exactly the same as when cooking for a crowd. You still need a sharp knife you can rely on, a chopping board, a few trusty wooden spoons and silicone spatulas, a wok, a box grater, an immersion blender, some tongs. And a spider strainer will be more useful than ever when cooking for one because the quantities will be smaller, so it makes even more sense to scoop pasta or vegetables from the water with a small strainer instead of bothering with a colander. But some of the extras I find especially helpful when alone in the kitchen are:

—A blini pan—I bought two of these after reading *How to Eat* by Nigella Lawson more than twenty years ago. I have hardly ever made blinis but I use the pans constantly for toasting nuts and spices and frying single eggs.
—A small ovenproof dish that you can brown stuff in and then braise it, either in the oven or on the stovetop. These are never cheap (unless you can find one second-hand) but pay for themselves over the years.
—A small saucepan for making things like béchamel.
—A few one-person pie dishes for making small soufflés (see page 302) or individual shepherd's pies.
—Lots of small containers for freezing one portion of the universal sauces (see page 243). I save plastic takeout containers and Greek yogurt containers with lids and use those.
—Freezer bags and brown paper bags for freezing things like bread (I try to keep good sliced sourdough in the freezer and toast it straight from frozen).

Using things up

When I spoke to friends who cooked alone about which ingredients they found hardest to use up, they all—to a man or woman—said the same thing: dairy products (especially cream) and fragile vegetables and herbs. So it makes sense to have a few delicious strategies for dealing with these. Everything I've said so far in the book about substituting ingredients is even more important when cooking for one. Use what you have, not what you think you ought to have. But with the best will in the world, when you are just one person, it can still be tricky to use up a whole carton of cream before it starts to sour or a big bag of spinach or kale. Here are a few ideas that have helped me and that I hope will help you too:

—Instant congee. Take leftover rice and blend it with twice the volume of water or chicken stock. Simmer for 5 minutes, or until porridge-like, then season well and serve with grated ginger, soy sauce, sesame oil, and perhaps a soft-boiled egg, some greens or a handful of shredded roasted chicken.

—Any-greens pesto. This is a good use for any oddments of both salad vegetables and herbs. Blitz the greens and herbs with a generous amount of olive oil, salt, a peeled clove of garlic, a handful of nuts. Taste and add a handful of any cheese you have in the fridge, grated. You can store this in a jar in the fridge for up to 5 days.

—Cook your salad. Lettuce and other salad greens such as arugula or radicchio are just as delicious cooked as they are raw. Shred them and wilt them into a risotto or add them to a soup.

—Make hard-to-use-up quantities of root vegetables, cabbage, and kale into little side salads. Almost any vegetable can be turned into a slaw: shredded or grated and combined with lemon juice, salt, and herbs. It always tastes better if you can let it sit for at least 5 minutes before adding olive oil to taste and perhaps some dried fruit or nuts.

—Freeze herbs. You can either freeze them whole or finely chop them and freeze them in ice cube trays, topped with a thin layer of olive oil. Turn the cubes out into a container with a lid and label carefully. These little herb cubes can be dropped, without defrosting, into a soup or stew or pasta sauce or dish of vegetables for added flavor.

—Use leftover dairy or coconut milk in your baking. Old milk? Make pancakes (for crêpe batter, blitz 1 cup plus 2 tablespoons/270ml milk with ¾ cup plus 2 tablespoons/110g all-purpose flour, 2 eggs, and a pinch of salt) or oatmeal. Old yogurt? Make cake (swapping it for maybe a third of the butter, which will also give you a healthier cake). Old cream or mascarpone? Make scones or biscuits. By the way, when I say "old," I mean cream that is a day or so past its best, not actually green with mold.

—Give cream a second life as a luscious fruit ice cream. The added bonus is you also get to use up some over-ripe fruit (another easy-to-waste food). Whip however much cream you have left. Make a fruit purée by blitzing over-ripe fruit with confectioners' sugar to taste. Combine the fruit and the cream and freeze in a lidded container for 4–5 hours or until frozen. Last time I made this with green grapes and the juice and zest of a leftover lime: a revelation.

As if by magic

"Why would I want to go to all that trouble just for me?
My answer is: If you like good food, why not honor
yourself enough to make a pleasing meal and relish
every mouthful?"
Judith Jones, *The Pleasures of Cooking for One*

One of the things that you miss out on when cooking every meal as a single person is that moment of solace when someone tells you to put your feet up and wait until dinner is ready. But it's possible to re-create this restful feeling with sheet pan or one dish cooking, except that you are that generous person who is telling yourself to relax and wait.

I find the sudden interest in sheet pan cooking over the past few years to be fascinating. Anything that can be cooked on a baking sheet in the oven now is, from full English breakfast to bibimbap.

Roasting dish food is the younger sibling of the 1990s roasted vegetable trend discussed on page 21. Most households have had baking sheets and ovens for many decades but—according to Google trends—it has only been since 2009 that the term "sheet pan" has risen in interest. At the time of writing, #sheetpandinner is a huge trend on Instagram.

"This is cooking I could actually do," said my sister, picking up my copy of *The Green Roasting Tin* by Rukmini Iyer, a book that every twenty-something I know holds dear because it makes cooking affordable vegetarian food so easy and yet somehow stylish.

Whether I am cooking for myself or for others, I turn to roasting-dish cooking on days when I feel overloaded and want a bit of peace. It's a way to get the taste and nutrition of homemade food without the effort of homemade food. It seems like a modern way of cooking but I am struck that it is actually a very old one. Until the twentieth century, to own your own oven was a relatively rare thing and people would take casseroles full of raw ingredients to the baker, paying a few coins to have them cooked in the baker's oven.

Cooking things all-in-one in the oven can feel like a kind of enchantment: as if the food has cooked itself. As Diana Henry writes in *From the Oven to the Table* (my favorite of all the sheet-pan cookbooks), "although I know I'm the one who has smeared the bird with butter, mixed the crumble with my fingers or halved the peppers and turned them in olive oil, I always feel, when I take food out of the oven, that someone else has cooked it." You get all the goodness of the cooking smells with a fraction of the effort. This is the kind of cooking I do on days when I want to avoid eating takeout. I often put a baking sheet of roasted vegetables into the oven alongside whatever else I am cooking, to get the most out of the oven's heat and to get ahead on tomorrow's lunch. The only thing to be said against oven cooking is that compared to stovetop cooking, it is not very energy efficient so it makes sense to stash a few things in the oven at a time, if possible. Having said this, human energy matters too and if switching the oven on is what will get you happily fed, I'm all in favor of that. These sheet-pan dishes all make two portions—one for tonight and one for tomorrow—but you can double the quantities if cooking for four.

Paneer jalfrezi with potatoes

One night, home alone and feeling tired, I wished that someone would come along and make me a dish of spiced jalfrezi with red bell peppers. Eventually, I realized that this person would have to be me. But the oven also played its part. This took me only two songs of prep followed by another song to clean up and after that I had 35 minutes clear to sit and wait as the scent of cumin, cinnamon, and ginger wafted from the kitchen. Adapt to whatever vegetables you have in the fridge.

Makes 2–3 portions

1 x 7-oz/200g block of paneer, cut into ¾-inch/2cm cubes

2 red bell peppers, deseeded and cut into strips

1 red onion, peeled and cut into wedges

3 large tomatoes, chopped

2 tablespoons pomegranate molasses (or leave it out and add
    1 tablespoon rice vinegar at the end)

10½ oz/300g new potatoes, halved or quartered if large

2-inch/5cm piece of ginger, grated

2 cloves of garlic, peeled and grated

½ teaspoon ground turmeric

¼ teaspoon cayenne

1 teaspoon ground cinnamon

1 teaspoon cumin seeds

2 tablespoons oil

To serve

Chopped fresh cilantro, yogurt, flatbreads, lime pickle

Put everything into a large roasting dish or on a baking sheet and add ¾ teaspoon of salt. Toss with your hands until thoroughly combined. Put into the oven, set it to 425°F, and roast for 30 minutes, or until the paneer is browned and the potatoes are tender. If you didn't use pomegranate molasses, sprinkle with 1 tablespoon of rice vinegar and toss gently. Serve sprinkled with cilantro, perhaps with some yogurt, flatbreads, and lime pickle on the side.

Roasting-dish chicken with fennel and citrus

This, adapted from *Bitter Honey* by Letitia Clark (a cookbook of Sardinian food that helped keep me sane during the first lockdown), is one of my most made roasting-dish meals. I find it comforting and uplifting at the same time. Crispy skin-on chicken thighs cook in a dish with fennel (both seeds and vegetable), white wine, citrus, and Dijon. The fennel becomes impregnated with the wine and the chicken fat until it is meaty and sweet and sour. If you decide to scale this up when cooking for more people, which is a great idea, don't scale up the liquid too much or the chicken will drown in it. If you triple the amount of chicken, only double the liquid.

Makes 2 portions
Zest and juice of 1 unwaxed lemon and 1 unwaxed orange
2 teaspoons Dijon mustard
2 tablespoons extra-virgin olive oil
1 teaspoon fennel seeds
¾ cup plus 2 tablespoons/200ml white wine
4 bone-in, skin-on chicken thighs
3 fennel bulbs, fronds reserved, bulbs cut into wedges
A handful of fat green olives

If you are feeling organized, start the day before or a few hours ahead. Whisk together the citrus juice and zest, Dijon, olive oil, fennel seeds, wine, and 1 teaspoon of salt and put into a zip-top bag along with the chicken. Chill for a couple of hours or up to 12 hours. This will help to tenderize the chicken. But in all honesty, I've often forgotten to do this and it still tastes great. Either way, put the chicken and all the marinade ingredients into a roasting dish. Add the fennel bulb wedges and the olives. Put into the oven and turn the oven on to 425°F for 1 hour, or until the fennel is meltingly soft and the chicken is bronzed (check after 45 minutes). Taste the sauce for seasoning. If the wine has all evaporated away, splash some water into the pan to make a simple gravy. Taste for seasoning. It shouldn't need much, because of all that citrus and wine. Eat with some crunchy green fennel fronds on top and good bread for mopping.

Two pearl barley stews

Spring: vignarola pearl barley stew with halloumi

Vignarola is a Roman spring vegetable stew. More than a decade ago, my sister spent a year in Rome, and some of my happiest food memories of all time are of the many artichoke meals we shared together that spring. This is one of the best uses I know for frozen artichokes, which I buy from my local Turkish grocery store, but if you can't find them, feel free to use jarred artichokes. The fried halloumi is not remotely Italian but its golden burnished texture reminds me of my very favorite way of eating artichokes in Italy, which is deep fried (as eaten in the Jewish quarter in Rome), so it feels right here. Another way to go would be to serve this with garlic aïoli.

Makes 2 portions
4 frozen artichoke hearts, quartered
A bunch of green onions, chopped
¾ cup/100g frozen fava beans or frozen edamame
2 tablespoons extra-virgin olive oil
7 tablespoons/100ml white wine or vermouth
¾ cup/150g pearl barley
⅔ cup/100g frozen petits pois
4¼ oz/120g halloumi
A couple of sprigs of mint
Preserved lemon slices or squeeze of lemon

Put everything up to and including the pearl barley into a deep roasting dish or Dutch oven, add ½ teaspoon of salt and 2⅓ cups/550ml of water, and stir well. Cover with foil or a lid and put into the oven and set it to 400°F for 1 hour. You are free! After the hour is up, open the lid to check if the barley is tender. If it is, add the peas and return it to the oven but switch off the oven. Slice the halloumi and fry it in a little oil in a large frying pan over medium heat until crispy and golden on both sides. Pick the mint leaves off the stalk and chop them. Check for seasoning and eat the barley with the halloumi and mint on top and a few slices of preserved lemon or a squeeze of fresh lemon.

Winter: mushroom and pearl barley stew

I adore the soft, earthy taste and almost gelatinous texture of pearl barley. My mother used it a lot in lamb stews as a way to make the meat go further. It's the perfect ingredient to turn into a one-pot dish in the oven because it looks after itself and you end up with something a bit like a risotto, only it feels heartier and more wholesome. It takes about an hour in the oven but that's no problem because it's an hour of freedom for you as the cook. I find that barley goes especially well with mushrooms, which pick up the earthiness in the barley. I would serve this to myself for warming cheer after a long wintry dog walk.

Makes 2 hearty portions
½ oz/15g dried porcini
9 oz/250g large flat mushrooms
2 tablespoons extra-virgin olive oil
¾ cup/150g pearl barley
1 × 14-oz/400g can of whole, peeled tomatoes, blitzed with an immersion blender
2 leeks, rinsed and thinly sliced
2 cloves of garlic, crushed to a paste or grated
1 bay leaf
1 oz/30g flat-leaf parsley, chopped—half to go in the dish, half to sprinkle at the end
A few sage or rosemary leaves, chopped

Put the porcini into a heatproof bowl and pour in 2 cups/480ml of boiling water from a kettle to soften. Meanwhile, coarsely chop the flat mushrooms and fry them over high heat in a large frying pan with the olive oil. The mushrooms need to be precooked or else they will become mushy and slimy in the oven. Put the pearl barley into a small ovenproof dish and add the tomatoes, leeks, garlic, bay leaf, ½ teaspoon of salt, half the parsley, and the sage or rosemary. Scoop the porcini out of their soaking water with a spider strainer, then rinse and chop them. Measure out 1½ cups/360ml of the porcini liquid. Add this liquid to the pan along with the porcini and cooked flat mushrooms. Now cover tightly with foil or a lid. Put into the oven, set it to 400°F and cook for 1 hour. Once the pearl barley is cooked, check it for seasoning and scatter the reserved parsley over the top.

Entertain yourself

"Sometimes I would go to the best restaurant
I knew about, and order dishes and good wines
as if I were a guest of myself, to be treated with
infinite courtesy."
M. F. K. Fisher, *The Gastronomical Me*

Some of the happiest evenings of my life have been spent eating out alone on
work trips, in various cities. A couple of years ago, on arriving in Milan, I spent
hours researching where I would go on my first night to eat osso bucco with risotto
Milanese: a rich veal stew with bright saffron-yellow rice. I settled on a trattoria in
a residential area near to a square where children were playing on swings. I sat at
the bar, watching the barman as he mixed Negronis for elegant Milanese women.
I ordered two glasses of wine, one white and one red, and ate my food slowly,
savoring each mouthful of that yellow rice and meltingly soft veal.

It is possible to be convivial all by yourself, if you get in the right mood. In her
book *Solo: The Joy of Cooking for One*, food writer Signe Johansen explains that she
sees cooking alone as "one of life's simplest and most therapeutic pleasures." Being
alone is no reason not to light candles or to bring out your nicest plates. It can feel
liberating to choose the most special ingredients you can imagine—ones you might
serve to an honored guest—and cook them just for you.

When we say that cooking for one is not worthwhile, what we are really saying, at
some level, is that we are not worth it. Many of us spend half our lives being slightly
unkind to ourselves. We berate ourselves for waking up too late, for gaining weight,
for failing to run 6 miles, for not saving enough money, for making mistakes, for
looking goofy. But none of these are things that we would chastise our friends for,
so why do it to ourselves? Giving yourself something spectacular to eat from time
to time is a way to remind yourself of your own worth.

When dining alone, we should be a bit more like Lucullus. Lucullus was an
ancient Roman general known for his extravagant hospitality. One night, his
chef presented Lucullus with a small and inexpensive dinner, because he was not
expecting any guests. The general exploded with rage. "What? Dost thou not know
that tonight Lucullus dines with Lucullus?" I can't say Lucullus is someone I'd want

to spend much time with. He sounds like what one of my friends calls "a big I am," by which she means "arrogant jerk." But "Lucullus dines with Lucullus" is still a great and rare sentiment. How many of us have the confidence to look after ourselves so well at the table?

Preparing a special dinner for one can actually be more of a treat than cooking for a crowd. You know your own tastes, so you don't have to spend ages second-guessing whether it will be a disaster if you include anchovies in a dish. You also don't do that thing I always do when people come over of panicking that what I have made isn't good enough and making two extra unnecessary dishes to compensate. When eating alone, the company is never disappointing; and if it is, you can switch on Netflix or read a book without offending anyone. Another bonus is that you can splash out on something really extravagant once in a while because everything costs so much less when you are buying a portion for one. When I am older, I aspire to be like Agatha Christie's Miss Marple, who treats herself to a *whole* partridge, despite the expense. Sometimes, in the same spirit, I steam myself a whole globe artichoke, the biggest I can find, and eat it, leaf by leaf, with a hunk of bread and a huge bowl of hollandaise sauce seasoned with lime and chives.

There is public cooking and there is private cooking and of the two, it is private cooking that is the truest and most visceral if you can allow yourself to relax into it. The food writer John Thorne writes of "intimate cuisine:" the kind of informal eating that is done when no one is watching. Such meals, Thorne writes, are an "oasis from our public selves." Intimate cuisine might include a meal made up of nothing but appetizers or meze. Or it could start with dessert. It could also consist of mostly vegetables: platters of roasted potatoes served with pickles, or masses of corn on the cob with butter. There are all kinds of dreamy meals that don't quite make it on to restaurant menus because they are too informal or too childish or too simple. I think of tomato sandwiches; and toad in the hole (an egg broken into a piece of bread in a pan); and the creamed mushrooms on toast that my friend Louise's dad used to make for breakfast when we were seventeen and had stayed up half the night. Eating alone, you can reclaim all these joys and more and serve them to yourself with as much or as little ceremony as you like.

When you can find a window in your diary, invite yourself to dinner. Welcome yourself in and pour yourself a drink. Ask how your day went and listen with rapt attention. Offer yourself a few choice dishes, the ones you would search for on a restaurant menu. Amaze yourself with soufflé, or cosset yourself with stew. Even though it is only you, take the time to make a single perfect portion of cheesecake and strew it with slices of fresh, perfumed peach. Tonight, You dine with You.

A whole miso-glazed eggplant

You can turn a whole vegetable into a feast for one. For a while, versions of these cross-hatched eggplants seemed to appear in every new cookbook.

Serves 1
1 medium-large eggplant
Neutral oil such as sunflower
½ cup/100g short-grain white rice, rinsed in a sieve
2 teaspoons miso paste (any kind)
2 teaspoons pomegranate molasses (or 1 teaspoon maple syrup and 1 teaspoon
    balsamic vinegar)
1 teaspoon soy sauce
2 teaspoons sesame oil
2 teaspoons mirin or sake

To serve
Sushi ginger
Black sesame seeds
Cucumber slices (optional)

Preheat the oven to 425°F. Cut the eggplant lengthwise and make shallow cuts into each half in a criss-cross pattern. Brush each half with neutral oil and put on a baking sheet in the oven for 20 minutes, or until tender all the way through. Meanwhile, cook some rice: Put the rice into a small pot with ¾ cup/180ml of water, bring to simmering point, turn the heat to very low, put the lid on, and cook for 12 minutes. Let stand off the heat for a few minutes.

When the eggplant is tender, mix together the miso, pomegranate molasses (or maple and balsamic), soy, sesame oil, and mirin or sake. Brush this liberally over each eggplant half and return to the oven for 5 minutes, or until browned. Eat with the rice, some sushi ginger, a scattering of sesame seeds, and maybe some slices of crisp little cucumber (for crunch!).

Scallops with watercress butter

This is one of my dream things to eat for dinner. The combination of green garlicky butter and sweet caramelized scallops feels like the most indulgent treat imaginable for one. You will end up with far too much watercress butter but this is happy news: keep it in a twist of foil in the freezer and use slabs of it to season any piece of fish or meat or to stuff a baked potato or melt luxuriously in a bowl of minestrone or toss into pasta instead of pesto. For years, I found it tricky to make compound butters such as these but then I found that if I zapped the butter for a few moments in the microwave, it would blend in moments with an immersion blender. If you don't have a microwave, just warm it very slightly in a saucepan.

Serves 1
7 oz/200g sustainable scallops, preferably with the roe intact
   (this is usually about 5 scallops if they are big ones)
A little olive oil

For the watercress butter
½ cup/125g unsalted butter
1 fat clove of garlic, peeled and grated
1¾ oz/50g watercress (or arugula or sorrel)
Zest of ½ an unwaxed lemon
2 teaspoons lemon juice

Put the butter on a plate in the microwave and heat it for about 20 seconds, plus another 20 seconds if you think it needs it. You are aiming for a semi-molten state. Put all the watercress butter ingredients into a large bowl with a pinch of salt and blitz with an immersion blender until homogenized. Taste for salt and lemon.

   To cook the scallops, heat a pan, preferably cast iron, until it is so hot that a drop of water will dance across the surface and immediately evaporate. While this is happening, dry the scallops with paper towels (they won't sear properly if they are wet) and season them on both sides. Add a little olive oil to the pan and give the scallops 2 or 3 minutes per side. You want them to have a caramelized outside and to be just cooked. Take them off the heat and cover with a lid. Take as much watercress

butter as you think you can eat in one sitting (don't stint) and gently melt it in a saucepan. Arrange the scallops on a plate and pour the butter over the top. Devour, perhaps with a glass of very cold white wine and bread for dipping into the green butter.

Take the rest of the butter and roll it up into a cylinder shape in a piece of foil. Label it and keep in the freezer.

Having said that we should make the time to cook when alone, there are also days when you want to eat something wonderful without switching an oven on. Here are a few ideas for no-cook assembly jobs on those days:

No-cooking treats for one

—Prosciutto and melon: half a ripe orange melon such as Charentais or cantaloupe, a few slices of the best prosciutto, a tiny pinch of cayenne, and a few basil leaves.
—A ripe Comice pear and shards of young pecorino cheese, plus a handful of walnuts.
—A few pods of raw fava beans and a soft, supple goat cheese with some mint leaves. And bread. Sit and shell the beans and pop them into your mouth, alternating with mouthfuls of bread spread with goat cheese and whole mint leaves.
—An improvised cheesecake made by mixing a couple of tablespoons of cream cheese or mascarpone with confectioners' sugar to taste. Serve in a bowl, topped with a ripe sliced peach, a drizzle of honey, and a few toasted walnuts or almonds or the instant praline on page 100, plus a couple of fresh oregano or marjoram leaves (this is all inspired by the famous cheesecake at Honey & Co in London).
—Fruit with cream and sugar. So obvious but very often overlooked. Strawberries are far from the only fruit that is dreamy with cream. Also consider thick whipped cream spooned over grated apples or pears with a drizzle of maple syrup; or with sliced sugared peaches; or dolloped over frozen blackberries, warmed with brown sugar. Eat from your nicest bowl and know that solitude is not the same as loneliness.

Welcome all eaters

"To invite a person to your house is to
take charge of their happiness for as
long as they are under your roof."
  Jean Anthelme Brillat-Savarin, 1825

The first rule of cooking for other people—whether it's low-key meals for friends
and family or more lavish entertaining for larger numbers—is to cook something
that you actually like eating yourself. That way, at least one person at the table will be
happy and, strangely, your happiness will be contagious. If you focus first on making
yourself feel at ease, this sense of ease will transmit itself to others at the table. Some
of us struggle even to know what it is that we most want to eat because we have
spent so many years suppressing our natural appetite through diets. When deciding
what to make, I sometimes find it helps to imagine I am ordering from a restaurant
menu on a cold evening when I am in search of simple comfort and this usually leads
me to figure out the answer. "All anyone really wants when they go over to someone's
house is spaghetti bolognese," said one of my friends the other day.

It has taken me a long time to get there but I find that if you offer someone
food in the spirit of "I think this is delicious and I hope you will too," it is likely to
receive a more positive response than food that is offered with doubts and apologies
or an anxious view to impress. Nadine Levy Redzepi—who is married to René
Redzepi, the chef of Noma in Denmark, which is widely considered one of the best
restaurants in the world—has cooked numerous dinners for top chefs, something
that many of us would find intimidating. In her cookbook *Downtime: Deliciousness
at Home*, Redzepi remarks that she has found that chefs are "happy and appreciative"
to be served an informal family meal rather than something pretentious with "fancy
garnishes." When she has a chef coming over, she might cook something like a
roasted chicken or roasted ribs and sweet potatoes. She has found that the most
relaxed approach to cooking is to try to blur the lines between food served for
company and food eaten in private.

The question remains of how you can happily share a table with people who
have radically different eating habits and tastes from yours. This question is at the
heart of all social cooking, whether you are making a meal for picky children or for

friends and family with very different dietary requirements or tastes to your own. Many cooks find it a downer when they have planned a meal only to have half the possibilities closed off because so many of the guests have food intolerances or they are vegan or on a diet or they simply have a series of foods that they very much dislike. But it's worth remembering that however awkward it may be for the cook in these situations, it is far more difficult to be the guest having to explain time after time that they can't eat gluten or meat or shellfish as the case may be without wishing to cause anyone extra trouble. The onus is on us as the cooks to make guests feel that their diet is no trouble at all and to cook for them with as much love as we can muster.

I found it helpful to discover that the root of the word hospitality is *hostis*, which is the Latin word for stranger or enemy (and which is where the word *hostility* comes from). It's in the very nature of being a good host that you are feeding someone with whom you may not initially have much in common. Part of hospitality is providing for a guest's needs even if you don't share or even understand those needs. By the end of the encounter, the enemy has become a friend. I've met couples where one of them is a strict vegetarian and the other feels that a meal is incomplete without red meat; yet somehow, they make it work.

As the great food writer Claudia Roden once wrote, in relation to the hospitality of the Middle East, "If two people have eaten together, they are compelled to treat each other well." It's a lovely idea, even if it doesn't fully ring true to anyone who has eaten tense family dinners where no matter how nice the food was, you could cut the atmosphere with a knife.

When you make the generous decision to cook for others, you are not expecting that everything will always be smooth sailing, but that doesn't mean it isn't worth it. The secret is to try to make yours a table at which all eaters are welcome, no matter how divergent they may be in their habits and inclinations: the ones who can't eat gluten, the picky ones, the vegetarians and the keto carnivores, the carb dodgers and the pasta lovers, the people who yearn for second helpings and the ones who feel happiest with small portions—come one, come all. Yes, it won't always work out perfectly. When eating together, people don't always see eye to eye over grapefruit (never mind over politics). Sometimes—mostly when feeding children—lovingly cooked food may even be hurled back in your face. But the attempt to carry on sitting at the same table sharing a meal despite our profound differences is one of the greatest of all human endeavors.

One meal to feed them all

"I like to make sure that everyone sitting at
my table can enjoy whatever I'm making."
    Julia Turshen, *Small Victories*

When I am invited to a dinner and asked for dietary requirements, I am one of
those lucky people who replies, "I eat everything." But as time goes by, I know ever
more people who have much more complex and particular food needs. Some of my
friends are celiac and some have type 2 diabetes and some have serious nut allergies
and when I see the world of food through their eyes, I see how frustrating it can
be to be the person who can't go out to dinner without explaining what they can't
eat and why. This is before we have even got on to questions of not eating whole
categories of food for religious and ethical reasons.

In a world of varied human tastes, there is no such thing as a dish of universal
acceptance. But I do think that it's not a bad idea, as a host, to come up with a
series of ideas for truly delicious things you feel happy cooking for various occasions
to suit different diets without leaving you feeling in any way resentful about the
process. The aim is that you will not feel thrown when catering for friends who have
no-go areas with food but will welcome them easily and confidently. I have made
a point of starting to collect recipes I really love that happen to be gluten-free or
dairy-free or low-carb or vegetarian or vegan as the case may be. Vegan recipes can
be handy to serve not just to friends who are actually vegan but to people following
a kosher or halal diet, who often choose to eat vegetarian when out.

As well as collecting recipes that work well for a range of dietary restrictions, it
also helps to think about ways to structure a meal that work well when people at the
table have different diets. Regardless of whether you are cooking Chinese food or not,
the Chinese system of serving dishes family style, with various dishes placed on the
table for people to help themselves, is generally much more accommodating than
the Western pattern of dishing everything up on individual plates. As Yan-Kit So
writes in *Yan-Kit's Classic Chinese Cookbook*, "As a Chinese meal is a communal affair,
a round table is usually used, being more conducive to sharing of the dishes." It's a
very tactful and accommodating way of serving food, which gives a lot of leeway for

different tastes and appetites. A hungry person might eat three bowlfuls of rice. A tofu sceptic can easily avoid a dish of bean curd and focus on the chicken or fish.

Another dinner format that works well when accommodating different diets and tastes is any kind of build-your-own meal. An obvious example would be a meal of tortillas with various fillings and salsas. This is the sort of meal that makes all the eaters at the table feel free, whether you are someone who likes to cram their tortilla with every possible filling, or you are a child of selective tastes who would rather have a few separate spoonfuls of vegetables and/or meat with a plain tortilla on the side.

On the side is a concept I find helpful for accommodating different palates and diets. In the rom-com *When Harry Met Sally*, the character of Sally (played by Meg Ryan) is forever ordering stuff on the side. When they finally get married, they have a coconut cake with rich chocolate sauce on the side. Harry explains it is "because not everybody likes it on the cake, because it makes it very soggy." Years of catering for children has made me very comfortable with the idea of on the side, whether it's sauces or spices. To take one example, I almost never add chiles directly to a dish because my son Leo won't eat it if I do, so I have gotten used to having a range of chile-based condiments on the table. But actually, almost anything can be served on the side, depending on the occasion. You can even serve meat on the side. If you are catering for a party of mostly vegetarians but know that you have one person—they do exist—who won't tolerate a dinner without meat, you could cook a small amount of steak or lamb chops to have on the side. I recommend the lamb chops on page 276.

Scattered sushi (gluten-free)

This is one of my favorite one-pot meals to make for friends following gluten-free diets, but it's also great when serving children who are going through that "nothing must touch" phase because you can separate out the various components. Almost everyone seems to find sushi a treat—except for low-carbists—and this is dreamily easy. The only remotely strenuous part is cooking and seasoning the rice. Instead of shaping the rice into individual pieces of sushi, you serve it in a generous communal bowl with the toppings scattered over the top. This is a popular thing to make for a home-cooked meal in Japan. You get all the flavors of sushi with a fraction of the effort. It's also very forgiving on the host because you serve it at room temperature. Here are three different ideas for toppings, one with smoked trout or mackerel, one with omelet and a vegan one with autumn roasted vegetables. If you were having a bigger party, you could make all three. Any leftovers are excellent in a lunchbox the next day. I buy huge bags of short-grain rice from a Korean grocery store and I always have rice vinegar in the house, so I know that I can make a version of this on short notice.

Serves 4, generously

For the rice
1½ cups/300g short-grain rice
3 tablespoons rice vinegar
1½ tablespoons sugar

Put the rice into a sieve and rinse thoroughly under the cold tap. Use one of your hands to gently massage the rice as the water runs through. Watch the color of the water that passes through the rice. You have rinsed it enough when the water runs clear or when you get bored, whichever is soonest. I usually make this in my Instant Pot: put it in the Instant Pot with 1¾ cups/450ml of water, set to high pressure for 5 minutes, and allow to slow release. But it is also easily made in an ordinary pan. Put the water and rice into a pan with a lid, bring to simmering point, immediately clamp on the lid, set it to the lowest possible heat, and cook for 12 minutes. Then switch off the heat and let it rest with the lid on for 10 minutes.

To make the sushi vinegar, mix together the vinegar, sugar, and 1 teaspoon of salt until the sugar and salt have dissolved.

Tip the warm rice into one of your biggest serving bowls. If you don't have a very big serving bowl, use a roasting dish. Using a spatula, a wooden spoon, or a rice paddle, gradually pour in the vinegar mixture and mix it gently until every grain is coated. Sri Owen writes that the motion you are looking for is not vigorous stirring but "more like the gentle tossing of a salad." Taste the rice as you go. Depending on your taste, you might not want all the vinegar. Cover the bowl until you are ready to eat—the rice can be eaten warm or at room temperature. Sushi rice is always most delicious when it hasn't been refrigerated. It can sit, covered, in a cool place in your kitchen for up to 2 hours (any longer than that and you should put it into the fridge—cooked rice is a breeding ground for bacteria).

Scattered sushi with smoked fish, avocado, and cucumber

This is a very likeable version that makes a small amount of smoked fish go a long way.

Serves 4
1 batch of cooked and seasoned sushi rice (see page 337)
7 oz/200g smoked trout or smoked mackerel
4 small Persian cucumbers or 1 large English one
2 ripe avocados
A squeeze of lemon
White or black sesame seeds
Pickled ginger and wasabi, to serve

Put the rice into a large serving bowl. Tear or cut the fish into bite-size pieces. Rinse and slice the cucumbers. Peel and slice the avocados and squeeze lemon over the slices so that they don't brown. Scatter the fish, avocado, and cucumber all over the rice, distributing it evenly. Finally, scatter some sesame seeds. Serve with pickled ginger and wasabi on the side.

Scattered sushi with miso-roasted beet and squash

This is a vegan version that is especially lovely in autumn.

Serves 4
1 batch of cooked and seasoned sushi rice (see page 337)
1 lb 2 oz/500g beets, peeled and cut into pieces 2 thumbs wide
1 lb 50 z/600g butternut squash or other squash, peeled and cut into pieces
   2 thumbs wide
2 tablespoons miso
2 tablespoons olive oil
A handful of chives
A handful of tarragon (optional)
A handful of walnuts
Pickled ginger and wasabi, to serve

While the sushi rice is cooking, preheat the oven to 425°F. Put the beet and squash on a baking sheet and toss them together with the miso and oil, then roast for 45 minutes or until tender and dark in places. Keep an eye on it because the miso means it may burn quicker than usual. Snip the chives with scissors and pick the tarragon leaves from their stems (if using). Put the cooked, seasoned rice into a big serving bowl and top with the roasted vegetables, followed by the walnuts and herbs. Serve with pickled ginger and wasabi on the side.

Scattered sushi with omelet, salty-sweet broccoli, and nori

This has a very high ease-to-reward ratio and you can make it even when there isn't much in the fridge except for eggs and a few vegetables.

Serves 4
4 eggs
Neutral oil
1 lb 5 oz/600g broccoli, sliced into small pieces about ¼ inch/5mm thick (obviously the sizes will vary)
2 tablespoons soy sauce
1 tablespoon mirin
1 teaspoon brown sugar
2 sheets of nori seaweed
1 batch of cooked and seasoned sushi rice (see page 337)
1 tablespoon black sesame seeds
Pickled ginger and wasabi, to serve

First, make the omelet. Crack the eggs and beat them with a bit of oil (and a dash of mirin if you like). Heat some oil in an omelet pan or nonstick frying pan over high heat. Pour in the eggs and swirl them around the pan to make an omelet. If you want to make a traditional layered Japanese omelet, search the internet for "how to make tamagoyaki using round pan." Otherwise, just make the omelet as you usually would. Transfer it to a plate and slice it into strips. To cook the broccoli, heat a couple of large spoonfuls of oil in a wok until very hot, then add the broccoli and stir-fry for a few minutes or until beginning to tenderize (add a splash of water to help it along if it needs it). Add the soy sauce, mirin, and sugar and cook until the liquid has reduced and is sticky. Slice the nori into small strips using kitchen scissors. Now put the sushi rice into a big bowl and scatter the omelet strips, the broccoli, nori, and sesame seeds on top. Serve with pickled ginger and wasabi.

Zucchini and basil moussaka with lemon béchamel (vegetarian and gluten-free)

Lasagne is one of the first things many of us turn to when looking for a dish that will please many people and be easy to prepare in advance, but moussaka is an even more universal crowd-pleaser. When I say moussaka, I am playing fast and loose with Greek cuisine: what I really mean is a lasagne-like savory bake centered on potatoes.

Moussaka is a useful concept to have up your sleeve when cooking for a group of people, some of whom are following special diets and some of whom are not. Moussaka has the comfort of lasagne except that it is gluten-free (or at least, it can be if you use gluten-free flour to make the white sauce). Everyone is happy the minute you set the burnished dish on the table.

Much as I love the classic version of moussaka made with a rich meat sauce and fried eggplants, these days I prefer to make it with vegetables instead so that it works for vegetarians and non-vegetarians alike. You can make it vegan by using olive oil instead of butter. I add lemon zest and juice to the béchamel to make it taste sprightly and fresh, an idea I got from a lasagne recipe in *Gennaro's Limoni* by Gennaro Contaldo.

Serves 4 (double or triple it for big parties)
2 lb/900g waxy potatoes (such as Yukon Gold), peeled and cut into thin slices about ¼ inch/5mm thick
14 oz/400g zucchini, cut lengthwise into long ribbons
14 oz/400g onions, peeled and cut into slices, or fennel, trimmed and sliced
2–3 tablespoons olive oil
3 tablespoons unsalted butter (or use olive oil to make it vegan)
⅓ cup/40g gluten-free flour (or use all-purpose flour, if you are not cooking for people on a gluten-free diet)
2 cups/480ml milk (use oat milk to make it vegan)
1 large unwaxed lemon
A few basil leaves
1 ball of fresh mozzarella, drained and sliced (optional)
¼ cup/30g grated parmesan (or vegetarian equivalent, or leave it out for the vegan version)

Preheat the oven to 425°F. Cook the potatoes in boiling salted water for 12–15 minutes, or until cooked through but not soggy. Drain in a colander. Meanwhile, brush the zucchini and the onions or fennel with the oil, arrange them on two baking sheets, and roast for 20 minutes or until sweet and tender, turning after 10 minutes. While the vegetables are roasting, make the lemon sauce. Melt the butter in a medium saucepan, add the flour, and mix very thoroughly with a whisk. Slowly, slowly add the milk, whisking all the while. Bring it to simmering point, stirring often, and simmer until it is thick and smooth. Season with salt and add the zest and half the juice of the lemon. Taste it to see if you think it needs more juice.

Now you can layer everything up in an ovenproof dish (the dish I use is around 9 × 13 inches/23cm × 33cm). First, put a layer of half the potatoes, then half the sauce, then the onions or fennel, then more potatoes, then the basil plus the mozzarella, if using, then the zucchini (arranged in lines), then the final half of the sauce. Top with the parmesan and bake in the oven for 15 minutes, or until bubbling and brown on top. Or, if it suits you better, you can assemble this ahead of time and refrigerate it, covered, for up for 3 days. If you bake it cold from the fridge it will need more like 30 minutes in the oven to heat through. Serve with a salad, and perhaps the carrot and panch pooran pickle on page 40.

VARIATIONS

This works with any vegetables you can think of instead of the zucchini and onions or fennel. Some good combinations are:
—Roasted slices of eggplant and sweet potato.
—Mushrooms sautéd with thyme and sage (in which case, leave out the basil).
—A jar of artichokes, drained, and some sautéd cavolo nero.
—Roasted butternut squash and wilted spinach.
—Roasted cherry tomatoes and butter-poached carrots (see page 37).

You can make a more traditional-tasting vegetarian moussaka by leaving out the roasted vegetables and instead layering the potatoes and sauce with Leo's lentil ragù on page 285, making it without the nutmeg and with an added pinch of cinnamon plus a few sprigs of chopped fresh oregano or thyme.

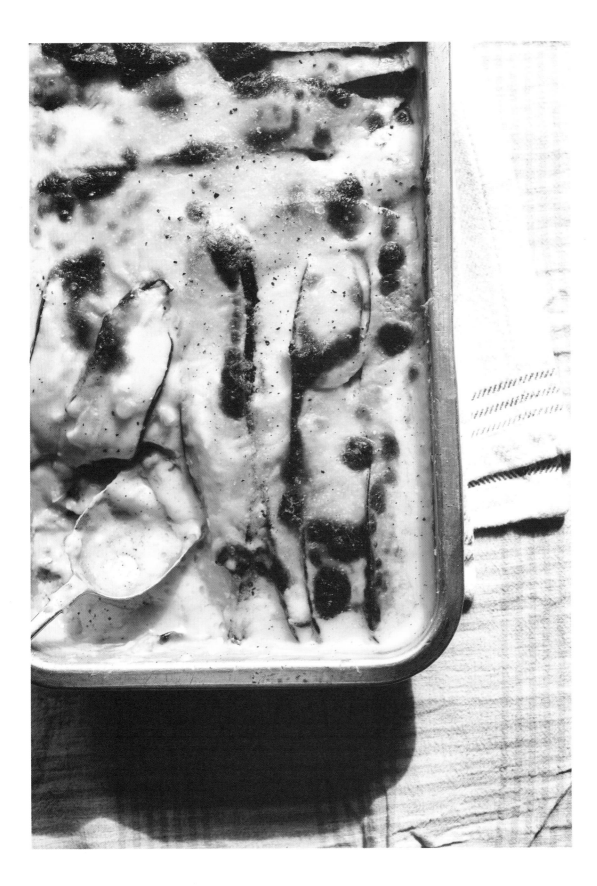

Universal desserts

I've started trying to build up a repertoire of gluten-free and dairy-free desserts that I can serve no matter who is coming over (unless they are completely off sugar, in which case I just serve fresh fruit or nothing but mint tea). As a lover of cream and wheat flour, the thing I have found surprising is that so many delicious sweet things can be made without a speck of either of them. Maybe this just proves that sugar is even more delicious than we thought. Some of these recipes can be found dotted around the book. See, for example, the chocolate mousse on page 118 (lactose-free and gluten-free but contains eggs), and raspberry ripple hazelnut meringue on page 389 (gluten-free), cherry and watermelon granita on page 401 (vegan and gluten-free), jammy plums with coconut cream on page 272 (vegan and gluten-free), Marsala pears with clove cream (gluten-free) on page 277, and Tasha's never-fail chocolate cake on page 404 (gluten-free).

Vegan pear, lemon, and ginger cake

Even though she is not vegan, I devised this cake for my mother, because pears have always been her favorite fruit and she is also crazy about ginger. Now that she has dementia, food seems to be one of the few things that still evokes clear memories for her (music is another). This is the kind of soft cake you might eat as easily with a fork for dessert as with fingers for afternoon tea. I adapted this from a Meera Sodha apple cake recipe. I make it in a square pan and decorate it with very thin slices of whole pear because I always feel that the pregnant shape of a pear is one of the most beautiful things in nature.

Serves 8
3 medium pears (total weight about 10½ oz/300g,
   but don't worry if it's a bit over or under)
¾-inch/2cm piece of ginger, grated
3 tablespoons brown sugar
1 unwaxed lemon

For the cake
1½ cups/200g all-purpose flour
3¾ teaspoons baking powder
¼ teaspoon salt
Packed ¾ cup/160g brown sugar
7 tablespoons/100ml light oil or olive oil
7 tablespoons/100ml non-dairy milk, such as oat or coconut
1 oz/30g crystallized ginger, chopped (optional)
Demerara sugar

Peel 2 of the pears, core them, and cut them into the tiniest dice you can manage. Put them into a bowl with the ginger, brown sugar, the zest of the lemon, and half its juice.

    Line a square (9½ × 9½-inch/24 × 24cm) cake pan with parchment paper. Preheat the oven to 400°F. Take the remaining pear, peel it, and cut off 4 thin slices, core and all, which show the full swollen-bellied outline of the pear. Keep going until you

have 4 very nice-looking slices. Eat the remaining scraps of pear.

In a mixing bowl, whisk together all the cake ingredients (except for the demerara) along with the remaining juice of ½ a lemon. Fold in the pears from the bowl. Scrape the mixture into the pan, decorate with the pear slices, sprinkle with a little demerara, and bake for 30 minutes, or until the cake is risen and a skewer comes out clean. Let it cool in the pan for at least half an hour before eating.

Chocolate and hazelnut macaroons (gluten- and dairy-free)

One of these dark fudgy macaroons—with or without sliced sugared peaches or berries and ice cream on the side—makes the perfect sweet end to any meal. They are based on François Payard's recipe for flourless chocolate and walnut cookies—as sold at his patisserie in Manhattan and as written about in *Food52 Genius Desserts* by Kristen Miglore. I swapped hazelnuts for the walnuts because I love the Nutella combination of hazelnut and chocolate. Assuming you have electric beaters or a stand mixer, these couldn't be easier, and they are dairy- and gluten-free (though not vegan). I suspect that the secret of why they taste so deeply fudgy and chewy is the vast amount of sugar. But just one of these is more satisfying by far than three lesser cookies. Anyway, I've halved the sugar content of each cookie by halving their size from Payard's original recipe (a trick that is always worth bearing in mind when you are craving sweet baked things but wanting to eat less sugar).

Makes 12 macaroons
1 cup/130g blanched hazelnuts
1⅓ cups/160g confectioners' sugar
6 tablespoons/35g cocoa powder
2 teaspoons vanilla extract
3 large egg whites

Set the oven to 375°F and line two baking sheets with parchment paper. Put the hazelnuts on one of the lined sheets and put it into the oven for 8 minutes. Remove the hazelnuts from the oven, let them cool slightly, and chop coarsely. Put the confectioners' sugar, cocoa, vanilla, egg whites, and a pinch of salt into a large mixing bowl (or stand mixer) and whisk on medium-low speed until slightly thickened. Add the hazelnuts and continue to whisk for 1 minute. Scoop out spoonfuls of the batter onto the two lined baking sheets. Aim for 6 cookies on each sheet. Bake for 10–12 minutes, or until the tops are shiny and cracked. If in doubt, they are ready (you want these soft). Let cool completely before removing from the parchment paper.

Eating with children:
a recipe for learning new tastes

"My child likes a kind of pattern to her meals:
I put raisins in rows, instead of willy-nilly, on a
slice of buttered toast..."
  M. F. K. Fisher, *An Alphabet for Gourmets*, 1949

Everyone tells you that you need to offer a child a new vegetable many times—maybe as often as thirteen to fifteen times—before it is accepted. But almost no one tells you *how* to go about doing it. This is about as helpful as being told to cook baked Alaska from scratch without being given a recipe. Without some kind of blueprint, the process of offering a child a food that they hate can be so painful for all concerned that it's easy to give up long before you reach thirteen attempts.

After my first child was born, I fell in love and out of love. I fell in love with him and I fell out of love with cooking, at least for a while. In my sleep-deprived state, I couldn't feel the same urgency in the kitchen. I no longer felt any motivation to embark on elaborate projects such as simmering shellfish stock or shaping home-made pasta. It was a win if I managed to eat anything more involved than toast. But at the back of my mind, I still had a dream of how wonderful it would be when he was old enough to try solid food. I wanted to share all the delicious things in the world with him.

It was a shock, then, to find that my son recoiled at many of the things that I considered to be most delicious. He couldn't stand fresh tomatoes, not even the sweetest smallest cherry tomatoes (though pasta sauce was OK as long as it was very smooth). He also loathed mashed potatoes and, oddest of all, chocolate. I soon started to see that I couldn't just give him my favorite foods and expect him automatically to love them as much as I did. And yet, of my three children, he was by far the most adventurous eater (from an early age he said his favorite food was squid). My daughter, born four years later, had a deep fear of what she called "spicy" food and liked things to be plain and separate where possible. She was suspicious of "bits" such as nuts or raisins. But her reluctance about new food was nothing compared to my youngest child, another boy, born ten years after my first, for whom food was a real struggle for several years. When he was eighteen months old, one by one he started to reject the varied foods he had enjoyed as a baby, from carrots to broccoli to lamb casserole. There were often tears at meal times (usually his). I felt a deep sense of shame and failure, both as a parent and as a cook, and the more anxious I was about his eating, the less—quite understandably—he wanted to eat.

Gradually, to my immense relief and gratitude, my younger son relearned his eating habits. Over a period of months and years, he broadened his horizons with food and learned to love a whole range of things I never imagined I would see him consume, from eggplants to fish.

The good news is that there are some concrete things that can really help. Every child is different, so you may need to experiment until you find the strategies that work for you. But try not to give up too soon or to brand your efforts a failure. Be kind to yourself and remove any element of guilt or judgement about the way you have fed your child. If your child has limited tastes, it doesn't mean you have done anything wrong. There's a strong genetic component to the way children eat and—as I discovered with my three children—some children find the whole business of eating much harder than others. Eating habits can also go forward and back again. A child may have learned to enjoy a wonderfully varied diet, only to unlearn it again, particularly after a stomach bug (anything that has once been eaten in a state of nausea may lose its appeal for a long time, even if it was once a favorite).

Here are some recipes for learning to love new foods (at any age). The three basic principles are 1) honesty about what is being tasted, 2) variety over quantity, and 3) no pressure (on you or your child).

Honesty

There was a vogue a few years ago for hiding vegetables in children's meals, for example, by smuggling beet into a chocolate cake or sneaking a bit of zucchini into a pasta sauce. If you enjoy adding beet to your chocolate cake, please don't let me stop you, but as a tool for changing tastes, it is very unlikely to work. If the child doesn't know that they ate any beet, all that happens is that serving them chocolate-beet cake will reinforce their liking for chocolate cake. Which is fine (who doesn't love cake?) but if you want your child to become someone who eventually chooses vegetables of their own free will, you need to be open and honest with them about what it is they are eating.

The end goal here is to get the child excited about the food itself. Keep reminding yourself that this is possible, no matter how reluctant they now seem. There are plenty of food cultures in the world where children enjoying vegetables is seen as a perfectly normal and everyday thing.

Variety over quantity

Why should you focus on the variety of foods being offered rather than the quantity? Dr. Keith Williams is the director of the Feeding Disorders Program at Hershey Medical Center in Pennsylvania. He has worked with dozens of families whose children eat an extremely limited diet. The parents are usually beside themselves with worry and quite naturally concerned with whether their child is eating enough. But what Williams has seen is that this worry about quantity can be counterproductive.

Some parents resort to giving their children a lot of milk to make up for the lack of nutrients from food, but the effect is to fill the child up so much that they have even less appetite for new foods. Others may pressure their child to clean their plate, but what this does—apart from creating an atmosphere of anxiety at dinner time—is to make a child learn to ignore his or her own internal cues for hunger and fullness. By contrast, if you trust that it is OK to focus on variety rather than quantity, children tend to end up eating more food—and, just as importantly, do so in a way that will set them up for a more varied diet for life. In the clinic, Williams and his colleagues found that increasing the variety of foods being served from three foods to six foods resulted in picky eaters having three bites more per meal or snack. That sounds like nothing but Williams points out that "over the course of the day, children ate an average of eighteen more bites (over three meals and three snacks) merely because they were offered a wider variety of foods."

No pressure

The next problem is *how* you offer these foods. How can you remove the pressure a child feels about trying disliked new foods? There are a few different strategies and you should pick and mix to find the ones that work for you, your child and your family. I found it helpful to bear in mind Ellyn Satter's Division of Responsibility in Feeding. Satter, who was a psychotherapist and expert in eating disorders, said that when it comes to eating, "The parent is responsible for what, when, and where. The child is responsible for how much and whether." In other words, it is not actually your job as a parent to make a child eat. You only need to provide the food and the venue and trust that your child will—eventually—do the rest.

Here is something I have seen working first-hand with hundreds of children: sensory taste education—a no-pressure method for exploring food with all five senses. If a child doesn't want to swallow something they dislike—and who can blame them?—you could just try looking and touching and smelling and even listening to it, as a first step to making it familiar and safe enough to taste. I once said this to an audience of Spanish people and they pointed out that children get sensory food education every time they go to a real food market: a good point. If you can take your child grocery shopping and ask them to point out the different colors and shapes and smells, you are halfway there.

A couple of years ago, I came across a remarkable method of food education called Sapere, which is used in Sweden and Finland, among other countries. What I found so appealing was the idea that children could best learn about food by playing with it and using their natural sense of curiosity. To cut a long story short, I wrote about Sapere in one of my books (*First Bite*) and then a couple of years later, I set up a British version of Sapere called TastEd (www.tasteducation.com) with a head teacher named Jason O'Rourke.

In TastEd, there are two golden rules that the teacher or parent reinforces at the start of each session: "no one has to like" and "no one has to try." These two phrases seem to have an almost supernatural effect on children's ability to relax and experience food in a more curious spirit. Obviously, the end goal is that you do want them to try the vegetables and to like them. But as soon as the child knows they will not be judged if they find the food disgusting, the whole exercise feels different. You can see them visibly relax. One of the most moving experiences of my life was watching a girl with sensory phobias who had previously been terrified of trying new foods daring to try a whole range of fruits and vegetables at school as part of a course of TastEd—and actually liking some of them.

Some games for trying new foods (or retrying hated foods)

One simple technique to make it easier for a child to taste new things is to decrease the size of the piece of food being tasted so that it is as small as a pea. For many children, the horror of new food comes as much from the texture as the flavor. If the piece of food being tried is small enough, it is almost as if it is not there at all. This technique was pioneered by a psychologist named Lucy Cooke who calls it Tiny Tastes. The idea is to do the tasting sessions away from meal times. Together, you and your child pick a vegetable to work on. Every day, at roughly the same time, they try a minuscule piece of the chosen food. If they manage to try it, they get a sticker. If not, nothing is lost: there is always tomorrow. Once your child actually starts to like the vegetable you can offer bigger pieces and stop.

If a child is a reluctant eater, try to teach them to use their other senses to get to know the food a bit better before they taste it. Stroke a pear, sniff an orange or a strawberry. Listen to the loud crunch of a carrot. Put raspberries on your fingers like finger puppets.

If you have a child who fears green vegetables, play a game that is all about looking (not tasting). Take three green vegetables and try to rank them in order of color ("the cucumber is the palest and the spinach is the darkest"). At the end, you can taste them and let your child know that they are welcome to join in.

If your child tastes something and doesn't like it, be unphased (or at least pretend to be unphased). Ask them, gently, "Why don't you like it?" and encourage them to form a sentence. "I don't like the peach because it is furry." "I don't like eggs because they are slimy." Also discuss why they *do* like something. "I like the tomato because it explodes in my mouth."

Serve vegetables—or other disliked foods such as fish or egg or cheese—as a starter rather than alongside the main course. Studies have shown that offering vegetables before the meal has begun increases the chance they will be eaten, partly because the child is hungrier then and partly because they are free to consume—or not consume—the vegetables without feeling the whole table is paying attention to them. Once my son started to be less scared of vegetables, we did this every dinner time. I would put some vegetables (cooked or uncooked) on a saucer in front of him while I finished cooking dinner. I would then remove the saucer without any comment and we would all sit down and eat the rest of dinner. Over time, he became totally conditioned to this veg-first thing and to this day, he always eats any vegetables on his plate first.

As a parent, you know that these feeding techniques have succeeded when you no longer need them. I was talking to the teenage daughter of a friend, who remembered that she used to be so picky that when she went to her family's favorite Indian restaurant, the chef would get a plate of fries and plain cucumber ready as soon as he saw her walk in the door. But now she is twenty-one and would happily eat almost anything on the menu. The greatest thing about your child becoming a less picky eater is that—finally!—you both get the joy back in dinner.

Family food

"My mother firmly believed that almonds were
brain food and that any child sent off to write
two examination papers for six hours unfortified
with almond balls was surely suffering from the
severest form of neglect."
   Madhur Jaffrey, *A Taste of India*, 1985

The whole idea of children's food—as a separate category from normal food—is flawed. Children are not pets. They do not need to be fed special products distinct from other humans (although the profits of the baby food industry depend on pretending that they do).

Having said this, I do think that a household's eating habits quite naturally take on different patterns when there is one or more young child at the table. The whole rhythms of the day change, to sync with nap times. I have never eaten dinner so ludicrously early as I did when my children were little. The obvious step, which I often fell into, is to do as the Victorians did, and to divide the household's meals into two completely different sittings, nursery food for children and proper dinner for the adults. Sometimes, because of working patterns, a divided sitting for dinner is the only way to get everyone fed. Equally, parents sometimes want the chance of a grown-up dinner without all the interruptions and mess of eating with toddlers.

But the more often you can manage to be at the same table as your children, eating the same food, the happier family eating becomes, even if it's only on weekends. You don't need me to rehearse the many benefits of shared family meals. Children who eat regular family meals are less likely to be depressed and less likely to suffer eating disorders and more likely to eat vegetables. What doesn't get discussed so much are the benefits of the family meal to the parents.

Yes, you have to cook the darn thing. But you also get to eat it. And the work involved in cooking a single family dinner is actually so much less than if you make yourself a short-order cook, producing endless separate meals for each family member over the course of an evening.

Family cooking doesn't have to be any more elaborate than sticking a dish of potatoes in the oven. I find that one hour at 425°F does it for medium-large potatoes. Oil the potatoes first and prick them with a fork. The beauty of a meal of baked potatoes is that different people at the table can indulge different whims without it feeling as if you are eating separate meals. I might put a bowl of tuna mixed with crème fraîche on the table, plus a bowl of grated cheese, a bottle of Tabasco, and—obviously—butter. Plus a handful of herbs on the side for anyone who wants them and definitely some kind of vegetable, often cooked simply by the method for Raymond's butter-poached carrots (page 37) or a tomato salad with a clove of raw garlic mixed into the oil. Or we might have some smoked fish on the side. In the spring, we might have our potatoes with poached eggs and green vegetables (except that I substitute a small omelet for my youngest, who still can't abide the wobble of a poached egg). Another excellent way with baked potatoes, if you don't know it already, is to bake them, halve them, mix the flesh with butter and grated cheese (with or without cooked bacon), and pile it back into the shells before returning it to the oven and baking until crispy on top. This was one of my Granny's favorite meals. It tastes like luxury but is very cheap.

When you are short on ideas for family dinner, don't forget pesto. I once edited a community cookbook of favorite family recipes for my children's school. We received so many recipes involving pesto, we had to create a whole chapter devoted to the pungent green sauce. It seems that many children have a surprising passion for this strong-tasting basil sauce. To make a quick, fresh pesto, whiz together a handful each of basil leaves and parmesan (or vegetarian equivalent) and a spoonful of pine nuts or sliced almonds (cheaper) with a small clove of garlic, salt, and as much oil as you want to make it as thick as you like, not forgetting you can thin it with a large spoonful of water. A meal in which broccoli is cooked along with pasta so it becomes pleasingly soft, mixed with a few spoonfuls of pesto, is a very nourishing and fast meal. Other than pasta pesto, you can eat spoonfuls with a piece of fish or a fishcake, stir it into rice, into mashed potatoes, or into a bowl of steamed vegetables.

The point of family food is not just to please the children at the table but to cosset the poor exhausted parents, who need someone to look after them too. If you manage to find a food that deeply comforts your child, the chances are that it will comfort you too, both in the moment and in the memory. Every time I cook spaghetti and meatballs, it takes me back to eating it at the kitchen table with my oldest son when he was only two and watching the look of surprise and delight on his face when he managed to suck up a whole strand of spaghetti in one go.

There are recipes dotted all over the book that would qualify as family food. Some examples that have been popular with children I know include:

—Kim's gyoza (page 149)

—Scattered sushi (page 337)

—The loveliest red curry (perhaps minus the chile for very young children) (page 245)

—Zucchini and basil moussaka with lemon béchamel (easily adaptable to the particular vegetables your child likes) (page 343)

—Zucchini and herb fritters (page 145)

—Leo's lentil ragù (page 285)

—Slow-start roasted chicken (page 75)

—Polenta-crisp oven fries (page 388)

Tiny vegetable-fried rice or noodles, with or without egg

When I used to take my children out to eat at Thai or Vietnamese restaurants when they were little, I was so grateful for the presence on the menu of vegetable-fried rice or noodles, because I knew that this would keep them happy while I ate something fierier. But when I tried to re-create these simple dishes at home, they never seemed to go down quite so well with my children. I suddenly realized that my knifework was to blame. The vegetables in the fried rice from a professional kitchen tend to be cut so much smaller than we usually do at home—the size of a pea—which makes them texturally so much easier for children to handle. This is a recipe for which it is really worth sharpening your knife. Fried rice was also the first dish that made my youngest son consent to eat eggs in any form because the pieces of omelet were so small. Slowly, slowly, he graduated from egg-fried rice to a whole omelet.

Serves 4
2 tablespoons light oil
4 cloves of garlic, peeled and finely chopped
A few handfuls of vegetables, finely diced no bigger than ¼ inch/5mm
    (for example, zucchini, asparagus, green beans, carrot, broccoli, cabbage,
    cauliflower, mushrooms; you could also include the kernels stripped from
    a cob of corn or a drained can of corn)
2 tablespoons soy sauce
1 tablespoon sesame oil
1½ tablespoons mirin
4 large portions of cooked rice or 4 portions of noodles, cooked as per package
    instructions and rinsed in a sieve
1 tablespoon rice vinegar
4 green onions, finely chopped
2 teaspoons sesame seeds, white or black (optional)

To serve
Lime wedges, Japanese pickles, sriracha, chile crisp oil, for anyone
    who wants them

Heat the oil in a wok or a large frying pan over medium heat and add the garlic and all the other vegetables, stir-frying for 4 or 5 minutes or until cooked through. Add the soy sauce, sesame oil, and mirin along with the rice or noodles. If using rice, you will have to stir it patiently with a wooden spatula or spoon, breaking up the clumps and making sure that every piece is well coated with the vegetable mixture. If using the noodles, stir more gently, not breaking them up too much, and adding a splash or two of water as you go to keep them slippery. When the rice or noodles are fully combined with the vegetables and hot all the way through, stir in the vinegar and green onions and sprinkle with the sesame seeds, if using. Eat with lime wedges for squeezing, Japanese pickles, and sriracha, chile crisp oil, or any condiments you like.

EGG VARIATION

For egg-fried rice or noodles, first beat together 2 eggs with a pinch of salt and a drop of sesame oil. Heat 1 tablespoon of light oil in the wok, pour in the eggs, and cook them into a fairly dry, pancake-like omelet. Transfer to a plate, wipe out the pan, and proceed as above. Chop the omelet into small pieces and add it when you add the rice or noodles.

Two stews for tired people

The oldest recipe, aka chicken stew

Chicken—like all meat—tastes better cooked on the bone. But tell that to a tired parent who hasn't slept properly in months. This is a pragmatic stew that uses skinless, boneless chicken thighs to make it much quicker to cook and prep but is nevertheless delicious: chicken stew for the soul.

This is much easier than most casseroles because instead of laboriously softening onions, you just throw in a lot of chopped leeks and carrots and potatoes, which happily cook in the broth without any sautéing. But I do think it tastes a lot better if you can spare a little time to brown the chicken thoroughly in butter before the vegetables go in. If you make a big batch of it, you can live off this for a couple of days and it tastes both restorative and comforting. It's a way to stretch a little bit of meat a long way. My mother taught me that meat stew should be more vegetable than meat and I think she was right, both on grounds of sustainability and taste. But if you are feeling meat-hungry, double the quantity of chicken.

The reason I call it the oldest recipe is that the oldest recorded recipes are on a group of clay tablets from Mesopotamia dating from four thousand years ago, give or take. Most of the recipes—twenty-one of them—take the form of various kinds of simple meat broths, with meat or poultry cooked in water and usually flavored with leeks and garlic, sometimes with herbs added and sometimes with barley. I'm pretty sure that modern chicken, even the free-range kind, is nothing like the game birds they ate in Mesopotamia. But I still find it extraordinary to think that when I take some chicken and cook it in water with leeks, I am more or less cooking the same way that people were cooking four thousand years ago.

Serves 6–10, depending on how many of you are children

1 lb 2 oz/500g boneless, skinless chicken thighs (organic and/or free-range)

1½ tablespoons unsalted butter

14 oz/400g leeks

1 lb 9 oz/700g carrots

1 lb 2 oz/500g baby new potatoes

1 cup/240ml white wine (the alcohol burns off so you won't make your children drunk, but if you are at all worried just leave it out and use all water, with a bit of extra lemon juice at the end)

6 cloves of garlic

1 oz/30g flat-leaf parsley, chopped (I add this because all my mother's stews tasted like parsley but if either you or your child object, leave it out or use different herbs such as dill, tarragon, chives, or oregano)

At the end: a squeeze of lemon plus some zest, a spoonful or two of heavy cream

Trim any big pieces of fat off the chicken thighs and cut each thigh into 4 or 5 pieces. If you are truly shattered, you can skip this stage and just chuck the meat from package to pan. In a large shallow lidded pan, heat the butter over medium-high heat and add the chicken and a light sprinkle of salt (leave out for babies). While the chicken is browning, clean your chopping board and knife and prep the veg. Cut the leeks in half lengthwise, rinse out any grit, and cut them into ½-inch/1cm pieces. Peel the carrots and cut them into thick coins. Halve the potatoes.

After each prepping job, check on the chicken in the pan and turn it to brown on all sides. Pour the wine into the pan. It will create billows of savory steam and pick up all the lovely brown chicken bits in the pan. Add all the vegetables including the unpeeled separated cloves of garlic, plus half the parsley, 1 teaspoon of salt (optional— if cooking for babies, just leave it out and season at the table), and 1⅔ cups/400ml of water. Cover the pan, turn the heat down, and cook for 30 minutes or until all the vegetables are tender (check a couple of potatoes). Taste to see if it needs lemon and add a couple of spoonfuls of cream and the remaining parsley (or hold this back to add at the table if you are feeding any parsley objectors). For babies, chop or blend to whatever texture they can manage. Eat in bowls and feel restored.

VARIATION

Sometimes I change the seasoning of this and the white bean stew on page 366, leaving out the cream, wine, and parsley and adding lime leaves and lemongrass along with the vegetables and lots of lime juice at the end and a spoonful of miso and cliantro plus chile for anyone who wants it (but not for babies).

Restorative white bean stew

This is the vegetarian equivalent of the chicken stew above. It was the brilliant chefs at Vanderlyle restaurant in Cambridge (Alex Rushmer and Lawrence Butler) who taught me that the broth in which white beans cook can be as soothing as chicken stock. In the past, I would foolishly rinse the beans after cooking them, thus throwing the best bit away. When you are tired, cooking dried beans can feel like too much effort, but you don't have to soak them. These can happily simmer away in the background while you play with train tracks. The hands-on cooking here is minimal and the results are pure comfort.

Serves 4–6 or more, depending on how many of you are children
1¼ cups/250g dried white beans, such as cannellini
1 oz/30g flat-leaf parsley, chopped (or any other herb of your choosing)
6 cloves of garlic
1 lb 5 oz/600g new potatoes
2 medium zucchini or 2 large carrots
3½ oz/100g green onions
⅔ cup/160ml white wine or vermouth
Lemon (zest and juice)
Heavy cream (or coconut cream to keep it dairy-free)

Put the beans into a medium-large saucepan, add half the parsley and the whole cloves of garlic, cover with masses of water, and bring to simmering point. Simmer for around 2 hours, or until the beans are totally tender. This is the unpredictable part, but it really isn't strenuous. Dried beans can cook in anywhere from 1½–3 hours without soaking. Just check them every half an hour and keep topping up with water as needed.

When they are tender, chop the potatoes and zucchini (or peeled carrots) and green onions into small pieces and add them to the pan along with 1 teaspoon of salt (leave it out if cooking for toddlers and season at the table for non-toddlers) and the wine. Put a lid on the pan and simmer for 15 minutes or until the potatoes are tender. Adjust the seasoning with lemon and add a big slosh of cream and the second half of the parsley.

Sicilian pork meatballs

For many years, these were a way of life in my family. Any time I was cooking in a slightly more leisurely way on a weekend, if I asked my oldest son what he wanted to eat, he would say "meatballs" in a voice of incredulity that I was even bothering to ask him because the answer was so obvious. *Well, duh.*

When you are a parent, dishes can taste like home in more than one way. There are the dishes that remind you of the food you grew up with and then there are the dishes that taste of the new imaginary home you want to create for your children. My mother never made meatballs. My vision of spaghetti and meatballs as a food representing family happiness owes much to the children's book *Bread and Jam for Frances* by Russell Hoban, in which Frances, a female badger, stops eating nothing but bread and jam because she sees the rest of the family eating spaghetti and meatballs and she wants to join in.

My meatball recipe was originally based on one by Clarissa Hyman, although I've changed the recipe by adding tepid water to the mix to lighten it, a tip from Food52. They are very lemony and bursting with flat-leaf parsley and make a change from the usual meatballs in tomato sauce, but if you want the classic tomato version (which in all honesty, my children always do, given the choice), I've explained how to do that too.

Serves 4–6 (but leftovers are always good)
3½ oz/100g slightly stale bread
1¾ oz/50g flat-leaf parsley
1 lb 2 oz/500g free-range ground pork
⅔ cup/75g grated pecorino or parmesan
Zest of 1 unwaxed lemon
2 cloves of garlic, peeled and grated
2 large eggs
All-purpose flour
2 tablespoons olive oil
½ cup/120ml dry white wine
4 fresh bay leaves

In a food processor, whiz together the bread and parsley to make very green breadcrumbs. Put them into a bowl, add 7 tablespoons/100ml of tepid water, and mix well. Now mix in the pork, cheese, lemon zest, garlic, eggs, and ¾ teaspoon of salt, mixing thoroughly. Using your hands, shape it into small walnut-sized balls, placing them on a plate as you go. Wash your hands. Sprinkle some flour all over the meatballs. Heat the oil in a large frying pan over medium-high heat, add the meatballs, and immediately move them around a bit to get them slippery from the oil. Then cook them undisturbed until the bottom half is brown and crisp. Carefully turn them and brown the other side. Add the wine and the bay leaves, followed by enough water to barely cover the meatballs. Simmer uncovered until the water has reduced right down, the meatballs are cooked, and the juices have become syrupy, 15–20 minutes.

Serve over cooked linguini or spaghetti or with white or brown rice or with the nutmeg mashed potatoes on page 212. And a green vegetable.

VARIATIONS

Meatballs in tomato sauce

If you insist on tomato sauce for your meatballs, make the all-in-one tomato sauce on page 20. You can make the tomato sauce while you are browning the meatballs, then lower the browned meatballs into it, and continue to simmer for 15 minutes or until the meatballs are cooked.

Meatloaf

Make the meatball mix but instead of forming it into meatballs, pack it into an oiled 9 × 5-inch/900g loaf pan and bake at 400°F or 35 minutes, or until browned on top and thoroughly cooked.

Quicker, lazier meatballs

If you are short on time, forget about browning the meatballs, skip the flour, and simply drop the raw meatballs into a simmering pan of the tomato sauce above. This creates a softer texture and a milder flavor but I like it just as much.

White fish and red bell pepper

This was one of the first dishes that persuaded my daughter, then age two, that food could taste better when the flavors intermingle, rather than being totally separate. It is an idea more than a recipe. You could apply it to any protein food and any vegetable. The key is that you cook them together in a pan, with olive oil, and oil carries the flavors of the vegetable to the protein and vice versa until the two become acquainted—but not alarmingly so.

For two children, you need 2 very small fillets of white fish, or one 5-oz/140g fillet cut in half (I favor hake, but choose anything that is fresh and sustainable), 1 red bell pepper, and a large spoonful or so of olive oil, and possibly a peeled, grated clove of garlic. Cut the bell pepper into long strips and sauté until soft in the oil in a small frying pan over medium-high heat. Turn the heat down a notch and add the garlic if using. Push the bell pepper to the side of the pan and add the fish fillets, seasoned with a light sprinkle of salt. Cover the pan and cook until the fish is just cooked through, a couple of minutes. The fish pleasingly takes on some of the color and flavor of the bell pepper, which should be now very soft, red, and sweet. This is especially good with new potatoes. Scale up if you are cooking for larger numbers.

Homemade frozen pizza with buttermilk dough

If you want to put everyone in the house (including yourself) in a better mood, simply utter the phrase "pizza for dinner." Making pizza dough isn't hard and nor is assembling the sauce and the toppings, but attempting both parts back to back can seem an impossible hurdle on those rainy afternoons when you are all stuck in the house and there's also laundry to do and urgent UNO games to play. My suggestion is to divide the two parts of pizza-making into stages. If you make the dough in advance and stash it in balls in the freezer, it is always there for when you need it. It's worth considering putting at least some whole wheat flour in the dough. Pizza is a great delivery system for convincing children that whole grains can be treat, not duty. You can turn the dough-making into a fun activity to do together; or make it by yourself and let some tension out. The buttermilk strengthens the dough and helps the crust to brown but it's not essential.

Makes enough for 4 large crusts, each of which would feed one very hungry adult or several children

4 cups/500g Italian 00 flour or all-purpose flour (or a combination of all-purpose and whole wheat)
1 x ¼-oz/7g envelope fast-acting dried yeast
A pinch of sugar
7 tablespoons/100ml buttermilk (or substitute water)
3 tablespoons olive oil

Put the flour into a mixing bowl with the yeast, sugar, and 2 teaspoons of salt. Pour in the buttermilk and ¾ cup plus 2 tablespoons/200ml of lukewarm water plus the olive oil and mix with a silicone spatula or wooden spoon until it comes together. Turn it out onto a lightly floured surface and knead for 5 minutes or until it feels silky in your hand. Kneading sounds hard when you have never done it before, but all you have to do is push the dough away from you using your hand, bring it back toward you then push it back again. Repeat this motion over and over. When the dough feels smooth, return it to the bowl, cover with a clean kitchen towel, and place it in a warm place for 1 hour or until it has risen.

Now knock the air out of the dough, divide it into four pieces and form into balls. Put each one into a labeled container or zip-top bag and transfer to the freezer. Any

time you and your child feel like pizza for dinner, transfer a ball of dough to the fridge in the morning or put it out at room temperature for a couple of hours. Or if you prefer, use the dough straight away.

Topping and baking
1–2 × 14-oz/400g cans of whole, peeled tomatoes
Olive oil
A clove of garlic
A couple of balls of mozzarella
Toppings such as thinly sliced mushrooms or thinly sliced zucchini, fresh oregano
    or basil leaves, sautéd onions, pitted black olives, capers, salami
Parmesan

For the easiest no-cook pizza sauce, simply take a can or two of whole, peeled tomatoes and drain the liquid off (you can save it to drink as tomato juice). Blitz with a couple of spoonfuls of extra-virgin olive oil and a peeled grated clove of garlic (I don't add salt here).

What you need to know about the cheese is that mozzarella can ooze white liquid and make the pizza soggy. To avoid this, slice the mozzarella and wrap it in a few sheets of paper towel in a bowl and allow it to dry out for anywhere between 5 minutes and all day. Or use low-moisture mozzarella if you can find it. The other thing that helps avoid pools of moisture is breaking the pieces of mozzarella very small before adding them to the pizza.

To turn the dough into pizza, simply set the oven to 450°F, dust your work surface with flour, and roll each ball of dough into a rough circle as thin as you can until it is a circle of close to 12 inches/30cm in diameter. For smaller child-size pizzas, divide each piece of dough in half before rolling. Place them on greased baking sheets (I use pizza pans with holes in the bottom, but a regular baking sheet works fine) and stretch the dough a little more.

Top each crust with a couple of spoonfuls of your sauce and spread out thinly. Add whatever toppings you like, followed by a grating of parmesan and a tiny drizzle of oil.

Bake for 10–15 minutes, or until bubbling and golden. Wait at least 5 minutes before eating to avoid mouth-burn. My main pizza tip is not to be too generous with the sauce or the cheese, or else you will end up with a molten mess. One of the secrets of cooking is knowing when to be generous and when to rein yourself in, and pizza topping, strangely, is a time for restraint. After it's out of the oven, you can always make a plain pizza more exciting by adding dabs of some kind of green herb sauce, such as the chimichurri on page 212 (I learned this from Helen Evans, the talented chef of Flor in London).

Complete frozen pizzas

Another way to go with this is to freeze whole pizzas pretopped with sauce so that you always have a last-minute dinner in the freezer. For this, I make the pizzas smaller so that they are easier to store. Roll out the dough as above but subdivide the dough into 8 circles not 4. Top each with sauce and freeze them uncovered on baking sheets lined with parchment paper. When they are frozen solid, wrap them in layers of parchment paper and store in containers or zip-top bags until needed. Freeze for up to 3 months. Add cheese and toppings and bake from frozen on a baking sheet in a hot oven for 15–18 minutes or until bubbling and golden.

Cook for the life you have (and make it better)

"Cooking is both simpler and more
necessary than we imagine."
   Tamar Adler, *An Everlasting Meal*, 2012

The secret of cooking is that there is no secret formula, no special sauce, no hidden element. The only universal secret is to find the recipes and methods that will make the person cooking feel more able to do it. Your comfort, ease, and pleasure in the kitchen must come first. What this means is that cutting corners is always a good idea, assuming you still like the end results. But it also means that spending more time and effort on cooking can be completely worth it if you will enjoy either the process or the end results (or ideally, both). As Albert Einstein said, "Everything should be made as simple as possible but no simpler."

No matter what your temperament, one thing that never improves the experience of home cooking is anxiety. When I was talking to the writer John Lanchester in the summer of 2021, he observed that much of modern Western food culture is driven by anxiety. "If we lived in a completely stable society where everyone ate the food they grew up with, would that society have cookbooks and a food channel? In an era of social change, cooking becomes a question of who am I trying to impress with what version of myself? It's asking a hell of a lot of food. Of course it will make you anxious and stressed and disoriented."

When deciding what to cook, the least important considerations are whether what you are making is fashionable or impressive. Instead, we should think more in terms of the pleasures that can sustain and lift us. The Danish cookbook author Trine Hahnemann, who is one of the wisest people I know, has written that the only rule in her kitchen is that "the cooking has to be done with love. So, no matter if it's feeding myself a simple salad, or cooking a meal for my husband, or hosting a party, I keep that rule." I like this approach. To cook with love is to cook with both freedom and care. You know you are on the right lines when you make a sandwich for yourself with the same care you might bring to cooking Christmas dinner; or when you cook a fancy dinner with the same freedom you bring to making a sandwich.

Cooking can't make you a different person, which is just as well since the person you are is fine already. But cooking can change the textures and the tastes of your everyday life, both on humdrum mornings and on feast days. As Trine Hahnemann writes, cooking is a space in daily life to "do something meaningful," to use your hands, and to establish repetitive rituals that mean something to you. It's a way to recall people you have loved and lost and to be generous to the people who are still here (starting with yourself). It's a chance to make the next day taste slightly better than the last. I sometimes think that this is as close as most of us will ever come to living the dream.

Fiesta

"The things that happened could only
have happened during a fiesta."
  Ernest Hemingway, *The Sun Also Rises*, 1926

This might sound like a strange thing to say in a book that is mostly about making cooking simpler, but most of us don't have enough feasts in our lives. I don't necessarily mean organized religious festivals such as Christmas and Eid and Passover and Diwali, when most of the script of feasting has been written in advance. Nor do I mean any meal involving obligation, such as dutiful dinner parties for work colleagues or for in-laws. The kind of feasting I am talking about is random just-for-the-heck-of-it celebrating at any time of year: maybe for a birthday or maybe just to remind yourself that you are alive. If you can put together food you actually want to cook with a big table of people you truly want to see, you have a pretty good formula for a celebration.

It can easily seem as if there is no time in our lives for this kind of cooking (and I'm certainly not suggesting you attempt it every day). But when you look back through the years, those feasts you thought you didn't have time for are among the bright spots that stand out in the memory, the moments that distinguish one blank repetitive year from another: the vignettes at a table when people and flavors came together and something changed. When the meal ended, maybe there was tequila and dancing; or maybe there was herb tea and conversation. Either way, the ripple effect of the meal extends into the next day and the next week because the people who were there that night carry it with them.

In the old books of secrets of Renaissance times, cooking is often seen as the key to staving off disease and the march of time. In a household book from 1695 (*The Family Dictionary*), the author suggests that a drink made from honey, blackcurrants, licorice, and figs can be used to cure a "slimy cough" and remedy "shortness of breath." The same book suggests that garlic can be used to ward off or cure "convulsions," blemishes, and "the bitings of Mad Dogs and other Venomous Creatures," and that hyssop can be mixed with cumin and salt to remedy "the poisonous biting of serpents."

Clearly, there is no recipe that can really save us from the inevitable, but I do think that these old books of secrets were on to something. Cooking is one of the few benign ways anyone can achieve immortality: not because we can cook up the elixir of life but because we live on through the dishes we made. Like the fruit in a jar of jam, the best part of our lives is preserved in the memories of those we cooked for. When I am gone, I hope that my children will sometimes stage a giant waffle frolic and think of me.

Of all the reasons to cook, one of the best is to be remembered. This is why we should enjoy fiestas while we can. My sister had a friend, a poet named Craig Arnold who died far too young, while hiking on a Japanese island at the age of forty-two. There are many ways to remember Craig. He was a loving father and friend. He wrote beautiful poems about grapefruits and artichokes. Some of his poems won prizes. But after his death, people also remembered Craig's cooking. "He stuffed vegetables," said one of his friends, with deep emotion, and went on to explain that the way Craig stuffed vegetables with rice and pine nuts and currants when he had people over was just the coolest thing.

Some say that home cooking is doomed but I am convinced that the golden age of home cooking is yet to come. Part of why I believe this is because of the countless conversations I hear people having about the celebration meals they have just cooked and the people they cooked them for. In this world of screens and anxiety, to talk about cooking feels like something that is real and honest and good. These conversations are everywhere once you start listening out for them: on the bus, at the hairdresser, in the street, at the school gates. An Italian-Scottish friend just described to me in loving detail every layer of a special lasagne she devised for a party for her husband's sixtieth birthday: a layer of chicken with the broth it was cooked in, then pasta, then a layer of roasted eggplants, then pasta, then a layer of sugo (tomato sauce with herbs from the garden), then pasta, then a layer of spinach, then pasta, then finally the white sauce and cheese. Love and thought had gone into every element. It wasn't lasagne as her Italian nonna would have made but something new.

Cooking for other people can seem daunting and it can be hard, but if you serve food you like to people you love, you can't go far wrong. Here are two of the meals I've celebrated with over the past year. They are designed for eating in the summer and spring or autumn. I hope they bring you as much joy as they brought me.

Summer fiesta

Stuffed vegetable party with slightly Italian flavors (vegetarian)

For 8 (with leftovers)
Restorative white bean stew (optional) (see page 366)
Tomatoes stuffed with basil-scented rice
Bell peppers stuffed with garlicky fennel potatoes
Zucchini stuffed with ricotta, lemon and pine nuts
A bowl of thick yogurt or Turkish beet dip (see page 270) or green tahini (page 117)
Green salad (see page 114)
Polenta-crisp oven fries
Manjula's preserved lemons (see page 94)
Olives
Bread
Raspberry ripple hazelnut meringue

Some insist that stuffed vegetables are a bad joke from the 1970s, one that should never be revived. But tell that to the Greek and Turkish and Italian cooks for whom stuffed vegetables are a way of cooking that dates back generations. As Arto der Haroutunian writes in *Vegetarian Dishes from the Middle East*, the tradition goes all the way back to the ancient Babylonians, who were already stuffing vine and cabbage leaves with delicious mixtures of wheat and spices or ground meat.

In Anatolia, in Turkey, there is a meal of mixed stuffed vegetables called Kizi-Inzi, meaning "one for you and one for me." The thought is that each person helps themselves in turn to a variety of stuffed vegetables: a pepper, a tomato, a zucchini, an eggplant. A platter of mixed stuffed vegetables served warm or at room temperature feels like a very forgiving and flexible way to have a vegetarian feast in the summer: forgiving both on the cook and on the eaters. As Sarit Packer and Itamar Srulovich have written, stuffed peppers are a great thing to cook "for a lot of people you don't need to impress, just nourish." Something magical happens to the vegetables in the oven. They become soft and wrinkly and very sweet.

As for the fillings, having experimented with many types of stuffed vegetables, I have decided that the ones I like best are the simplest, with Italian flavors. There are three variants here. All are vegetarian and two are both vegan and gluten-free. There are tomatoes stuffed with rice and basil, bell peppers stuffed with potatoes and fennel seeds, and zucchini stuffed with a rich mixture of ricotta, pine nuts, and breadcrumbs. One for you and one for me.

Potatoes feature twice in the menu, once in the bell peppers and once as oven fries on the side to give the meal some much-needed crunch. If you feel that is too much potato for one meal, you could swap sweet potatoes for the potatoes, or other good side dishes here would be the burned finger lentils (page 102) or the bulgur and eggplant pilaf with pistachio and lemon (page 271). Or save yourself the bother of either and just get some good bread.

If you want a starter, I'd go for small bowls of the restorative white bean stew on page 366 but served with some torn basil at the end. Don't double the recipe unless it will reassure you to do so—it will stretch to 8 as a starter.

To follow, I've suggested a pavlova-like hazelnut meringue with raspberries, which looks and tastes deeply festive. But this menu would also go very well with the orange and cardamom shortbread squares on page 28 or just a big bowl of strawberries and a slab of halva. If you are cooking for smaller numbers, any of the stuffed vegetables by themselves would make a meal for 4, with salad and bread and a bowl of garlicky yogurt or tahini.

If you have room in your oven (or a double oven), you should be able to bake all three kinds of vegetables at once, but know that they sit quite happily once they are out of the oven so there is no panic about timing. Hot from the oven, a stuffed vegetable has no charm (maybe this is where the 1970s versions went wrong). It needs an hour or so to cool and settle into itself.

Tomatoes stuffed with basil-scented rice

This was the recipe that converted me to the merits of stuffed vegetables as a comfort food. The perfume of the basil and garlic cooking inside the sweet tomatoes with rice and oil smells like summer. I first made it following Rachel Roddy's recipe in the *Guardian*. The main change I have made is to parcook the rice slightly, which cuts down on the cooking time.

Serves 4 as a stand-alone main course or 8 as part of a feast
¾ cup/160g risotto rice
12 ripe medium tomatoes
4 cloves of garlic, grated or crushed to a paste
1 cup/20g fresh basil, chopped, plus more to serve
⅓ cup/80ml olive oil

Boil a kettle. Cook the rice in boiling salted water for 5 minutes. Drain. Meanwhile, cut the top off each tomato. Using an ice cream scoop or a spoon, scoop out the flesh and seeds of the tomatoes and put them into a large bowl. Put the tomato shells upside down on a plate to drain. Blitz the tomato flesh, juice, and seeds with an immersion blender. Mix it with the rice, basil, and oil and a decent whack of salt.

Preheat the oven to 400°F. Put the tomato shells into a large roasting dish, sprinkle them with salt inside, and fill them with the rice mixture, making sure that each one has a good ratio of liquid to rice. Put the lids back on the tomatoes. You will almost certainly have quite a lot of the stuffing mixture left over. Put this into a small baking dish. Put the dish of stuffed tomatoes plus the baking dish of stuffing in the oven and bake for 40 minutes, checking after 30, until the tomatoes are soft and wrinkled and the rice is cooked. If the rice seems raw or is drying out, add a splash more water to each tomato and give it a bit longer. When the tomatoes come out of the oven, remove the lid of each one and top up with the extra stuffing from the baking dish. Add a final sprinkle of basil and replace the lids.

Bell peppers stuffed with garlicky fennel potatoes

I got this idea from *The Almost Vegetarian Cookbook* by Josceline Dimbleby, except that she seasons her potatoes with dill seeds, not fennel. I had never seen the idea of stuffing bell peppers with potatoes before. It's a good one and these are also the quickest stuffed vegetables I've ever made.

Serves 4 as a stand-alone main course or 8 as part of a feast

1 lb 10 oz/750g waxy potatoes (such as Yukon Gold), peeled and cut into very small cubes
8 bell peppers, preferably yellow
6 cloves of garlic, peeled and chopped or grated
7 tablespoons/100ml olive oil
2 teaspoons fennel seeds

Start by par-cooking the potatoes. Bring a big pot of water to a boil, add salt, and boil the potatoes for 2 minutes before draining well in a colander. Prep the bell peppers by slicing off the tops. Scoop out and discard any seeds inside. Cut the tops of the bell peppers into very small cubes.

Heat the oven to 400°F. Put the cubed potatoes into a bowl with the cubed bell pepper, and add the garlic, oil, fennel seeds, and a good couple of pinches of salt. Mix well. Spoon the potato and bell pepper mixture into the empty bell peppers. Drizzle with a little extra oil and bake for 1 hour, checking after 45 minutes. They are done when the potatoes are tender and golden and the bell peppers are softening.

Zucchini stuffed with ricotta, lemon, and pine nuts

Serves 4 as a stand-alone main course or 8 as part of a feast
4–6 medium zucchini (about 1¾ lb/800g)
1 cup/250g ricotta
A handful of marjoram, chopped
A handful of chives, chopped
Zest and juice of 1 unwaxed lemon
½ cup/60g grated parmesan or vegetarian equivalent
1 cup/80g fresh breadcrumbs (whiz white bread in the food processor)
⅓ cup/40g pine nuts
A grating of nutmeg
Olive oil

Preheat the oven to 400°F. Cut the zucchini in half lengthwise and lay them on a baking sheet cut side up. Bake them for 10 minutes. Meanwhile, mix together the ricotta, herbs, lemon juice and zest, parmesan, breadcrumbs, pine nuts, and nutmeg in a mixing bowl. When the zucchini are cool enough to handle, scoop out most of their flesh using a melon baller or small spoon. Chop this and add it to the ricotta mixture. Check the mixture for seasoning and add salt and pepper. Sprinkle a little salt and a smidge of oil in the bottom of each zucchini half. Fill each one with the filling. You can pile this one quite high without coming to any harm, so you should be able to use up all the mixture. Return the zucchini to the oven and bake for 20 minutes, or until crisp and golden on top.

When all the stuffed vegetables are done, allow them to cool for at least half an hour, preferably an hour or more. Serve with a big bowl of yogurt either left plain or mixed with a grated clove of garlic and some chopped herbs, plus a green salad. Lots of the other things on the table are quite oily and garlicky, so I would keep the dressing for the salad relatively astringent and plain: raw apple cider vinegar, oil, and a little salt. Put the leaves into a big bowl and toss with this dressing. It would be nice to have some olives and a dish of preserved lemons or some other simple pickle (see the pickled carrots on page 40) on the table. As mentioned on page 382, you could absolutely skip the potatoes and just have a loaf of good bread alongside.

Polenta-crisp oven fries

Serves 8

4½ lb/2kg potatoes (or sweet potatoes if you prefer), peeled and cut into thick fries
3 tablespoons polenta
Olive oil

Put the peeled and cut potatoes into a bowl of cold water and let soak for 10–30 minutes (or longer if that suits you). Drain very well and pat dry with a clean kitchen towel. When you are about an hour away from eating, preheat the oven to 450°F. Spread the fries out on two baking sheets. Scatter each sheet with the polenta and a little salt and drizzle with oil. Toss with your hands to make sure the potatoes are all coated with some polenta and oil. Put into the oven for 30–40 minutes, or until well crisped and golden.

Raspberry ripple hazelnut meringue (gluten-free)

If you feel you have enough cooking on your hands with the stuffed vegetables, there's no need to cook dessert. No one would be disappointed with a big bowl of raspberries or strawberries, a bowl of whipped cream, and a bowl of sugar. But this meringue is spectacular and very easy—a pavlova flavored with toasted hazelnuts and filled with cream rippled with raspberries. I got the idea from Jeremy Lee, the chef proprietor of Quo Vadis restaurant, who makes a similar meringue but with almonds and whom I am not alone in considering the king of desserts. The addition of the nuts makes the meringue twice as nice, in my view, but obviously if you are serving the meal to anyone who can't eat nuts, you can just leave them out and it's still a thing of splendor.

The meringue itself can be made ahead of time (even 1–2 days ahead), and then all you have to do is whip the cream and assemble it with the fruit.

Serves 8
Scant 1 cup/120g blanched hazelnuts
5 large egg whites (save the yolks to make pasta or custard)
¼ teaspoon cream of tartar (optional, but helps the egg white to hold its shape)
1¼ cups plus 2 tablespoons/275g granulated sugar
3⅓ cups/400g raspberries
Confectioners' sugar
1⅔ cups/400ml heavy cream

Line a baking sheet with parchment paper. Heat the oven to 375°F. Scatter the hazelnuts on the baking sheet and roast in the oven until their color is just starting to deepen and they smell wonderful (about 10 minutes). Tip them into a food processor and grind them very coarsely (there should still be some big pieces). If you don't have a food processor, chop them by hand.

Using electric beaters, beat the egg whites with the cream of tartar in a large, clean mixing bowl until they are stiff and very white. Slowly add the granulated sugar and continue to beat until glossy. Fold in most of the ground nuts, reserving a large handful, using a large spatula or metal spoon. Tip the meringue onto the lined sheet and spread it out to make a rough circle shape of approximately

9½ inches/24cm. Scatter the remaining hazelnuts on top. Bake the meringue for 20 minutes, then lower the oven temperature to 275°F and bake for 40 minutes. It should look a divine pale cookie-brown: the color of a fawn whippet. Allow to cool out of the oven.

While the meringue is baking, take 1 cup/125g of raspberries and press them through a sieve to make a purée. Mix this with 3 tablespoons of confectioners' sugar to sweeten. Whip the cream with 1 tablespoon of confectioners' sugar until it reaches soft peaks. Swirl half the raspberry purée into the cream to make a ripple. Dollop the cream over the meringue, followed by the rest of the whole raspberries. Drizzle the remaining sweet raspberry purée over the top and dust with confectioners' sugar. At this point, according to Jeremy Lee, the cook should "take a bow."

Spring or autumn fiesta

Chinese fish feast for Tom

For 6
Shrimp, chive, and black sesame toasts
Whole baked fish with ginger and green onion
Oven-baked jasmine rice
Stir-fried greens and asparagus with oyster sauce
Cherry and watermelon granita
Tasha's never-fail chocolate cake

Since I was a child, I have always thought of going out to eat Chinese food as the ultimate treat. I remember the excitement of dishes served sizzling-hot and the elegance of eating rice from tiny bowls. When my oldest son, Tom, spent a year in Nanjing, his reports and photos of everything he ate made me all the more in awe of the genius of Chinese cooking. This menu is designed for him, although it owes more to my memories of British-Chinese restaurant food of the 1980s than to the food of modern-day Nanjing.

It would be more authentically Chinese to steam the fish instead of baking it but I find that putting both the fish and the rice in the oven is a more relaxed way of doing things. The only real work for the main course is then stir-frying some greens and some last-minute seasoning of the fish with ginger, green onion, and hot oil.

In China, meals do not normally end with dessert, only fresh fruit. But this is a fiesta, so I've suggested not one but two different desserts. One is a cherry and watermelon granita, which is the cheeriest-looking deep pink color I've ever seen, and the other is the chocolate cake my daughter, Tasha, often makes when people come over. You don't need to make both desserts by any means. A bowl of fresh lychees with or without a plate of store-bought baklava would be a fine way to end things. If you only want to make one dessert, the granita is the easier of the two, and with some sweetened whipped cream it makes a very fine and festive end to the meal. If you layer up the granita and the cream in small drinking glasses it looks like a neon-pink glass of beer from the future.

Shrimp, chive, and black sesame toasts

I'd forgotten just how good these are—a retro dream: the crisp comfort of fried bread coupled with the succulence of garlicky shrimp. If any of you are on a gluten-free diet, you can skip the toast, double the cornstarch, and drop the mixture into the hot oil in small spoonfuls. I've added chives to the toasts because I can never resist shrimp and chive dumplings when I go out to eat dim sum. If you want a second starter, make the gyoza on page 149.

Serves 6
12¼ oz/350g raw shelled shrimp (defrosted if frozen and patted dry)
A handful of chives, chopped
A smaller handful of cilantro, finely chopped (optional)
2 cloves of garlic, peeled and finely chopped or grated
1 tablespoon cornstarch
1 large egg, beaten
7 oz/200g white sandwich bread cut into triangles, or baguette, cut into thin slices
¼ cup/40g black sesame seeds
Light oil for frying, such as sunflower
Lime wedges or vinegar (Chinese black vinegar or Japanese rice vinegar),
    to serve

Finely chop the shrimp and mix with the chives, cilantro (if using), garlic, cornstarch, egg, and a big pinch of salt. Refrigerate the mixture in a bowl for 30 minutes or so. Spread it thickly on small triangles of bread or slices of baguette, sprinkle these with the black sesame seeds, and put them on a plate in the fridge for another half an hour to firm up. If you are skipping the bread, simply mix the black sesame seeds, into the mixture and return it to the fridge until you are ready to fry it.

Heat a generous amount of oil in a frying pan over medium-high heat and shallow fry the toasts in batches for 1 minute per side or until gorgeously bronzed and crisp. Put them into the pan, gingerly, shrimp side down and after 1 minute, flip them with an offset spatula or fish spatula. Turn the heat down if they show any sign of burning. Drain them on paper towels on a plate while you cook the remaining batches. Eat with lime wedges or a little vinegar mixed with slivers of fresh ginger on the side.

Whole baked fish with ginger and green onion

I've suggested sea bass here because it's usually the most readily available big fish to buy on the bone. But ask your fishmonger for advice. A whole sea trout would be amazing in late spring if you can get one. The fish is baked in the oven, stuffed with green onions, smothered with a simple paste of garlic and ginger. You then cover it with more green onions and ginger cut into thread-like shreds, and pour hot sizzling oil over the top to cook the onion and ginger slightly. This technique is borrowed from the famous Cantonese dish, clear-steamed sea bass. For something so delicious, this couldn't be easier.

Serves 6

1 whole 3-lb/1.4kg sea bass, gutted and scaled (the weight is approximate, you may
    have to buy a fish as small as 2½ lb/1.2kg or as large as 4 lb/1.8kg)
1½ inches/4cm fresh ginger
6 cloves of garlic
5 tablespoons/75ml sunflower or olive oil
3½ oz/100g green onions
1 tablespoon rice vinegar
¼ teaspoon sugar
2 tablespoons soy sauce

Preheat the oven to 400°F. Line a big roasting dish with a double layer of parchment paper. Slash the skin of the fish on both sides, making about 4 or 5 deep slits. Fish skin can be surprisingly tough. Make sure your knife is sharp. Peel and grate half the ginger and all of the garlic. Massage this into both sides of the fish along with 1 tablespoon of the oil and a little salt. Pour the vinegar over the top of the fish. Stuff the belly of the fish with all the green onions except for 5. Put the fish into the oven for 30 minutes, then check for doneness by poking the flesh near the bone. If it looks translucent and not white, it is not quite done—give it more time in the oven, 5 minutes at a time.

    While the fish is in the oven, cut the reserved 5 green onions and the second half of the ginger into fine lengthwise threads. The Chinese term is "silken threads." My knife work is not the most precise and I never fully manage this. But the basic idea is to chop the green onions in half and then to cut each of these halves in half lengthwise before cutting each half into shreds. Shred the ginger to similar-size threads. When the fish is out of the oven, put it into the dish you want to serve it in. Sprinkle with ¼ teaspoon of salt and the sugar, then cover the fish with the strands of ginger and green onion. Heat up the remaining 4 tablespoons/60ml of oil in a small saucepan until it is very hot. Pour it, sizzling, little by little, all over the green onion and ginger. Then pour the soy sauce on top and serve with the jasmine rice and the stir-fried greens.

Oven-baked jasmine rice

When I already have the oven on for something else, this is one of my favorite ways to cook plain rice because it removes all the guesswork.

Serves 6 with this menu (or 4-6 if part of a smaller meal)
1½ cups/300g jasmine rice, rinsed

Preheat the oven to 400°F. Put the rice into a Dutch oven with 2½ cups/600ml of boiling water from a kettle and put the lid on. Put into the oven for 30 minutes. Let stand out of the oven for 10 minutes or up to 1 hour.

VARIATION

This basic method is completely unseasoned, which is how I like it for this particular menu but depending on my mood, I might add a few knobs of butter and a few pinches of salt before the rice goes in the oven; and if serving with other dishes I might add some bay leaves, or cumin seeds, or nigella seeds, or a scattering of cardamom pods and whole cloves, or all of the above.

Stir-fried greens and asparagus with oyster sauce

Serves 6

2 tablespoons oyster sauce

2 tablespoons soy sauce

1 tablespoon rice vinegar

1 teaspoon sugar

1 tablespoon neutral oil

7 oz/200g asparagus, tough stalks removed and tender spears cut in half

1 lb 5 oz/600g bok choy or any tender greens, rinsed and cut into quarters

1 teaspoon cornstarch mixed with 2 teaspoons water

Stir together the oyster sauce, soy sauce, rice vinegar, and sugar. Heat the oil in a wok until shimmering hot. Add the asparagus and the greens and cook for just a couple of minutes or until slightly wilted. Add a spoonful of water and cook for 1 minute more. Now add the soy sauce mixture followed by the cornstarch mixture and simmer for 1 minute or so more until the sauce is just thickened and glossy. It should look shiny and smell delicious. Arrange it on a serving plate and eat with the fish and rice.

Cherry and watermelon granita

Watermelon granita, as Jacob Kenedy writes in *Bocca: Cookbook* is "possibly the one thing in the world more refreshing than a big slice of watermelon." But much depends on the quality of the watermelon. Some watermelons are so dull-tasting that your granita would end up tasting of nothing but sugar. As insurance against disappointing melons, I tried adding some frozen cherries to the watermelon granita mix one day. It worked! The cherries heighten the melon both in color and in flavor. So if you open up your melon and it tastes boring, don't despair. This granita will still be sublime.

Serves 8

2 lb 2 oz/1kg or so of watermelon

1⅓ cups/300g frozen cherries (I buy frozen sour cherries from the supermarket or from a health food store)

½ cup plus 1 tablespoon/110g sugar

Cut all the green and white rind off the watermelon. Whiz the watermelon with an immersion blender and then strain the juice through a sieve to get rid of the seeds. You should have 2½–3 cups/600–700ml of juice. Add the cherries to the watermelon juice and again whiz it with an immersion blender to purée the cherries. Add the sugar and stir to dissolve. Taste the vivid pink liquid for sweetness, remembering that ice cream and granita mix should always taste too sweet when unfrozen because the cold dampens your sense of sweetness. Pour it into a shallow container (I usually use a ceramic baking dish). Place it in your freezer and check after 1 hour. Once ice crystals start to form, mash them to a slush with a fork. Keep mashing every half an hour or so. It should take around 4 hours to freeze in total. I like to make the final mashing of the granita a communal affair. Bring the dish to the table and let each guest have a go at mashing it with a fork until it looks like beautiful pink slush, as airy as snow.

You can have this plain, pure and refreshing or—my preference—you can eat it with lots of whipped cream. Take 1¼ cups/300ml of heavy cream and whisk it with 1 tablespoon of confectioners' sugar until it forms very soft peaks (if you are in doubt, stop—whipped cream can easily turn into butter if you overwhisk).

Tasha's never-fail chocolate cake (gluten-free)

Serves 6
7 oz/200g dark chocolate
¾ cup plus 2 tablespoons/200g unsalted butter
6 large eggs
Packed 1 cup/200g brown sugar
1 cup/120g almond flour
1 teaspoon vanilla extract
Cocoa powder for dusting and whipped cream to serve

Line a 9-inch/23cm cake pan with parchment paper. Preheat the oven to 375°F. Break the chocolate into small pieces and chop the butter. Put them together in a medium metal bowl balanced over a saucepan a quarter full of water. Place this over medium heat to melt the butter and chocolate. Watch it carefully and stir from time to time with a silicone spatula. As soon as it is melted, take the bowl off the pan.

While the chocolate is melting, break the eggs into a large mixing bowl. Add the sugar and beat with electric beaters until very airy and increased in volume—about 4 minutes. You can still make this if you only have a whisk but it will take you longer—8–10 minutes of solid whisking. Pour in the chocolate-butter mixture and whisk again. Finally, sprinkle with the almond flour plus a pinch of salt and the vanilla and whisk one more time to combine. Pour into the cake pan, using the spatula to help you get every drop of the rich chocolatey mixture. Bake for 30–35 minutes, or until the top is just firm and not jiggling with wetness (but you want it still moist inside, so the skewer test won't work). Give it 5 more minutes if you can feel liquid under the crust. Let cool in the pan for at least 20 minutes. It will store well in an airtight container and is, if anything, best on the second day, so do make this ahead if it helps.

When you serve it, dust the top of the cake with a little cocoa pushed through a sieve and eat with whipped cream sweetened with a little confectioners' sugar. Make the cream-whipping a communal activity. Pass around the bowl filled with cream and sugar plus a whisk and let everyone have a go at whisking. Or another way to go, especially if it's anyone's birthday, is to top it with the ganache on page 203 and sprinkle with crystallized roses.

A few thoughts on organizing a fiesta

If you want tips on elegant entertaining, you will have to look elsewhere. It's your house and your rules. Do it your way. Everything I've already said elsewhere in the book about making yourself feel relaxed as a cook applies double when you have people over. But remember that if you can cook for 8 as naturally as you cook for yourself, people will probably love it, no matter what you serve. Here are a few random thoughts.

Get as much as you can ready in advance so that you can enjoy the meal and be a part of it too.

Don't worry too much about the temperature of food (or another way to put this is: choose mostly dishes that won't be ruined if they are served warm or room temperature rather than piping hot). Apparently the great food writer M.F.K. Fisher served all her food at room temperature when entertaining. Your own temperature and mood matter far more than that of the food.

Having plenty of candles to light up the room never hurts (unless you spill wax on yourself).

If you serve cocktails for bigger parties, one way to go is to make the default version non-alcoholic so that people can add as much or as little alcohol as they like. As Katharine Whitehorn observed, some people get nervous not knowing how much alcohol is in a drink.

Include at least one tiny element of communal cooking in the meal—for example, shelling peas or passing around a branch of lemon verbena and some scissors so that everyone can make their own tisane. If nothing else, I usually pass around a bowl of cream and a whisk when it is time for dessert (see Tasha's never-fail chocolate cake, page 404) so that everyone can help with whipping it. In days gone by, feasts often centered around communal food gathering of some kind or other, such as the culmination of harvest. A feast assembled from the grocery stores does not carry quite the same weight, but there is something about adding a tiny element of group cooking that reconnects people with their senses and with the group.

What to eat when

Sometimes, the hardest part of cooking is deciding what to cook, especially when you are catering for mixed audiences with differing tastes (or different dietary needs). Here are a few ideas to get started but you should, of course, feel free to combine anything in the book in any combination you like. I haven't given numbers here, in the hope that you will improvise and scale the recipes up or down depending on how many you are catering for.

Special weekend breakfast
Shakshuka(page 184)
Heavenly overnight waffles
  (page 157)
Maple syrup, berries, coffee

*Low-risk, low-stress dinner for someone
  you don't know very well (gluten-free)*
Roasting-dish chicken with fennel
  and citrus (page 320)
Polenta-crisp oven fries (page 388)
Olia's tomato, cucumber, and radish
  salad (page 168)
Four-ingredient chocolate mousse
  (page 118)

*For a night when you are craving takeout
  noodles (vegetarian)*
Yogurt-fried onions with lemons and
  sage (page 224; serve with chile crisp
  oil or other condiments of your
  choice)
Sort-of pad thai with Burmese tofu
  (page 191)

One pot or sheet-pan dinners
Paneer jalfrezi with potatoes (page 318)
Roasting-dish chicken with fennel
  and citrus (page 320)

Vignarola pearl barley stew with
  halloumi (page 322)
Mushroom and pearl barley stew
  (page 323)
Chicken stew for tired people (page 363)
Restorative white bean stew (page 366)
Magic pasta with mushrooms, garlic,
  cream, and wine (page 25)
Magic pasta with leek, seaweed,
  and ginger (page 27)

Midweek meals conjured from the freezer
Chicken curry (page 248; or any of the
  variations)
Lemon-yellow laksa (page 259; defrost
  the sauce and use it with whatever
  vegetables you have in the fridge)
Celery root and white bean
  bouillabaisse (page 252)
Leo's lentil ragù (page 285)
Homemade frozen pizza with
  buttermilk dough (page 372)

*Extremely easy dishes to revive you when
  your cooking energy is gone*
Gochujang carrots (page 43)
Sausage, greens, and polenta (page 305)
Mushroom noodles with peanut
  dressing (page 166)

Grated tomato and butter pasta sauce
(page 143)

Mellow soup for frayed nerves (page 16)

Buttery lima bean stew with kimchi
and sausages (page 309)

Ten-minute chana masala (page 265)

*Winter vegan dinner that will also please
non-vegans*

Crispy cauliflower with pasta and
mustard croutons (page 296)

Grated carrot salad (Moroccan
variation, page 36) or green salad
with drinkable vinaigrette (page 114)

Vegan pear, lemon, and ginger cake
(page 347)

*Summer vegan dinner that will also
please non-vegans*

Kim's gyoza (page 149; or any of the
variations)

Green pumpkin curry with potatoes
and green beans (page 258; serve with
rice or rice noodles plus wedges of
lime)

Jammy plums with coconut cream
(page 272; make with nectarines or
peaches and apricot jam if nectarines
or peaches are in season)

*Low-effort but special dinner for meat
eaters*

Bread salad with zucchini and grapes
(page 171)

Smoky lamb chops with not-romesco
sauce (page 276)

Polenta-crisp oven fries or new potatoes
(page 388)

Crisp spiced apple strudel (page 106)

*Prepare in advance vegetarian and
gluten-free comfort dinner*

Zucchini and basil moussaka with
lemon béchamel (page 343; make it
with gluten-free flour)

Burmese carrot salad (page 36) or green
salad with drinkable vinaigrette (page
114)

Tasha's never-fail chocolate cake (page
404; make the day before)

Curry feast

Pickled ginger lamb keema (page 283)

Red cauliflower and shrimp curry (page
250)

Paneer jalfrezi with potatoes (page 318)

Ten-minute chana masala (page 265)

Rice and flatbreads

Carrot and panch pooran pickle
(page 40)

Manjula's preserved lemons (page 94)

Aphorisms

It's much harder to remain furious with someone when they have cooked you something wonderful. This is also true when you cook for yourself.

No fancy ingredient you can buy feels as soothing as a clean fridge.

If you want to eat better food, you need to care for the cook.
That probably means you.

Time your cooking by songs instead of by the clock and it will start to feel like dancing.

Many people believe they dislike cooking when what they really dislike is washing dishes.

There is always another way of doing something in the kitchen. Pick the way that doesn't drive you crazy.

Every element in a recipe is optional—including the decision to cook it in the first place.

It doesn't matter how authentic or healthy or otherwise virtuous a dish is if you don't like it.

An easy meal made by a relaxed person is better than an elaborate meal cooked in a state of stress.

Apologizing for its shortcomings never made a meal taste better.

Cooking eggs is the closest that most of us will ever come to performing magic.

Pots and pans are like friends. Try to pick the ones that are so lovable you will forgive them when they let you down.

If in doubt, add more butter. When that fails, add more garlic. (I am not talking about desserts.)

Sometimes you think that a dish needs more salt when it really needs a touch of water.

Through cooking, you can not only recover old memories but make newer, happier ones.

When feeling unmoored, hold onto a wooden spoon. It will steady you.

Your own mood is one of the missing ingredients in every recipe.

No measuring device yet invented is half as brilliant as the human hand.

The hardest part of cooking is not the cooking but the grocery shopping.

The best knife sharpener is the one that you use.

You may believe you can't cook but if you know how to eat, you are halfway there.

Acknowledgments

There were many stages during the writing of this book when I thought it just wouldn't happen. But so many people buoyed me up that I feel the book has been the most collective effort of any book I've written.

First and foremost, I must thank my three children, Tom, Tasha, and Leo, for being my favorite people to cook for and with and also my favorite people full stop. During the months of pandemic lockdowns, Tash and Leo were my recipe testers-in-chief and I am so grateful to both of them for eating multiple versions of so many dishes good-humoredly while I struggled to get them right. Their company at the table kept me going when I wasn't sure if I could. I'm also especially grateful to Tom for reading drafts of the chapters and telling me things to cut but also occasionally writing "fab" in the margin, which made me very happy.

I must also thank the valiant friends who read early drafts and tested recipes for me, sometimes during lockdown when it was impossible to eat together. Caroline Boileau, Hugh Boileau, Miranda Doyle, and Catherine Blyth went so far above and beyond the call of friendship in their recipe testing that I can never properly thank them. You made me feel I was not alone at the table—thank you all. Huge thanks, too, on the recipe testing front to Angus MacKinnon, Deirdre Black, Katherine Bunke, Bee Boileau, Gabi Lemos, Hugo Lemos, Abby Scott, Mark Turner, Lily Scott Turner, Freya Scott Turner.

For help or ideas of various kinds, I am grateful to (in alphabetical order) Faraj Alnasser, Lucy Antal, Shahidha Bari, Kimberly Bell, Ellie Birne, Duncan Boak, Freya Brackett, Psyche Brackett, Nadia and Nick Brown, Catherine Carr, Miranda Carter, Rachael Clay, Rozy Dunn, Ruby Eastwood, Claire Edwards, Theo Fairley, Roberto Flore, David Foreman, Frankie Gil (you are the pavlova queen), Gonzalo Gil, Luke Gil, Emily Gowers, Charlotte Griffiths, Robert Hanks, Christopher Hawtree, Lara Heimert, John Lanchester, Anne Malcolm, Miriam Manook, Elizabeth McDermott, Harold McGee, Alison McTaggert, George Morley, Emily Nunn, Sarah and Nick Ray, Manjula Rajan, Ranjita Rajan, Ryan Riley, Leo Robson, Gary Rosen, Imogen Roth, Cathy Runciman, Lisa Runciman, Ruth Runciman, Alex Rushmer, Ruth Scurr, Peter Stothard, Max Strasser, Inigo Thomas, Mark Tinkler, Jo Vincent, Chris Wallace, Shaun Whiteside, Emily Wilson, Arash Zeini. And to Charlie, who (among so many other things) is a much better cook than I will ever be.

I am hugely grateful to all my colleagues at TastEd—Fran Box, Gurpinder Lalli, Jane Lockie, Jason O'Rourke, and especially to Kim Smith and Rosina Borelli for so generously giving me a sabbatical from the charity to write the book.

It always feels deeply reassuring to know that Zoe Pagnamenta, Sarah Ballard, and Eli Keren are my agents, and I couldn't be more grateful for everything they do on my behalf.

I couldn't have wished for a better photographer than Matt Russell, the "master of daylight," assisted by Matthew Hague. Matt seemed to be able to summon light on the drabbest London day and to make even a box grater look mysterious. I am so grateful to the wonderful food styling of Kitty Coles, assisted by Susannah Unsworth and Florence Blair. Kitty taught me so much about cooking and late in the process made me finally rethink my longstanding fear of the mandoline (the utensil, not the musical instrument) and Susanna gave me the crucial tweak I needed for the focaccia recipe. Huge thanks, too, to Rachel Vere for the inspired props and to the ceramicist Lucy Rutter.

At 4th Estate, I would like to thank my marvelous editor Louise Haines as well as Mia Colleran, both of whom worked so hard on every aspect of the book (with special thanks to Mia for her meticulous work and for being so encouraging about the mushroom noodle salad). I have been aware for years that Louise is one of the best and cleverest cookbook editors in publishing and it has felt like a dream to work with her on a cookbook at last. Grateful thanks are due to Annie Lee for her brilliant copy editing and to Alex Gingell for some great spots.

Also at 4th Estate, I am indebted to the creative work of David Pearson, Gary Simpson, Julian Humphries, Patrick Hargadon, and others. And thank you to Annabel Lee for the stunning illustrations.

At Norton, it's been a joy to work with Melanie Tortoroli for the first time as well as Maria Zizka (thank you for having such great kitchen knowledge) and the rest of the team.

Some of the section on homemade spice mixes first appeared in *The Wall Street Journal* ("Traveling the World with the Power of Spices" by Bee Wilson, February 11th 2021).

Some of my thoughts on braised asparagus first appeared in *Market Life* magazine for Borough Market (edited by Mark Riddaway).

Index